BY PAUL JACOBS

THE STATE OF THE UNIONS   1963

OLD AGE AND POLITICAL BEHAVIOR   1959
(WITH FRANK PONNER AND PHILIP SELZNICK)

LABOR IN A FREE SOCIETY   1959
(EDITOR, WITH MICHAEL HARRINGTON)

THE
STATE
OF
THE
UNIONS

THE
STATE
OF
THE
UNIONS

Paul Jacobs

ATHENEUM

NEW YORK

1963

Some of the material for this book has appeared in
AWARE, COMMENTARY, DISSENT, THE REPORTER, HARPER'S,
THE CALIFORNIA LAW REVIEW and
booklets issued by the Fund for the Republic.

TO ROBERT M HUTCHINS

ACKNOWLEDGMENTS

S O M E of the material in this book appeared first in *The Reporter*. It was there that I first began trying to discover the state of the unions. The magazine was a fine place to begin the search and I shall always be grateful to its editor, Max Ascoli, for his enthusiastic encouragement of my initial writing efforts.

The Center for the Study of Democratic Institutions, with which I have been, and still am, happily associated, has generously allowed me the opportunity to continue that inquiry, as does the Institute of Industrial Relations of the University of California at Berkeley. The intellectual stimulation I have received from my colleagues at the Center and the Institute is the most important contribution made to this book. I am especially grateful to my very close friends, Daniel Bell and Philip Selznick, from whom I have learned so much so enjoyably. My secretary, Laurel Fujishige, was of great assistance in a variety of ways and I found her editorial comments always very useful.

As for my wife, Ruth, only she would have had the patience to put up with me during the discouraging hours when writing stops and self-doubt begins. It would be foolish to thank her merely for the encouragement she gives to my writing, since this is the story of our whole life together.

PREFACE

THE FLOUR MILL took on the outlines of a turreted castle in the darkening fall twilight. It seemed far, far away from where I stood, clumped together with half a dozen others, nervously shifting around on the hard cinders of the wide railroad yard that separated the mill from the highway. High above us arc lights swung gently in the night breeze, protected from rifle shots by heavy wire netting. Someplace in the shadows behind us a big truck was parked near the heavy pole that carried one of the main electric lines into the railroad yard and the mill. Two thick cables were in the back of the truck, ready to be looped around the pole and attached to a steel ring that protruded from each side of the truck cab. Then the truck would pull away and jerk the pole down with it so that the lines could be cut by an electrician, waiting in the truck with the driver. I shivered with fright and felt an uncomfortable pressure in my bladder.

It was 1936, in Minneapolis, Minnesota. I was eighteen years old and scared, because soon all of us in the group were going to drop flat on the ground and crawl across the expanse of paralleling and criss-crossing railroad tracks toward the flour mill. Alongside the mill wall we were going to join up with other groups who were coming in from different parts of the yard and, together, all of us were going to force our way into the mill, either to beat up the scabs inside it or drive them out of the building. And we knew that we might ourselves get shot while crawling across the tracks or slugged inside the mill by the guards who were protecting the strikebreakers.

But, although we were frightened and uncertain of how the night was going to turn out, we were confident we knew what it was all about. Even as I scuttled on my belly across that endlessly long railroad yard, the cinders harshly abrasive to my hands, the low tracks like high mountains I had to force myself to climb, I was arrogantly certain of our general mission.

One day, more than twenty years later, I lounged comfortably in a chair pulled up to a big, glistening table in the air-conditioned board room of a huge oil corporation. I was a union official negotiating the renewal of a union contract with a vice-president of the company sitting opposite me. He was flanked on both sides by well-dressed officials, and on either side of me were well-dressed union members.

We had been in the contract discussions for three or four weeks and that morning I was arguing that the company should give a twenty-five-cent increase to the $1.50 meal allowance paid its employees when they had to work overtime on drilling operations out in the oilfields. The company, initially, had refused to grant the demand, but I was sure we would get it because overtime in the fields occurred only rarely and the total amount of money involved would be very small—the company could give it up easily in exchange for some other more expensive union demand.

So I sat, unworried, certain that the vice-president would eventually cede the point. But, as I heard my voice confidently arguing about the meal allowance, an uncertainty far back in my mind came into sharp focus: I no longer knew what the union was all about.

Many people, in and out of unions, seem to share that uncertainty. Now, as never before in recent times, basic conceptions about unions are being questioned. The nature of American unions, their role in society, the relations between union members and leaders, the internal life of the organization—issues such as these are engrossing the attention of wider and wider groups. And the public attention being directed at unions today comes at a time when automation and unemployment have presented unions with more difficult problems than those they have had to face in many years.

What is the state of unions? That question can't be answered by itself for unions cannot be understood apart from the society in which they exist. Thus, looming behind any inquiry into the state of the unions are larger questions about the state of the union.

The intention of this book is to make some analysis both of the most significant problems unions face today and of the way in which union leaders are coping with these issues. Although most of the material in the book appeared, originally, as separate articles over a six-year span, a common theme dominates them: the search for the meaning of the unions in America and to America. For this book, all of the articles have been studied in the context of current events and I have added commentaries to them. They are now all linked together by these comments and by the final section of the book, which focuses on the future of the unions in the United States.

Approximately one-fourth of this book is devoted to Jimmy Hoffa and the reader might legitimately ask: "Why give so much space to him?" Well, there are a number of reasons for this seeming disproportion. Hoffa symbolizes, in many ways, some of the basic dilemmas of American unionism. He is the prototype of the union leader who sees his union as a business and himself as a businessman. His union is the largest in the United States, and his relationship to its members, their support for him despite the public disapproval that surrounds him, sharply raises the whole question of union democracy. In addition, Hoffa also happens to be a very colorful and interesting person to write about—someone who, in an age of pallid and dull union leaders, "comes on" very strongly indeed. Another reason for the lengthy discussion of Hoffa in this book is that I happen to know a good deal about him.

CONTENTS

THE
STATE
OF
THE
UNIONS

INTRODUCTION

B L O O D   F E U D S are pervaded with a sense of horror and a quality of doom, inescapably fascinating to many people. For nearly seven years the whole country has watched, intently, the relentless stalking of Jimmy Hoffa by Robert Kennedy, who is determined to jail Hoffa—somehow, somewhere, on some charge.

Unfortunately, though, the pursuit of Hoffa and his fantastic ability to avoid conviction, again and again, obscured the much more significant issues involved in the Teamster leader's rise to power. The story of Hoffa is only partially the story of how a brilliant, amoral, fiercely ambitious man achieved power; equally important is the context in which that success was possible and the values which sustain his power. For no one, not even Bobby Kennedy, can deny that, whatever Hoffa is today, the great majority of Teamster members like him that way. Even if he goes to jail, as it seems he must, eventually, for no one can defeat indefinitely a major commitment of the U.S. government to convict him, Hoffa will still be his membership's popular choice for union president.

The case of Jimmy Hoffa is a most instructive one in analyzing the state of the unions. In the fall of 1956, when I began interviewing him, he was not the notorious figure that the Mc-Clellan Committee investigations made him six months later. Very few people outside the unions, or Detroit where he lived, had ever heard of him. But, even then, Hoffa was suspicious of journalists, for some of his operations had already been investigated by a congressional committee and he had been grilled by a district attorney about his financial dealings.

Gradually, as I went back and forth to Detroit, and watched him operate in Los Angeles, New York, and Washington, his suspicion of me diminished, although he never did come to trust me—nor was there any reason why he should have. Early in our relationship, he discovered that we had been in Minneapolis at the same time: I as a young Trotskyite, on the edges of the big Teamster local there, then controlled by the Trotskyites, and he as a member of a strong-arm group sent in by Teamster headquarters to help smash the Trotskyite hold on the local. He knew also that I had been a union organizer and that common link helped in opening him up to my questions. After the first two articles appeared, Hoffa told me that although I had attacked him unfairly I had neither misquoted him nor treated him as if he were a simple thug. Three months later, the McClellan Committee opened its investigations, focusing on the Teamsters Union and Hoffa became notorious.

THE
WORLD
OF
JIMMY
HOFFA
(1)

(1957) Nearly a fifth of all the freight that moves between the cities of the United States is carried by motor trucks—82 per cent of the country's livestock shipments, practically all its poultry and eggs, more than half its fruit and vegetables, and at least four-fifths of its automobiles. Yet less than a quarter of the sprawling giant that is the trucking industry is subject to anything like the Federal control imposed on railroads and shipping. By far the greatest influence on the trucking business—in fact, an integral part of it—is the International Brotherhood of Teamsters, Chauffeurs, Warehousemen, and Helpers of America, generally known as the Teamsters Union.

With upwards of 1,330,000 members and an insatiable thirst for expansion, the powerful Teamsters Union is one of the keys to the distributive economy of the nation. And inside the union the most dynamic force is James R. Hoffa, ninth vice-president by title but rapidly becoming its dominant figure—and thereby a figure of national prominence as well.

Jimmy Hoffa is a man of undisputed power and, to say the least, controversial reputation. Since 1951, five congressional committees have investigated him, his activities, or his associates in connection with racketeering, but he has never been prosecuted specifically on such a charge. The district attorney of Philadelphia recently described a union campaign in which Hoffa was involved as "the attempts of the racket mob" to take over the city, but Detroit once proclaimed a Jimmy Hoffa Day to do honor to his "valuable sense of civic duty."

A group of Eastern truck operators have demanded that their industry be saved from him, while the head of a national truck employers' association has applauded his contribution to the "stability and progress of the industry." George Meany, president of the AFL-CIO, has attacked some of his activities, and within his own union he is bitterly opposed by a group of officers who claim he is trying to win total control of the organization; but Dave Beck, president of the Teamsters, whose job Hoffa is sometimes charged with coveting, says of him, "There is no man who has a greater future in the trade union movement and in the Teamsters. . . ."

Jimmy Hoffa is forty-three years old and not worried about his future. "I know where I'm going," he says. "I know what I'm going to do. I've been around forty-three years and nobody's been leading me by the hand."

Within the Teamsters' national organization, Hoffa's sway already extends to about four hundred locals with nearly 650,000 members. "There's only two unions in the U.S. that are bigger," he points out. Yet many Americans don't even know his name, much less the nature of his power.

All a man needs to be considered a truck operator is one truck, either owned or, commonly enough, merely leased. Thus, in spite of the industry's huge size—in 1955, truckers carried 226 billion ton-miles of freight between cities, not to count the unknown billions carried within cities by local drayage companies—it is still a rough, brawling, extremely competitive battle royal among small units with a remarkably high percentage of business failures. There are only 2,600 freight carriers covered by Interstate Commerce Commission regulations in the country whose annual operating revenue is more than $200,000.

In recent years there has been a marked tendency toward

consolidation among these thousands of operators, and a growing number of bigger companies are emerging. Yet the Denver-Chicago Company is still the only coast-to-coast freight trucking organization. Within cities, too, the competition is harsh and ruthless as the smaller companies are forced to prey on each other in their struggle for survival. "While I'm negotiating with the union," the president of a trucking employers' association once complained, "the truckers I represent are out stealing my own accounts."

Stealing customers is characteristic of the industry. Not until 1935 when Congress passed the Motor Carrier Act, was there any Federal regulation of trucking at all. More than seventy-five per cent of the industry still escapes even the minimal regulation by the ICC laid down under the Act.

Another characteristic of the industry is that, unlike many other businesses, no clear line of demarcation separates management from labor. Thousands of operators are former drivers who have accumulated enough capital, or enough credit, to procure one or two "rigs" of their own. If, as often happens, they go broke in the vicious competition, they generally climb into someone else's truck cab and go back to the long, nerve-racking runs, straining their eyes to peer through the rain and fog of mountain grades or baking on the sweaty seat as the desert heat shimmers on the roadbed ahead. If they are local draymen who have failed, they go back to fighting city traffic. Even when a freighter owns his own truck, he is frequently its only driver and, as such, a member of the Teamsters Union. There are no reliable statistics on how many thousands of such owner-drivers are operating trucks, and there is very little the union or any other national agency can do to regulate their working hours or conditions.

There are still discernible traces in the industry of the rumrunners and bootleggers who, during prohibition, were among the first big-scale users of trucks. With repeal, many of these men began carrying legitimate freight, but their methods often remained the same as they had been in the days when hijacking a competitor's load was considered a normal business technique.

The Teamsters' jurisdictional claims reflect the loose nature of the trucking industry—and then some. To quote the union's constitution, these claims extend to "all teamsters, chauffeurs, warehousemen and helpers; all who are employed on or around horses, harness, carriages, automobiles, trucks, trailers, and all other vehicles hauling, carrying or conveying freight, merchandise, or materials; automotive sales, service, and maintenance employees; garage workers and service station employees; warehousemen of all kinds employed in warehouse work, stockmen, shipping room employees, and loaders, that is, persons engaged in loading or unloading freight, merchandise, or other materials on, to, or from any type of vehicle; all classes of dairy employees, inside and outside, including salesmen, brewery and soft drink workers; workers employed in ice cream plants; all other workers employed in the manufacture, processing, sale and distribution of food, milk, dairy and other products; all truck terminal employees, cannery workers. . . ."

And, as if this were not enough, there is a final clause in which the union says it also has jurisdiction over "other workers where the security of the bargaining positions of the above classifications requires the organization of such other workers."

In short, everyone except real teamsters. There are now only a few hundred men who drive teams of horses still left in the Teamsters Union. When Jimmy Hoffa talks about himself as a teamster, he is describing an attitude toward the world, not a job that involves teams of horses or even tractors and trailers.

A union's jurisdiction is its very life, and the history of the American labor movement is a chronicle of contradictory jurisdictional demands, overlapping claims, and ambiguous decisions by authorities unwilling or unable to enforce them. In this struggle, the Teamsters Union, which has almost tripled its membership in the past fifteen years, has generally come out on top. "What we want we try to get," says Hoffa. "What we get we keep."

The problem of rivalry was theoretically solved by the constitution of the merged AFL-CIO, which provides that its president and executive council "shall seek to eliminate such

conflicts and duplications through the process of voluntary agreement or voluntary merger between the affiliates involved."

Jimmy Hoffa, too, believes in the voluntary approach. "We
can work things out O.K.," he says, "but it's got to be that our
jurisdiction is recognized." Further, Hoffa feels that real labor
unity won't be accomplished "until the problem of jurisdiction is solved." How does he think it will be solved? "By fighting. That's how we expect to do it."

Always poised for a fight, Hoffa is quite capable of conducting one, with or without Queensberry rules. "A union isn't
a social club," he says. "As long as they allow strikebreakers,
as long as they allow employers to get injunctions, we'll have
to remain strong physically, economically, and financially to
survive." Although Hoffa seems here to be limiting the use of
"muscle" to disputes with employers, the same strong-arm approach has been used to settle jurisdictional disputes with other
unions. He and his staff once broke the strike of a CIO union
against a soft-drink bottling company in Detroit by driving
trucks through the picket lines and operating the plant. "Muscle"
has even been used by the Teamsters to prevent other unions
from organizing. In Detroit, Hoffa was once identified as one of
four men who beat a CIO organizer with tire chains to keep him
from organizing an optical plant in which an AFL official allegedly had some interest.

There is a posture of hardness and violence about the man
that is found in many teamsters, although it is not always expressed so openly. As a way of life, toughness is important to
Hoffa. Once he described to some of his associates how he had
put his son, then six years old, alone in a duck blind for six
hours with a gun and a bottle of pop. Since Hoffa received his
early union schooling in an atmosphere of gang warfare and
violence, "muscle" seems quite natural to him, something he
neither refrains from using himself nor especially resents when
it is used against him. "In the old days, we ran a union differently," he says. "We met with some rough, tough guys."

Hoffa was recently involved in a fist fight when he and two
associates were jumped by a group of disgruntled union mem-

bers in North Carolina after a meeting to ratify a contract. His grinning comment on the fight was: "The other guys got the worst of it. They got a few knots on their heads. I can get along." Pride in this ability to get along is reflected in his boast, "I don't have to walk around with no goddamn bodyguards."

Hoffa works out of a large but not elegantly furnished room on the second floor of a building owned by the Teamsters in Detroit. He sits behind a semicircular desk that he shares with his "partner," Bert Brennan. Many Teamster officials have such partners—lieutenants to whom they delegate some union responsibilities and with whom they share the profits of various extra-union activities, Hoffa and Brennan have been associated for many years. "Jimmy's got the brains in this team," says Brennan admiringly. "All I've got is muscle."

Hoffa's desk is heaped with papers and crowded with telephones into which he snaps orders. A photograph of his two children, both now teen-agers, faces him as he sits in a big chair with one foot and leg tucked underneath him. When he walks around the room, which is decorated with a large mounted game fish on one wall and on another a Rembrandt reproduction presented to him by his "Teamster friends in Ohio," he gives the impression of a tightly coiled spring, ready to fly open at any moment. The power is packed solidly in a stocky 180-pound frame about five foot five in height.

Hoffa is always a man in motion. He comes to his office early in the morning and leaves late at night. The three two-week vacations he takes each year are spent hunting and fishing. He rarely reads, except for newspapers, and the bookshelves built into one wall of his office are clearly more for decoration than education. They contain one set of unused labor reference books and a report on industrial relations given before Congress in 1912.

Hoffa is not a man to waste time. Ever since he started working as a youngster to help support his family, he has had no doubts about his capabilities. "I came up because enough people had less than I who wanted more." He is ascetic in his approach to power. "Drinking is a waste of time," he says, "and so is smoking." Hoffa does neither.

His phenomenal rise within the Teamsters can be attributed to his ambition, his energy, the keenness of his unschooled mind, and his ruthless concentration on the accumulation of power at almost any cost. But beyond all such personal qualities it has been made possible by the peculiar structure of his union, an instrument of power which he has turned to his own uses.

Back in 1937 Hoffa was elected president of Detroit Truck Drivers Local 299, a post he still holds, although he never drove a truck. He soon became president of the Michigan Conference of Teamsters; by 1946 he was head of the powerful Detroit Joint Council No. 43, and by 1948 a trustee of the International Union. The 1952 convention elected him ninth vice-president, and a year later Dave Beck made him head of the Central Conference of Teamsters. From the heights to which he has already risen, Hoffa looks out on a very different trade union from the one he entered as a young man in the early 1930's.

In those days the union's name did not even include the word "Warehousemen." Members were almost exclusively drivers and their helpers, organized in small, isolated, and autonomous locals scattered throughout the country. There was no thought in those days of recruiting aircraft workers, whiskey salesmen, and thermostat production employees. There were barely a hundred thousand members in the entire International. Dan Tobin, then the union's president, believed devoutly in keeping the membership within narrow craft lines.

But between 1933 and 1935 a remarkable change took place in a Teamster local in Minneapolis, a change that fundamentally affected the nature of the entire union. Local 574 in that city had come under the control of a group of Trotskyites, who in the short span of a few years established a wholly new pattern for the organization of Teamster unionism, one that has guided it to its present size and success.

The leaders of 574 during that period were the Dunne brothers—Vincent, Miles, and Grant—and Farrell Dobbs, all Trotskyites. (Dobbs has been the Socialist Workers Presidential candidate in the last three elections.)

In 1933, after Vincent Dunne was fired from a coalyard for political activity, he began to concentrate on a long-standing pressure campaign to get coalyard workers admitted into the local. The Teamsters then had less than a thousand members in Minneapolis, but the Minneapolis Trotskyites had frequently discussed the unrealized latent force of the Teamsters and their key role in the economy. The coal workers were allowed to enter the local at the end of the year. Two months later, a successful coal strike was conducted by Local 574, and immediately following it the membership shot up. An industrial union within a craft international, Local 574 was one of the first Teamster locals whose deliberate policy was to expand its jurisdiction.

Jimmy Hoffa, who had started his own Teamster career by organizing produce warehouse workers, watched the successes of the Minneapolis Trotskyites with great interest.

The expansion of Local 574 and its new methods of organization were bitterly resisted both by the employers and by Tobin, who once described as "rubbish" all workers who joined industrial unions. Employer opposition to Local 574 resulted in two bitter and bloody strikes later in 1934. Both were publicly attacked by Tobin, but both were won.

Immediately thereafter, Local 574, with a membership now in the thousands, moved out beyond the city limits of Minneapolis and started the first organizing of over-the-road drivers into the Teamsters Union. The Trotskyites believed that it was impossible, as their newspaper explained, "to have an island of truck-drivers, isolated in one place like the workers of a coal tipple or a woolen mill." They understood, better than Dan Tobin, that with "the trucking industry rapidly replacing the railroads in the handling of freight, the truckdrivers union becomes the dominating factor in labor organization."

Local 574 controlled the truck terminals in Minneapolis and through that control could extend its jurisdiction "by seeing that every driver pulling into our terminals has a union button." Thus began the "leapfrogging" that was later to become stand-

ard procedure for the entire union. This process consisted of
the unionization of a terminal, followed by the organization of
all the drivers coming into it, with the unionized drivers then
going on to organize the next terminal.

In spite of Dan Tobin—at one point he demanded as the
price of returning the local's charter that it rid itself of all
members who did not drive trucks 51 percent of the time—
574's influence spread throughout the Northwest. It had organized many different kinds of workers and then turned them
over to appropriate AFL unions. Its own membership was
growing, reflecting the appeal of the new industrial unionism,
which, encouraged by the passage of the Wagner Act in 1935,
was racing through the country, to culminate in the establishment of the CIO later that year.

To capitalize on this development and in the hope of de-
cisively influencing the character of the newly emerging labor
movement, the Trotskyite Teamsters, under Farrell Dobbs, had
begun the formation of a District Drivers Council, coordinating
Teamster locals throughout the Northwest: they later set up an
eleven-state area committee in the Mississippi Valley. The
Council brought many workers who were not drivers into the
union, a practice hitherto confined to the Minneapolis district.
The area committee negotiated a uniform contract for all over-
the-road drivers. Together they formed the foundation for the
four national Teamster Conferences that exist at present.

Back in the 1930's, Jimmy Hoffa was still operating on a
fairly limited scale. The Dunne brothers and Farrell Dobbs saw
that Hoffa was smart and extremely energetic, and he in turn
was impressed by their activities.

Another teamster with a future was Dave Beck, whose career
is inextricably linked with Hoffa's. Beck has come a long way
from the days of his boyhood poverty in Seattle to his post as
president of the Teamsters. As a teen-ager whose father was
unable to provide for the family, Beck went to work with his
mother in a laundry. He has been striving ever since to erase
those years from his memory and to achieve social status and
financial security.

Eighteen years older than Hoffa, Beck had been a Teamster international representative since 1925, but the most important factor in his rise was his work in establishing the Western Conference in 1937. This was his variation on the Trotskyites' Drivers Council. Although it did not become an official part of the Teamster machinery until 1947, the Conference device provided the base for Beck's increasing power, just as it was later to be the foundation of Hoffa's strength.

The Conference idea, all-important in the development of the union, went through several metamorphoses. The Drivers Council had been designated by the Trotskyites to implement their Marxist belief that unions were instruments of the class struggle. Beck, devoted as he was to the ideology of the business community, merely utilized the same structure to increase the size and power of the union and, at the same time, to extend his own influence within it. Out to capitalize on the spread of industrial unionism, which had aided the growth of the Minneapolis local, Beck began setting up locals whose membership ranged far outside the traditional Teamster jurisdiction. These new locals were then grouped into separate trade divisions established on an industry-wide basis. He then brought all these diverse groups together in the Conference. At present the Western Conference has twelve such separate divisions and represents a structure ideally adapted to a union both craft and industrial in character.

Hoffa carried this process a significant step further. Where Beck's contracts were limited to city-wide negotiations, Hoffa insisted on uniform area-wide agreements. These he negotiated himself, fixing terms for all employers within the area. It took Hoffa years to persuade local unions to give up their local autonomy for these area-wide agreements with uniform-contract provisions. It also took years and an occasional strike to persuade some employers to accept the arrangement. He succeeded, however, and has thus consolidated his great power throughout the Eastern, Central, and Southern states where his influence extends.

The only significant limitation on Hoffa's power within the

union today is imposed by his relationship with and perhaps even dependence upon Beck, who, as president since 1952, reigns over all eleven vice-presidents—with authority to rule if he sees fit. Like the other ten, Hoffa is given great freedom in his own domain. But the ultimate power is in Beck's hands, even if he often chooses not to use it.

The president has "authority to interpret the constitution and laws of the international union and to decide all questions of law thereunder . . ." He alone determines whether strike or lockout benefits will be paid. The bylaws of local unions are subject to his approval. He appoints and may remove all the international organizers. And the president appoints the four chairmen of the conferences, the most important informal power bases within the international.

In special circumstances, moreover, the president has the right to appoint a trustee to "take full charge of the affairs of a local union or other subordinate body," with authority to remove its officers or take any other action he thinks necessary.

There is no time limit specified for the period of such trusteeships, and the trustee, once appointed, can only be removed by the president—obviously an extremely effective device for controlling local unions. Almost 12 per cent of the Teamster locals —105 out of 897—were under such trusteeships at the end of 1955.

Trusteeships are established in a variety of situations, and for reasons both good and bad. In Missouri a trustee was appointed to wrest control of a local from hoodlums, but in Michigan a trustee was appointed to help keep convicted extortionists in the leadership of a local. This was Pontiac Local 614, and the trustee is Hoffa. Accusations have been made against both Beck and Hoffa that they have at times sent trustees to take over locals simply because their leadership had actively fought the top brass. As Hoffa puts it, "We're not theorists but practical people!"

Except to say that vice-presidents are members of the general executive board, the union's constitution is silent on their duties and responsibilities. In practice, an informal, reciprocal relationship of mutual protection and dependence exists between them and Beck. Coming to the aid of the International Longshoremen's Association, which had been expelled from the AFL, Beck agreed that the Teamsters would lend $400,000 to the ILA to help them fight a rival union set up by the AFL, but it was not suitable to pay the sum directly out of the international's treasury. Hoffa allowed the union's money to be siphoned to the longshoremen by way of this Central Conference. For weeks, he took the rap in public for the loan, never letting it be guessed that the Central Conference was opperating at a deficit and thus was hardly in a position to lend $400,000 to anyone.

In his turn, Beck kept hands off when Hoffa wanted a man named Gerald Connelly, who had been convicted of taking bribes from employers, returned to the payroll of a Teamster local in Minneapolis. Even when Connelly was convicted on two more charges, again for taking an employer's bribe and for bombings, Beck did not interfere. Hoffa has changed his mind and is no longer supporting Connelly, but not out of squeamishness. When he was asked in 1955 why he had supported Connelly, who had earlier been questioned by a House special subcommittee about possible involvement in the attempted murder of a union official in Florida, Hoffa replied, "Jerry isn't as young as he used to be. He had to run out of Florida. He can't keep on running forever. If he doesn't stay in Minneapolis, he'll have to move and it isn't so easy to start again."

One powerful reason for Hoffa's support of Connelly was the fact that three other important Teamster officials were closely tied up with the culprit in one of these episodes. All had shared with Connelly a five-thousand-dollar "tip" from the Archer-Daniels-Midland Company of Minneapolis to organize a Teamster local and thereby free that employer from the unwelcome attentions of John L. Lewis's catchall District 50, which had been making trouble for the company. The officials involved had questionable records in the union—one had taken "an advance" of $10,000 from welfare funds to open a bar—but among them was a good friend of Hoffa's, and in such cases

Jimmy is long on personal loyalty.

Just as Beck does not publicly criticize his vice-presidents in such delicate matters, nor they him, there are rarely public disputes among the vice-presidents themselves. Hoffa, for example, said nothing when the Western Conference of Teamsters, under the chairmanship of Frank Brewster, fifth vice-president, signed a mutual-aid pact with the International Union of Mine, Mill, and Smelter Workers, which had been expelled from the CIO as Communist-dominated. Even though there is no liking between the two men, Hoffa recognizes Brewster's regional sovereignty.

Occasionally, however, a conflict between the vice-presidents does break into the open. The attempt by Hoffa to take over the New York Teamsters Joint Council No. 16, for example, brought angry words and participation in a court action by Thomas Hickey, sixth vice-president in the New York area. (Martin Lacey's decision not to run for re-election as head of the Council has definitely cleared the way for the election of Hoffa's candidate, John J. O'Rourke.) On another occasion Brewster issued public statements that the Western Conference would withdraw from the international if racketeering and Communist influences threatened the union with expulsion from the AFL-CIO—an odd pronouncement considering Brewster's own pact with the Mine, Mill, and Smelter Workers, not to mention his questionable uses of the union's welfare fund.

To Hoffa as to Beck, the labor movement is a business. He talks about "the labor business" and his "friends in the labor business." In the absence of any other ideology, it is not surprising, therefore, that he should embody the ethics of the industry in which he operates.

Last summer he arranged a $200,000 loan to the J. W. Thomas Company in Minneapolis despite a bitter strike that had long been waged against that department store by a local of the Retail Clerks International Association. Asked about the propriety of a loan from a union welfare fund to a business involved in a labor dispute with another union, Hoffa answered: "The loan that the Michigan Conference Health and Welfare Fund made to the Thomas Company was made as a business deal. The strike had nothing to do with the loan one way or the other. This was strictly an investment. We would make a loan to a non-union company if it was a good investment. We would look at it just from the point of view of the return and the soundness of the investment."

Financial involvement with corporate enterprises is not new to the Teamsters, which once lent a million dollars to the Fruehauf Trailer Company. This loan was the basis of charges filed against Beck by Martin Crouse, then recording secretary of a Yakima, Washington, local, which is now under trusteeship. Crouse charged that the loan was made to Beck's friend Roy Fruehauf, then involved in a proxy fight, in order to help him keep control of the company. Beck is still president of the Teamsters; Crouse is now a real-estate salesman.

During the fight between Sewell Avery and Louis Wolfson for control of Montgomery Ward, the Teamsters purchased some million dollars' worth of stock from welfare funds. Although this hardly represented a decisive block of shares in the struggle, Avery, who had resisted unionization for many years, abruptly agreed to sign a contract with the Teamsters. Beck then jovially announced that the union shares would be voted in support of Avery.

Although both Hoffa and Beck pride themselves on running the union like a practical, efficient business, they differ in the way they use their power. Beck, perhaps because of his poverty-stricken childhood and youth, seems intent on utilizing his position to build a fortune for himself and to achieve status in the community. His election as president of the Seattle Elks and his position as president of the board of regents at the University of Washington are sources of great pride to him. Hoffa, although very much interested in money, is apparently motivated primarily by a desire for power itself.

In keeping with his pursuit of wealth, either outside the union or through it, Beck has varied and extensive business interests. The Teamster president's operations have at various times included real-estate holdings, auto financing, beer distribution, and a filling station. One of Beck's fliers in real estate was financed, at remarkably low rates, by the insurance company that wrote most of the union's health policies. Nearly $2 million was loaned directly from the union treasury to a business operation in which Beck allegedly holds an interest.

Beck's friends, too, have profited from his autocratic control over the resources of the International. A case in point was the windfall gathered by Nathan Shefferman, a Chicago management consultant, and his son Shelton through the sale of toy trucks to Teamster locals. Sale of the toys as an "imaginative way to promote interest" in the union was launched in the December, 1953, issue of the *International Teamster,* the union's monthly magazine. Four models were offered, ranging in price from $14.95 to $19.95 for the tractor-trailer combination. A letter from Beck, printed in the magazine, stated that the secretaries of all locals had been advised of "the shipments of model trucks for the promotion campaign." Obviously there was to be no choice in the matter.

Hundreds of the toy trucks were sold through Shefferman to the local unions at a markup of approximately 50 percent, according to the manufacturers, who incidentally had to convert their plant into a union shop for the occasion, though without benefit to their employees. The expenses for carrying out the operation were minimal, since the local unions were instructed to channel their orders through the AFL Union Label and Service Trades Department, at the same Washington address as the Teamster headquarters. Shelton Shefferman used Beck's office facilities there to carry on the operation.

Together, Beck and Hoffa make a powerful combination and will probably continue to do so at least until Hoffa feels that the time has come to move onward and upward. For the moment he is content to put the rhetorical question, "Why should I be nervous?" And then to answer himself: "If after Beck goes the boys want me—I'll assume my responsibilities."

THE
WORLD
OF
JIMMY
HOFFA
(2)

(1957) IN THE WORDS of James R. Hoffa, ninth vice-president of the International Brotherhood of Teamsters, head of its Central Conference, and by general consent the Brotherhood's most dynamic figure, the Teamsters are "the most clannish labor union in the U.S. Either you're in or you're out." To quote a member of the union's public-relations staff, "The Teamsters are a race apart," and like any race apart, they are extremely suspicious of the outside world. "My friends in the labor business are mostly all Teamsters," says Hoffa. "The rest you gotta watch with both eyes."

It is out of this suspiciousness that the union has developed one of its most characteristic, if dubious, concepts—the rejection, so far as that is feasible, of any sort of restraint upon it by an outside force. Courts in particular are looked upon with a jaundiced eye. Congressional committees and investigations, too, are regarded as an interference with the rights of the leaders in the conduct of union affairs.

Hoffa merely voices an article of the Teamster faith when he says: "We got guys all over the country, and when there's a rumble someplace we hear it right away. We don't 'holler cop,' we just get them in here and straighten it out." Thomas Flynn, chairman of the Teamsters' Eastern Conference and a friend of

Hoffa's, once challenged the president of a Teamster local who had given evidence in a trial, "Since when does one Teamster go into court to testify against another?" For years it was a fairly open secret in the labor movement that a West Coast Teamster official had been accused of stealing thousands of dollars from a union political group that he headed but had gone untried in court because no one in the organization was willing to "holler cop."

Hoffa reflects this same attitude when he says, "If we have any trouble, we might bring the guy in here, especially if he's one of my own guys, and straighten it out here. We might have to send him away very unhappy, but we'd get it straightened out."

An atmosphere of close personal and business relationships between employers and Teamsters Union officials, both unrestrained by institutional controls and both sharing the same standards of business ethics, distinguishes the curious netherworld of industrial relations in which Hoffa has become a key figure.

In the Teamsters, more than in most unions, the business agent is the cement that holds the organization together. He negotiates contracts, almost invariably without representation from the employees themselves. He listens to the members' complaints and acts on their grievances. Like the officials of many similar unions, he is more vulnerable to corruption than the officials of large industrial unions, just as the workers he represents are more vulnerable.

It is easier for a loader in a brewery, in collusion with a driver, to throw a few extra cases of beer on a truck and then split the proceeds than it is for an assembly-line worker in an auto plant to walk out the gate with a new bumper for his car. In the same way it is likelier that a trucking-industry employer will offer a bribe to a Teamster business agent, with whom he deals alone, than that the president of an oil company will attempt to bribe a representative of the oil workers union, who does his negotiating flanked by a committee of refinery employees.

In the labor movement as a whole, opportunities for union officials to conduct business on the side are many and varied. For the most part, such opportunities are made available by employers in the hope of establishing good personal relations. There is the business agent who services fire extinguishers in plants with which he negotiates, and another who buys scrap metal at a low price from a company with which he has contractual relationships. The Admiral Radio Corporation recently paid $30,000 to the manager of the electrical workers local union with which it had a contract, just for the right to act as a sponsor for the girls' baseball teams of which he was an owner. Insurance companies have given kickbacks and hired "favored brokers" or union officials' relatives as agents.

This sort of activity, limited in the labor movement in general, is more widely prevalent in Teamster-employer relationships. Hoffa's telephone in Detroit rings constantly with requests for favors from "management consultants." He has been wooed by management attorneys who represent trucking companies; he is fawned upon and lavishly entertained by insurance-company representatives attracted by the money in the huge welfare and pension funds he controls, and he is an extremely important person to a group of people hanging by their fingernails to the fringes of the labor movement.

These are the new middlemen of industrial relations who, like magicians pulling different colored handkerchiefs from their sleeves, do a business in making tame and malleable unions available to companies seeking a "good deal." In this group also are business "operators" whose stock in trade is their personal relationship with union leaders. Then there are officials of the "available" unions and their lawyers, who sometimes represent both labor and management.

Among these men, who smoke enormous cigars, wear suède and calf shoes, expensive custom-made suits, silk shirts, and hand-painted ties, who carry fat rolls of bills in diamond money clips and drive always-new Cadillacs to expensive steak houses —among them Jimmy Hoffa moves alertly, restlessly, arrogantly, wearing a not very expensive suit ("Covers me up, doesn't it? I don't need to impress anybody"), an old tie, cheap shoes, and white socks. Hoffa knows most of the people of this world, their weaknesses and strengths.

These furtive emissaries often seek his favors. "We get all kinds of people in here," he says, "and you know who sends them in? The employers, that's who. Guys send us whiskey and flowers and candy. We give them to the girls and then we send them something back worth twice as much. That stops that."

It is not this traffic that keeps Hoffa on top, however. The economic foundations of his growing power are the area agreements he has negotiated, extending his control over an ever broader territory. A typical agreement covers all over-the-road drivers employed in "Michigan, Ohio, Indiana, Illinois, Wisconsin, Minnesota, Iowa, Missouri, North Dakota, South Dakota, Nebraska, Kansas, and Louisville (Ky.), and operations into and out of all contiguous territory." The agreement was negotiated for fifteen employer groups representing about 260 freight companies. In effect its provisions apply to drivers employed by all carriers in the area. Two men on the employers' negotiating committee have long been involved in private business operations with Hoffa.

It is with such contracts that Hoffa maintains his basic hold over the membership rather than with the threat of potential violence or the use of the trusteeship device, whereby the president can appoint a trustee to take full charge of a local union that may be stepping out of line. Hoffa's real strength rests on the contracts he negotiates for his members. "We've got the best contracts in the country," he boasts. Whether or not this is accurate, they are certainly as good as those negotiated by any Teamster local in the United States.

Hoffa claims to be familiar with the details of almost every contract, and none of them is signed until he has decided that it meets the requirements set up by his research staff. He cares about his organization as if it were his own property and speaks of the union's staff as *my* men" paid from *my* payroll" to run *my* business."

Maintaining this feudal relationship within his local, No.

299 of Detroit, Hoffa prides himself on being available to the membership at any time. His office in the Teamsters Building opens directly into the corridor, and when he is in town the hallways are usually crowded with men "waiting to see Jimmy."

The members look upon him as their mediator with the outside world, the intercessor to whom they can come with their complaints and requests. He serves the same function for his membership that the political boss once served for immigrant groups and the poor people of his district. A member seeks his help in getting adequate medical care for his cancer-stricken wife; Hoffa calls up the City of Hope, a free hospital near Los Angeles supported by the Teamsters and other unions. The son of another member is in difficulty with the police; Hoffa uses his influence with city officials to help the boy.

In return the members are content to leave the running of the union in Hoffa's hands. He has been authorized in the past to spend whatever amount of the $1.5 million in the Local 299 treasury "he thinks necessary" in elections or other situations requiring the expenditure of funds.

Occasionally a member will come to Hoffa to complain about a business agent's activities or lack of them. Hoffa appears to be rather strict about his business agents' carrying out their work and claims to be absolutely opposed to any of his staff taking "tips" in exchange for contract concessions. "If one of my men doesn't service the members, he'd get fired. That's because he's letting a member down and myself also. There's no reason for any one of my men to have to accept gratuities from anyone. The same goes for any business agent who would make any agreement to violate the contract for any reason whatsoever." In fact, however, he has been known to allow men convicted of extortion to return to the payroll.

One reason Hoffa feels there is no reason for any of his men to accept gratuities is that he believes in giving them a good salary, a generous expense account, and a good automobile. A "business agent's no different from an executive." On the other hand, he doesn't see "anything wrong" with somebody giving a Teamster agent "some token of appreciation like a watch, a ring, a brooch," which he says is a standard practice among businessmen. Each of Hoffa's agents costs the local union about $300 a week—$200 in salary, plus expenses and the car, which is owned by the local.

Besides the usual pension and welfare benefits, the agents enjoy certain perquisites. They have the use of a private steam bath, a massage room with diathermy equipment, and the services of a barber and skilled masseur, all maintained for their use (and Hoffa's) in the building occupied by the Michigan Conference of Teamsters, just across the street from his local union headquarters. The Seattle Teamster headquarters, under President Dave Beck, has similar facilities.

This air of lavishness, pervading the entire union's official-dom, is especially marked at the top. Beck's home was purchased out of union funds. What is more, the constitution provides that "The General President, for the purpose of promoting the interests and welfare of the International and the making of diplomatic contacts with other organizations and institutions, and for the purpose of conserving his health, may in his discretion travel in this country or abroad and may take periodic rests," all on union funds and with full travel expenses for his wife and secretarial help thrown in.

Personal loyalty is rewarded and seniority observed by Hoffa in dealing with his staff. "There isn't a man on my payroll who didn't come up from the ranks," he says. (One who didn't, it turns out, is William Bufalino, president of a juke-box and vending-machine local in Detroit, who joined the labor movement after being an employer in the juke-box business.) "You can't buy loyalty," Hoffa says, "but also you can't keep loyalty if you don't give the wherewithal to maintain loyalty and respect. . . . I'm not worried about my men. They're my men. I pay good wages, have good working conditions, and I've never lost a man. If a promotion comes along, I give it to the man most entitled to it. He may not be the smartest guy, but if he knows the business and has been loyal, he gets promoted up."

Knowing "the business" is an extremely important requirement for remaining on Hoffa's staff. He keeps a running profit-

and-loss account on both the business agents and the locals. If a local shows a continuing loss, as between costs of operation and income, some adjustment takes place in personnel or in policy.

Almost every office in the building, which is occupied by a great number of locals, has a sketch or a photo of Hoffa on the wall. He is obviously The Boss, and when he snaps a request, it is taken as a command to be instantly obeyed.

Hoffa encourages his staff to become businessmen. "I don't object to my men having businesses outside of the union as long as it doesn't interfere with the union activities. That way they get to understand the employer's problem as well as the employee's problem."

Hoffa's own business enterprises have provided him with ample opportunity to "understand the employer's problem." He has reduced his operations considerably of late, but even with this reduction, he says, "I'm doing all right." His salary from the Teamsters Union is $21,000 a year; $15,000 from the local and $6,000 as a vice-president of the International. But, he says, "If I didn't have outside investments, I'd need more money."

His present business interests, he says, are restricted to a girls' camp, which he owns in partnership with, among others, Allen Dorfman (the son of Paul Dorfman, one-time head of a Chicago waste handlers' union who was recently suspended from the AFL-CIO for unethical conduct); a concern that leases trucks to freight companies; and an oil-lease corporation, now being liquidated. In the past, however, his enterprises were more diversified.

One of his early business ventures was a truck-leasing company set up for Hoffa and his partner and union lieutenant, Bert Brennan, by Albert and Carney Matheson, two Detroit attorneys who represented a large number of trucking companies and employer associations. All the company's stock was transferred to Mrs. Hoffa and Mrs. Brennan, under their maiden names. It then leased trucks to freight carriers in which the Matheson brothers owned substantial interests. Over a period of years, the brothers, as employer representatives, negotiated contracts with Hoffa, the union representative, in what appeared to be an extremely cozy arrangement.

The Mathesons were also direct business associates of Hoffa in at least three other enterprises: a brewery in which George Fitzgerald, Hoffa's attorney, was a stockholder; a corporation that owned a freight terminal; and a loan-and-investment company. Albert Matheson, while a lawyer for employers, was also secretary of the corporation that published the Michigan Teamster newspaper.

Like the Mathesons, Commercial Carriers, Inc., a Michigan trucking company, also set up a truck-leasing concern, again for the benefit of Hoffa's and Brennan's wives, and again under their maiden names. Neither of the ladies performed any functions for the companies they ostensibly owned, although they did request and receive generous dividends. In one case, a $4,000 investment yielded them more than $60,000 in dividends within four years.

Mrs. Hoffa and Mrs. Brennan were also carried at one time on the payroll of a juke-box servicemen's local. According to Eugene ("Jimmy") James, the official who ran the local, he had borrowed $2,000 from Hoffa and Brennan to start the local and then paid the two ladies approximately $6,000 from the union payroll to return the loan. The extra $4,000 was disbursed by James from the union treasury "out of the goodness of my heart" and because Hoffa and Brennan were "big men, they could help me a lot." Perhaps James felt he needed help since his local was being accused of having been set up in collusion with a juke-box operators' association in order to control all juke-box operations in Detroit. James was recently "suspended indefinitely" from the international leadership of the Laundry Workers International Union for complicity in a $900,000 embezzlement of welfare funds.

Under their own names, Hoffa and Brennan were once in the Columbus Trotting Association, a harness-racing track. Hoffa has also been associated in a lake-property development with Oren De Maas, once chief administrator of the Michigan Liquor Commission, who also put up the money for Hoffa's and Brennan's shares in the terminal property.

The girls' camp of which Hoffa is a part owner has been the subject of some discussion. It has occasionally served as the site for meetings of the trustees of the Teamster Central States Welfare Fund. In Drew Pearson's column of September 3, 1956, it was charged that the camp was used as "a blind for labor officials and gangland characters to meet," a charge vigorously denied by Hoffa. Interestingly, the part of the column that dealt with Hoffa was expunged in the Detroit *Free Press*.

Hoffa's business and personal relationships with the Dorfmans, father and son, and Dr. Leo Perlman, head of the insurance company that handles the Central Conference account, have come under severe congressional and press scrutiny. Hoffa and Perlman were partners in the oil-lease company, and Allen Dorfman became the Chicago agent for Perlman's insurance company. Thanks largely to the Teamster account, the company grew into a multimillion-dollar operation.

The public attention currently being directed toward Hoffa is probably a good reason for the reduction of his business activities. He is certainly alert to the fact that his operations are being watched constantly. His only new business enterprise appears to be Sun Valley, Inc., a real-estate promotion in Florida fifty miles south of Daytona Beach. At present twenty-eight hundred acres are under development, with an option on three thousand more. Financing for the project, which has been subdivided into twelve thousand lots, is being handled by the Bank of the Commonwealth in Detroit, and most of the lots are being purchased by business agents of the Teamsters or other unions. Salesmen for the operation work out of Hoffa's office. Hoffa claims that neither the Teamsters nor he personally will profit from this future retirement paradise, where business agents will be able to reminisce about the hard old days in the labor movement.

Partly accountable for the curtailment of Hoffa's outside activities, it is believed, and for other changes in the pattern of his administration, is Harold Gibbons. Formerly a director of the CIO United Retail, Wholesale, and Department Store Employees Union, Gibbons headed a four-thousand-member local that had disaffiliated from the CIO in 1948, and a year later brought them into the Teamsters. Now secretary-treasurer of the Central Conference, president of the St. Louis Joint Council No. 13, and secretary-treasurer of St. Louis Local 688, Gibbons is one of Hoffa's closest associates and one whose talents run to brains rather than muscle.

For many years, Gibbons's local was considered to be a model trade union. Its eight-man education committee, its stress on stewards' participation in a wide range of union affairs, its health center covering more than fifteen thousand members and their dependents, its participation in community and civic life, its political-action program, and its uncompromising position on civil rights—all these have been the subject of much publicity and discussion. A book was written about the local, and when European trade-unionists came to the United States, Local 688 was always on their itinerary as an example of the finest type of union to be found in the country.

Today Gibbons, who entered the labor movement as a Socialist, is committed to Hoffa and admires him greatly. In turn, Hoffa respects his lieutenant's capacities and assigns to him many extremely important functions. "Gibbons doesn't practice being a longhair," he says. "He's a practical Teamster."

Being a practical Teamster has made some great changes in Gibbons according to some of his old friends and co-workers. They feel that he, too, has a power drive that may yet take him a long way from the ideals he once held for the labor movement. One role Gibbons plays vis-à-vis Hoffa is to improve the ninth vice-president's public and community relations. It was he, for example, who arranged the dinner honoring Hoffa at which $280,000 was raised for a children's home in Israel.

Privately, Gibbons says that he thinks Hoffa is one of the most competent trade unionists in the country, that he believes Hoffa will be the next Teamster president, and that it *is* possible to broaden his perspective of the world. Most observers would certainly not question the first two opinions, whatever doubts they may have about the third.

* * *

In the struggle between trucking and the railroads, fought out in congressional committees and on the floors of state legislatures, the union has automatically identified its welfare with that of the truckers. When Jimmy Hoffa says, "In politics all we want to do is elect people who won't hurt us or the people in the industries with whom we do business," he is voicing the viewpoint of the entire union. The trucking industry needs all the political help it can get. For years the railroads have been its active enemy, fighting it wherever possible.

Truckers feel that their taxes are high. In one state, California, it is estimated that a single transport truck pays as much in taxes as eighty automobiles. Even though trucks comprise only 13.4 percent of all the motor vehicles in California, the carriers complain that they pay almost 30 percent of the highway-user taxes plus additional city taxes.

Unlike the railroads, the trucking industry is too young to have sunk deep roots into national community life. No well-known individuals are accepted as spokesmen for the industry. Not even the American Trucking Associations, Inc., claims to represent all the thousands of operators. And the public-relations problem of the ATA is further complicated by the resentment of many American motorists toward the monsters of the highway.

Politically, Hoffa is a powerful ally of the truckers. "I don't want to change the world," he says, but he is very much concerned with changing that portion of it directly affecting what he conceives to be his interests. Hoffa's main political focus, as is generally true of the Teamsters Union, is on the local, municipal, county, and state levels. He is more interested in judges than in the President, more concerned with highway and traffic commissioners than with Cabinet members.

The salient feature of his political activity is the expenditure of money—in large sums. "There are two ways to play politics," he once said. "You either make speeches or else you spend dough. We spend lots of dough. We got connections in the right places. We expect to keep them."

Hoffa's "connections" were the basis of a charge that the Republicans had called off a congressional investigation of him in 1953 in exchange for his promised support of Senator Homer Ferguson. Drew Pearson's column carried a story that Hoffa and Postmaster General Summerfield had made a deal on these terms. Hoffa did support the Michigan Republican, even though he was running against Pat McNamara, a former AFL official, endorsed by almost the entire AFL and CIO with the exception of the Teamsters.

To this day, Hoffa denies the story, saying, "No meeting was ever held with Summerfield on that Ferguson business. There's absolutely no truth in the Pearson story. I supported Ferguson from the time he started out as an assistant district attorney I always supported Ferguson in the past."

Party labels mean very little to Hoffa or to most Teamsters. He says that he supports "some Republicans because they've done as good a job as the Democrats did. The Democrats passed the Hobbs Act and the Republicans passed the Taft-Hartley Act and they haven't shown any signs of changing it." Similarly, out on the West Coast, the Teamsters supported Goodwin Knight when he ran for governor on the Republican ticket in 1954, partly because of Knight's commitment that he would veto any right-to-work bill that came out of the legislature.

In the State of Washington, on the other hand, the Teamsters supported Senator Warren Magnuson for re-election. A Democrat, Magnuson is chairman of the Senate Interstate and Foreign Commerce Committee, a position that enables him to give much help to the trucking industry. Reciprocally, Magnuson appeared for William Langley, the Teamsters' choice for District Attorney of Multnomah County, Oregon, which includes Portland. Langley is now under a grand-jury indictment on charges of malfeasance in office and conspiring with Teamster figures to permit gambling.

Because of their marginal role in society, certain businesses have come to be almost completely dependent on the Teamsters for political assistance and for help in discouraging competition. These are the pinball-machine and juke-box industries and concerns that collect garbage and waste, over whose employees the Teamsters have been exercising jurisdiction. These businesses operate under even fewer restraints than other industries involving the Teamsters, and their billion-dollar grosses make them extremely attractive to underworld elements.

When Jimmy Hoffa pleaded *nolo contendere* to a charge that he had "knowingly . . . engaged in a combination and conspiracy unreasonably to prevent" competing firms from selling wastepaper for shipment out of Detroit, he did not deny following a practice common to the Teamsters. The plea, he said, "is nothing against a man. Even General Motors has pleaded *nolo.*"

In Portland, Oregon, a U. S. court held in 1955 that an association of coin-machine operators and owners had illegally joined with the Teamsters Union, in restraint of trade, to prevent a tavern owner from purchasing a shuffleboard machine for his bar from outside the Portland area. It was also in Portland that the employer members of a coin-machine operators' association themselves joined the Teamsters Union in order to have political allies in the fight they were waging to legalize the pinball devices.

In Westchester County, New York, and in Los Angeles, Teamster officials have been involved in the garbage- and waste-carting business. Two Teamster officials are under indictment now in Los Angeles for perjury in denying collusion with employers to establish a monopoly, and in Westchester an internal fight within the Teamsters over which company should have the most business finally erupted in the murder, as yet unsolved, of one of the officials involved.

The juke-box business is one of the ways that Hoffa's name has been linked by persistent rumor to the underworld. If he has any direct financial tie-in with that world, he has thus far succeeded in keeping it very well hidden. No such specific charge has ever been substantiated against him in spite of all the investigations.

Nevertheless he maintains relations with the underworld, if

for no other reason than loyalty to his friends. He wears this kind of allegiance like an ensign. In his mind "friendship" obviously excuses a great deal. "You're no good if your word is no good or if your friendship is lukewarm. I have very few new friends. I have the same friends today that I had when I started organizing, and I have been fortunate in being able to make some additional friends as I go along."

When Hoffa started organizing, he soon found himself involved with shady figures. Some were employers. "I'd be a fake if I didn't associate with the people I do business with," he says. "I won't be that kind of a guy." Others were in "goon squads," hired by employers. And some were union "muscle men." All this occurred during Hoffa's basic training period—the time when his trade-union beliefs were being established.

One of his friends is a man named Sam Feldman, who recently began "organizing" restaurant workers in Philadelphia. Feldman, who believes that a man "learns to respect people" who "break his neck for him," served three years in jail for safecracking, followed by an additional four months for parole violation on a narcotics charge. Persons unknown attempted to murder him in 1934 but he escaped with a slight thigh wound. Asked why he had interceded with the Hotel and Restaurant and Bartenders International Union to get a charter for Feldman and his group, Hoffa explained, "Feldman is my friend." He added, by way of justification, "I believe the issuance of the charters is proper because independent unions can make a lot of trouble, especially with Teamsters unions, who become involved whenever there are picket lines."

Hoffa's friendship with Johnny Dio, now awaiting trial in the Victor Riesel acid-blinding case, has also been the subject of public attention. Hoffa met Dio when the latter was a representative of the United Automobile Workers-AFL (not to be confused with Reuther's UAW-CIO). Today the union is called the Allied Industrial Workers and was one of those investigated by the AFL-CIO Ethical Practices Committee. It faces the prospect of possible suspension from the AFL-CIO.

Dio, hired as an organizer for a UAW-AFL local of taxi drivers in New York, was no stranger to the labor movement. He and his uncle, James Plumeri, also known as Jimmy Doyle, had both gone to jail for extortion in the garment trade. He is said to have been at one time a strong-arm man for the International Ladies' Garment Workers' Union; he subsequently became an employer in the dress business.

There is no certain explanation why Dio wanted to become an official of the UAW-AFL. His own operations brought him a sizable income, but he told a number of people that his interest in the "labor business" was a desire to achieve the respectability that went with the title of a union representative. Whatever his motives, Dio was soon active in the UAW-AFL along with a number of other leaders with police records, including several officials of Teamster locals.

Hoffa's connection with this dubious group emerged when a number of the unions with which Dio was connected decided to switch over to the Teamsters. Mostly these are of the "paper" variety, and Hoffa's interest, allegedly, was to use them to extend his control into the New York Teamster Joint Council No. 16, and eventually to the entire eastern seaboard.

While there is no doubt that the "paper" locals were established by Hoffa, he naturally has another explanation. "Prior to the merger" of the AFL and CIO, he says, "I tried to switch as many locals as possible into the Teamsters. That's how come we had those locals chartered in New York. . . . Johnny Dio had nothing to do with the local unions agreeing to come into the Teamsters Union."

Nevertheless, at least seven officers of the newly chartered locals are also officials of the unions Dio was connected with and are on their payrolls. (Some of these officers were among those who refused to testify or pleaded the Fifth Amendment before the McClellan subcommittee currently investigating labor racketeering.) Their appearance at the New York Teamster Joint Council in quest of admission to that body was the signal for a labyrinthine battle between Martin Lacey, the Council president, and John O'Rourke, who sought to replace him with the help of the new locals—and of Jimmy Hoffa. O'Rourke won.

Hoffa will now be a key figure in the New York Teamsters. He also exerts great influence in the International Longshoremen's Association, which he supported after it had been expelled by the AFL.

Because the Teamsters are frequently a decisive element in strikes called by other unions, Hoffa has been able to build up a network of informal relations with many labor groups. If the Teamsters refuse to cross its picket line, a union like the Hotel and Restaurant Workers, for example, is in a strong bargaining position. When Hoffa asks a charter for his friend Feldman in Philadelphia, the Hotel and Restaurant Union officials are accordingly disinclined to antagonize him by refusing it. Other unions, like the Laundry Workers, are almost completely dependent upon the Teamsters for their existence.

It is almost impossible for any union to maintain a prolonged state of warfare with the Teamsters and not have its own resources depleted. As a result most labor organizations have attempted to work out a *modus vivendi* with them—some way of preserving their own jurisdiction while avoiding the kind of war with the "Teamos" that the machinists union once waged for two years over jurisdiction of the Boeing Airplane Company in Seattle, only to sign a mutual-assistance pact in the end. A similar pact has been signed with the butchers' and bakers' unions, extending still further the hegemony of Hoffa and his Teamsters.

In his relationships with the rest of the labor movement, Hoffa says he has "no set standards of judgment." He claims: "I judge 'em on the basis of the guy and the proposition. Sometimes two guys will come in here with the same proposition and I'll do it for one and not for the other." But in a sense he does have standards. He judges the merits of unions, for example, almost totally on the basis of their contracts. If a union has achieved good wages and conditions, and the industry is completely organized, Hoffa thinks it a good union, no matter what relationships exist between the leaders and the members or between the leaders and society as a whole.

Those close to Hoffa report a discernible shift in his attitude toward the community at large. Where once he would ask, "Who gives a damn what the public thinks?" he is now the subject of a glossy biography, defending him and glorifying his role in American life. Prepared by a member of Harold Gibbons's staff, the pamphlet was distributed by the thousands throughout the country, and was first displayed at a banquet held for the remarkable dual purpose of honoring Hoffa and raising funds for a children's home in Israel.

That affair was remarkable for the light it threw on Hoffa's growing prestige and on his influence in diverse circles of society. The Most Reverend Bernard J. Sheil, Auxiliary Bishop of Chicago, delivered the invocation, and Rabbi Aaron Decter of Temple B'Nai Aaron, Philadelphia, gave the benediction. The speakers were Dave Beck and Walter Mullady, past president of the American Trucking Association. Master of ceremonies was Nathan Feinsinger, professor of law at the University of Wisconsin and former chairman of the National Wage Stabilization Board.

From the realms of industry and labor, twenty-eight hundred people, including a fair proportion of top brass, paid $100 a plate to attend. The guest list included such diverse people as Samuel Feldman, the Philadelphia advocate of promoting respect by breaking necks; Roy Fruehauf, of the Fruehauf Trailer Company; and Louis ("Babe") Triscaro, a noted Detroit hoodlum. A. J. Hayes, president of the International Association of Machinists, was a sponsor, though probably not in his role as chairman of the AFL-CIO Ethical Practices Committee. Another of the 164 sponsors was Joseph O'Neill, president of the distillery workers union, one of the group that was under investigation by Hayes's committee.

Tables were purchased by companies like Ford, General Motors, the Bank of Commonwealth, Montgomery Ward, and Sears, Roebuck; by dozens of truck carriers; and by a great many unions, including the UAW-CIO. Some were genuine admirers of Hoffa. Some no doubt attended or were sponsors because of the object for which the funds were being raised. But many, it may be assumed, were there because they were either already dependent on Jimmy Hoffa or mindful of his future power.

Hoffa's status today and the promise of greater power to come are part of the changing pattern of labor-management relations. Today, the existence of organized labor as a permanent fact of our business life has gained general acceptance on the part both of government and of the major employers. Conflicts are of short duration and center on negotiable issues—issues of wages and working conditions, of dollars and cents to be paid to the workers while they hold jobs and when old age or accidents beyond their control prevent them from holding jobs. Labor has been successful in achieving its economic goals without inflicting any serious damage on the business community. The business community, with rare exceptions, has accepted the idea that unions not only are here to stay but have become a useful segment of the business system.

The more it considers itself as a business, whose prosperity depends on the success of business, the more labor is inclined to follow—sometimes with a vengeance—the practices of the business community. The chief incentive of many unions is to grow larger, faster, and more powerful—the same incentive, in short, as that of their business and industrial counterparts. In an economy characterized by bigger and bigger corporations, labor, to maintain its advantages and gain new ones, seeks to match corporate size. The relationship becomes that of two giants vying for economic power or collaborating in its joint exercise.

The resulting harmony has its risks. Unions, like all other organizations, tend to grow bureaucratic and rigid as they achieve stability. The trend toward long-term contracts tends further to reduce the area of disagreement between employers and union leaders to mere differences of interpretation. As a result, the labor leader today is likely to view his business counterpart as a fellow professional in the highly specialized field of industrial relations. Like diplomats, they both often find it necessary to arrive at a joint solution to a problem and then convince their respective constituencies of its correctness. The broader constituency—the nation's economy—which both labor and management are supposed to serve, is frequently lost sight of.

There is something different about Jimmy Hoffa, for he does more than just mold his union on the image of the trucking industry. He leads it—on the way to greater and greater concentration. Unlike the Auto Workers, which had to deal with a highly concentrated industry, the Teamsters began with a fragmented industry. By insisting on area agreements, Hoffa forces employers to band together on a wider and wider scale. "The future of labor-management relations," he says, "is big labor and big business, for there is no room for the small business or the small union." Therefore, Hoffa sought and found his allies among the bigger companies.

The Teamsters Union has thus played a role in stabilizing the trucking industry by promoting uniform wages and conditions, and at the same time it has powerfully contributed to driving the smaller and fringe operators out of business.

But as the industry—mostly because of Hoffa—becomes more corporate and less of a province of the freebooting entrepreneur, some dilemmas are already confronting the Teamsters' ninth vice-president. It can be safely predicted that these dilemmas and embarrassments will become more and more acute in direct relation to the success that has made Hoffa a national figure. It must already be difficult for him to reconcile the James R. Hoffa who recently lectured at Harvard with the Jimmy Hoffa who has no qualms about putting ex-convicts in favored positions in the labor organization.

Congressional investigations, the possibility of Federal regulation of the trucking industry, and the growing sobriety of the labor movement itself are all likely to act as curbs on the rambunctious Teamsters. Oddly enough, it was Dave Beck who complained: "We feel as if we are orphans in this industry. We are the only major transportation industry in America without its own regulatory body. The railroads have the Interstate Commerce Commission. The airlines have the Civil Aeronautics Board, and ships have the Maritime Board. Yet our industry must be regulated by the railroad-dominated Interstate Commerce Commission. We have pleaded for years for the appointment of someone on the ICC who comes from the industry and who knows trucking, but our efforts have been in vain." Beck's "orphan" may yet be adopted by the government, with all the restraints attending that relationship.

Within the united labor movement, the Ethical Practices Committee of the AFL-CIO can scarcely avoid coming to grips with the questionable alliances and business practices that feed the power of a Beck and a Hoffa.

For the time being, however, Hoffa remains one of those imperious rugged individualists whose actions make more and more difficult the self-assertion of other individuals. So far, the growth of his power has been enhanced by all attempts to check it.

"I learned a long time ago," he says, "that whatever you can do to me, I can do to you, only more."

INTRODUCTION

BY THE FALL of 1957, when I saw Hoffa again, Robert Kennedy and the McClellan Committee had succeeded in making his name a synonym for evil in America. Hoffa was attending a meeting of the Teamsters Union executive board which I was reporting for an Eastern newspaper, and he had asked me to dinner.

Two other men were with Hoffa the night we ate together: George Fitzgerald, one of his Detroit lawyers, and Nate Stein, one of his Los Angeles flunkies. Today Fitzgerald is no longer employed by Hoffa and Stein is under indictment in Los Angeles.

The relationship of Hoffa to Stein, a fat, squat, little man, has never been clear. When I first met Stein, he was employed in some vague capacity by a big gambling hotel in Las Vegas, and was also doing all kinds of odd jobs for Hoffa. I assumed then that Stein was one link, although probably not an important one, between Hoffa and the mysterious world of Las Vegas, to which he is somehow connected. Certainly, Hoffa has always spent a fair amount of time in Las Vegas. When once I asked him why he went there (since he says he's not interested very much in gambling) he answered, "I like to watch the action." What the "action" is that Hoffa likes to watch has never been made clear.

(40)

A
STEAK
DINNER
WITH
JIMMY
HOFFA

(1957) **W**E MET AGAIN, Jimmy Hoffa and I, a few weeks ago, in the patio of the very same hotel in Los Angeles where I had originally been introduced to him. It was our first meeting since the publication in *The Reporter,* at the beginning of the year, of the two articles I had written about him.

For Hoffa, the six months that had elapsed had been crowded. He had been indicted, tried, and, miraculously it seemed to most people, acquitted of a charge of attempting to obtain information through bribery from the files of the Senate committee. He had been indicted on a wiretapping charge. He had been summoned to a grueling four-day questioning by the committee that resulted in forty-eight charges being tabled against him.

Now he was the dominant figure at the union's board meeting, conceded almost certain to be elected president of the Teamsters at its September convention, and I was once again a reporter covering the board meeting.

We shook hands, and he introduced me to his two companions. One of them was his personal attorney, George Fitzgerald, who had been at his side at the Senate hearing. The other was someone I'd met before, a kind of combination guide, press agent, and steward called Nate. After a moment's conversation, Hoffa invited me to join them at dinner.

As I slid into the back seat of a Cadillac next to Hoffa, I noticed his white socks, in sharp, incongruous contrast to his black shoes and dark suit. But still he looked nattier than when I had seen him last year.

It wasn't only in his clothes that Hoffa had changed, though, I discovered while we drove to the restaurant. He seemed more cautious in his speech, more conscious that millions of eyes and ears could be quickly focused on him. Once, after making an especially pungent and witty remark about an opponent, he asked me, somewhat apologetically, not to quote him because "It might be bad for public relations."

We talked about his recent difficulties. He complained bitterly about the wiretaps to which he had been subjected. He seemed chastened rather than angry about his experiences before the McClellan Committee. But when he spoke of being followed by police and of his indictment on the bribery charge, the scorn in his voice brought me back to the earlier Hoffa.

At the restaurant Nate kept urging us to try the steak Sinatra —"It's steak fixed with peppers just like Sinatra likes it. It's gorgeous."

"O.K.," said Hoffa, who obviously couldn't have cared less.

We talked about Johnny Dio and Hoffa's reported offer to take care of Dio's family while he was in jail. "I'd do that for anyone," Hoffa said. "If you went to jail, maybe I'd take care of your family. Besides, I'm not so convinced he isn't getting a bum rap. Maybe he wasn't guilty."

Hoffa and I started talking about the Teamsters and their forthcoming executive-board meeting. He spoke as if he were already president of the union, predicting what would happen at the sessions. He discussed some of the constitutional changes that would be recommended to the convention, explaining that they "will take away some of the president's authority and give it back to the executive board, where it really belongs."

We talked of the possible expulsion of the Teamsters from the AFL-CIO. "I don't think the AFL-CIO wants an inter-union fight any more than the Teamsters," Hoffa said, "but if they do, we'll give it to them."

He told me in detail all the things the union was doing to avoid expulsion. Brennan, the vice-president convicted of extortion, probably wasn't going to run again; Beck was retiring and so was no longer an issue, he explained; and if the Ethical Practices Committee filed charges against him (as it did a few days later) he was prepared to answer them. The union would adopt all the ethical-practices codes except those prohibiting union office to men who used the Fifth Amendment or had past criminal records. But Frank Brewster, the vice-president convicted of congressional contempt, and Frank Matula, the Los Angeles Teamster official convicted of perjury, were to be supported. "Those are only technical convictions, not like a morals charge, or selling dope, stealing union funds, or taking dough from an employer for signing a lousy contract. Plenty of our guys have technical convictions. We built this union with muscle, and I'm not turning my back on the muscle like some other union leaders who use it and then pretend they never did."

The steak and peppers arrived. "Gorgeous, huh?" said Nate. "Just like Sinatra likes it. The boss went into the kitchen and fixed it himself for you."

Now we began discussing the "paper" locals in New York, allegedly chartered to help Hoffa get control of the New York Teamsters Council. "I'm going to bring up the question of those charters at the board meeting. If those guys did what they're accused of doing, they're out." He added contemptuously, "They're nothing but a bunch of drugstore cowboys, anyway." I remembered that he hadn't always talked about them that way.

Nate paid the bill, and we left the restaurant and got back in the car, Hoffa and I again in back. We stopped to get the morning newspapers from a vendor at the curb. "Gimme three sets!" hollered Nate.

Hoffa took the papers from Nate, shoving them aside with

hardly more than a glance, although the big headlines shouted about the Teamster meeting and his picture was featured prominently on the front pages. "Who cares?" he said indifferently.

But I think Hoffa does care now.

INTRODUCTION

N O O T H E R S I N G L E area of Hoffa's activities has caused him as much public difficulty as his continuing relationships with men of the underworld. All sorts of theories have been advanced to account for Hoffa's keeping convicted extortionists on the Teamster payroll and his refusal to condemn the racketeers inside the union. It is suggested that he is so indebted to the underworld for its help in his rise to power that he is its prisoner. The hypothesis has also been advanced that Hoffa's personal code of private loyalty is much more important to him than his public reputation, especially since most Teamsters seem totally uninterested in what the world thinks of their union leader. It's very possible that no satisfactory explanation can yet be given.

In my own experience with Hoffa, sharp questions about his relationship to men of the underworld are almost sure to evoke an outburst of anger from him.

Yet, the links that hold Hoffa to the garishly lit but still very shadowy worlds of Las Vegas and Chicago, for example, are most relevant in analyzing the relationship of the union to the business community in which it operates. No oil company ever offered me a bribe and I have never heard of an official of the steelworkers' or auto workers' unions who had any "deals" going for him with U. S. Steel or GM. But such corporations are a far cry from the marginal employers who once made up the bulk of the trucking industry. Since most unions reflect the patterns of the industry in which they operate, it's not likely that the teamsters will change except as the industry changes too, moving from marginality to respectability.

HOFFA
AND
THE
UNDERWORLD

(1959) I T W A S A L L very odd, even eerie, as
if by some trick one of my youthful political fantasies had come
true in a perverted form. There I sat, in a union hall jammed
with cheering truck drivers, listening to their union president
denounce the capitalist press, radio, and TV as instruments of
the bosses and shouting at the tough, burly teamsters that they
could never expect anything from their employers and that without the union they were helpless.

The reality of that meeting was tinged with fantasy for me
because it took place not during the hectic thirties, in Minneapolis, when the Dunne brothers, leaders of Teamster Local
544, were the heroes of the Trotskyite movement, but in 1959.
This meeting was in Detroit and the speaker was Jimmy Hoffa,
talking to his own local union while a CBS crew filmed him for
TV.

Now, obviously Jimmy Hoffa is not committed to over-
throwing the capitalist system. Indeed, quite the opposite is
true—Hoffa is a staunch defender of American capitalism
(after all, it's been very good to him) and his speech was a
singular exercise in vulgar demagogery. But at that union meeting Hoffa symbolized, as he does in general, some of the most
crucial problems facing the American trade unions.

Except in one extremely important way, I consider Hoffa a
characteristic product of the old AFL tradition. I've known
Hoffa for only three years, ever since I went to Detroit to write
about him for *The Reporter,* but during this time I've seen him

(47)

in a wide variety of circumstances, behaving in many different ways. In spite of these opportunities and though I've frequently talked to him at length, followed the McClellan Committee's hearings rather carefully, read a great deal about him and often discussed him with his subordinates, as well as with employers, public officials, and knowledgeable newspapermen, Hoffa remains an enigma to me.

Hoffa is still pretty spontaneous, although growing more cautious in his public speech. He exudes cockiness and ebullience; he has a great sense of native wit; he can be absolutely charming as he smiles with a boyish, dimpled grin; he's exceedingly smart and he works very, very hard at his job of running the Teamsters. Indeed, that's all he does. There is little overt hypocrisy about Hoffa and a great deal of apparent forthrightness.

But there is another side to him as well, a more frightening one. When Hoffa becomes really angry, his gray-green eyes get incredibly cold and menacing. It's then that his ruthlessness, his obvious belief in physical violence as an instrument of power, shows through as an important element in his personality. Usually the quest for power is but one motivation in a leader's life, but in Hoffa's case, power, linked with a desire to be feared rather than loved, seems an obsession. He has great contempt for and distrust of most people. He is tied, by strange cords, to the brutal men of the underworld. Still, other union leaders grow angry when crossed; others are avaricious for power; others use violence. It is Hoffa's attitude to the underworld that sets him apart.

Whether or not Hoffa has alliances with the underworld, he is certainly very tolerant of it. It is not enough of an explanation for his attitude to say that from a moral viewpoint he does not really recognize the underworld's existence. To Hoffa almost all of society is peopled by businessmen looking to make a fast buck; politicians who, like ex-Senator George Bender, say,

"If cats and dogs could vote, I would shake hands with them.
. . . You don't have to become a prostitute yourself but sometimes you have to get their votes"; police officers on the take;
respected insurance companies willing, indeed anxious, to give
kickbacks to union officials in exchange for welfare and pension
fund accounts; lawyers willing to make payoffs to get "good
deals" for their business clients; and employers who try to
cheat their workers while stealing from their customers.

But even this cynical view of the world, in which personal
loyalty and not squealing to the cops become the basic vir-
tues, does not totally explain Hoffa's ties to the underworld.
For Hoffa must also know that this area is where he is most
vulnerable, if not as yet to the law, at least to the blows of
public and private opinion. Nevertheless, he has continually resisted purging the Teamsters of those elements that only with
the greatest charity can be described as being even on the
fringes of decency.

And while the presence of criminal elements in the union may
be explained by the fact that the trucking industry has always
been the kind of marginal business which hovers between ir-
respectability and crime, it does not explain Hoffa's willingness to permit the continued access of criminals to Teamster
locals. It is true that even when the Trotskyites controlled the
Minneapolis Teamsters there were mysterious underworld relationships that occasionally rose from beneath the surface. A
local Teamsters Union president in Minneapolis was once mur-
dered under strange conditions and gangster elements once attempted, unsuccessfully, to muscle into one of the locals. It was
the revolutionary ideology of the Trotskyite leadership, their
commitment to use the Teamsters Union for a larger political
purpose, that most effectively prevented the underworld from
getting a foothold, either through force or collaboration, during
their tenure of office.

It is (as we would have said once upon an ancient time) by
no means an accident that Hoffa's power base, his home local,

is a drivers' local. These are men who generally have little formal education in a period of American life when high school
has been extended another two years through the creation of
the junior college. These are men physically isolated from each
other at work, frequently away when union meetings are held,
dependent upon business agents rather than fellow members
for the protection of their rights, working in an industry to which
respectability has been late in coming and where the police, on
highways and in towns, are rarely thought of as friends.

The industry tradition of toughness, the isolated conditions
of work and the special characteristics of the drivers help define
the loose boundaries of the moral territory in which Hoffa
roams without great complaints from his union membership.
In a hostile and dangerous work world, where toughness for
both employers and employees is essential to survival, where
the union contract is necessarily complicated, where it is expected that an employer will try to cheat his employees and
vice versa, it is only natural for the members gladly to abdicate
responsibility to the toughest and smartest of them all—Jimmy,
who may be a son of a bitch but is, after all, "our" son of a
bitch. And if he makes deals with the underworld . . . well,
that's the way of the world.

Hoffa's possible underworld relationships seem to me the
most important questions thus far posed about him. Indeed,
many of the Teamster procedures, which seemed so extraordinary to the McClellan Committee, are common to other unions
and have significance only when related to substantive problems. But Hoffa's underworld ties do mark him off from many
other union leaders with whom he otherwise has much more in
common than is generally admitted. Unfortunately, the Mc-
Clellan Committee staff came to their work unequipped to
make distinctions between matters of substance and of in-
significance.

In addition to Robert Kennedy's obvious obsession with the
pursuit of Hoffa, what was primarily lacking in the McClellan
Committee was a sense of judgment. As a result, the real problems of the American trade unions have become obscured by

masses of sensational triviality, dredged up by the committee staff. This is not to suggest that the committee's task would have been an easy one, even if Kennedy has been less naïve than he was about trade unions and business. Once the ethics of American business society are accepted as normal, only fine lines separate "proper" practices from "improper" ones.

Quite apart from the particular case of Hoffa, I do not believe that the general problem of the relationship between the underworld and other segments of our society has been explored with sufficient seriousness. Gus Tyler of the ILGWU has been pointing at the problem for some time and I agree completely with him that we must look into this aspect of American life far more searchingly.

It is true that there are enormous handicaps facing such an enterprise—the lack of access to information; the fact that, unlike government, business, or the unions, there are so few ex-radical comrades in the underworld, able to have some perspective on it; the overwhelming truth that the price for betraying the underworld is almost always death or something just short of it; and the fact that important political interests are linked to the underworld. Nevertheless, there has been surprisingly little serious attention paid to this phenomenon. Perhaps if a serious study were made, we would learn a great deal about the development of the underworld in general, rather than only in individual unions. One trouble, of course, is that no one in the modern underworld writes his memoirs. Lepke's view of American society would have been fascinating and Frank Costello's even more so.

In the case of unions, it is easily understandable why, until recently, less attention has been paid to the underworld than to other problems. There is a general disposition on the part of writers sympathetic to the stated aspirations of the unions to ignore the underworld's presence even if they are aware of it. I also suspect that, in spite of the adverse newspaper publicity, there is much less underworld infiltration of unions than of business. The unions in mass production industries are less vulnerable to underworld operations than are business enterprises, and there are still very many union leaders whose radical pasts or middle-class presents act as barriers to underworld infiltration.

Since so little is actually known about Hoffa's possible relations to the underworld, it is extremely difficult to compare him, on this score, with other union leaders who have also had some connections, by choice or necessity, with either the true underworld or the prosperous demimonde of American society. I suspect, as I've indicated, that here there may be a marked difference between Hoffa and other union officials, but, fascinating as the subject is, a discussion about it must inevitably peter out in gross speculation.

In other ways, however, Hoffa is much more comparable to one fairly large group of union leaders. Since he's franker than most of the others and more willing openly to state his real beliefs about the role of American unions and union leaders, he provides a most useful model, albeit of extreme design, which can be used as a comparison check for one type of union leader in America.

How much of Hoffa's apparent candor is a pose and how much is truly a reflection of his conviction is an intriguing question. Almost all of the journalists who have spent time with him are quickly shaken by the discrepancy between his public image and what appears to be the private reality, as revealed by his hard work, lack of hypocrisy, and strange quality of frankness. These attributes are so refreshing and appealing in comparison with the worn-out jazz, boringly repeated *ad nauseam,* by some of the sanctimonious, self-righteous, and stupid monomaniacs in union leadership, that there is a tendency, which one must guard against, to gloss over some of Hoffa's faults.

It may also be that what disturbs many people, in and out of trade unions, is Hoffa's unwillingness to play the game, making a buck here and there, getting fat on the expense account, and still keeping a civil tongue in his cheek by talking like everyone else. For some reason, perhaps rooted in his past and in his own image of himself, Hoffa, except when forced to by a consciousness of public-relations problems, refuses to live up to the surface standards of American society. My hunch is that this flows from (as also we would once have said) his contempt for most people. But if in these personal characteristics he is different from most American union leaders, in many other ways he is far more like them.

Hoffa's completely paternalistic attitude toward the Teamsters is one common denominator he shares with other union leaders. The members of the Teamsters Union are Hoffa's constituency: he takes care of them, and in Hoffa's case this is done personally, through direct contact. Hoffa is probably the only international president who still runs the affairs of his own local while carrying out his other work. He is on the phone every day from Washington to Detroit, conducting local business, and he attends local meetings at least every six weeks, settling shop grievances, giving contract interpretations, speaking to new groups of workers as they are being organized, and generally behaving as an extremely active local leader.

In return for his work on their behalf, Hoffa demands total loyalty from the union members and his staff. He is probably more accessible to them than the president of any other international union in the U.S. Since Hoffa's feeling that he is the key element in the success of the Teamsters Union is also shared by his staff and followers, he rarely faces palace revolutions or even the threat of them; his staff and much of his membership share his belief that they are dependent upon him for survival.

But is any union leader more paternalistic than Dubinsky? Does Reuther permit any less personal loyalty than Hoffa? When for the first time McDonald faced opposition from within the steelworkers' union, wasn't his administration's entire machinery put into high gear to smash the possible revolt? Paternalism, the leader's identification of the union with himself, and the demand for personal loyalty are hardly unique to Hoffa and the Teamsters; all that is unique is that Hoffa has been more gauche about doing what other union leaders have learned to do with finesse. "I've had to do everything myself to make this union a success," he once told me, openly stating, without modesty, what many others believe true but do not say of themselves.

Like some other union leaders, Hoffa views the union as his personal property, a resource available to him for his disposal as he sees fit, restricted only by the bothersome limitations imposed upon him by law plus some vague and undefined attitudes of doing "good" for the membership. He always speaks of the Teamsters as "my union" and the "my" here carries the connotation of personal property in addition to that of pride.

To Hoffa dues money is akin to the operating capital of a business. This view of the union as an institution whose resources can be *incidentally* used for the personal financial benefit of its leaders is reinforced by those institutions that seek business from unions. Certain insurance companies, for example, hot in pursuit of the vast sums of money now available in welfare and pension funds, have always sought to persuade union leaders that the choice of which insurance carrier got the union account was fundamentally a matter of the leader's personal preference, a preference which they then tried to affect in a variety of ways.

There is a wider range of attitudes among trade union leaders and members on this question than on the identification of the union with its leader, but I think that at least a few other union leaders secretly share Hoffa's attitude toward the union treasury. They feel restrained from acting out their beliefs by fear of exposure, by the internal controls of the unions, or by the carryover of attitudes formed when their organizations were struggling to survive.

When, however, one examines the far less important but curiously troublesome problem of expense accounts, the distinctions between union leaders grow less sharp even among those who reject Hoffa's view of the treasury as a vehicle of personal power. I am not here concerned so much with the possible financial rape of a union treasury through the exploitation of expense accounts (though this is possible in rare cases) as I am with the "legitimate" use of expense accounts while on union business, or the practice, not at all restricted to unions, of manufacturing a reason to take a trip and then justifying it by the excuse of "business." Neither the McClellan Committee nor anyone else has examined, at any great length, the use of expense accounts by unions or industry. To do so would have raised the entire question of the role played by the expense account for nearly everybody in society—for the businessman who goes to Las Vegas with a customer, for the corporation which spends thousands of dollars entertaining foreign buyers, and for the defense industry that flies high-ranking military officers to lush Bahamian islands for "conferences."

This is only one instance of practices now common in all of our society, practices which to union leaders like Hoffa are built into the very matrix of the world. One of the reasons for Hoffa's deep cynicism is that he continually contrasts the stated ideals of society with the actions of its members and then concludes from the comparison that the only common denominator for all people is hypocrisy.

A case in point was the recent meeting of the AFL-CIO executive council in Puerto Rico. Traditionally, before the merger with the CIO, winter meetings of the old AFL council had been held in Miami Beach. George Meany wanted last winter's meeting of the AFL-CIO council again to be held there, but the council, under goading from some of its members, either more ascetic or more conscious of public pressure, voted against Florida as the site for the meeting.

It was then that Meany "arranged" for the council to be invited to Puerto Rico, which is also a very pleasant place to be during the winter. As for Hoffa, he went ahead and held his board meeting in Miami, as usual, giving no explanations, using no subterfuges and feeling no need to justify his decision.

Let me make clear that what concerns me here is not whether other union leaders are more hypocritical than Hoffa. Some are, some are not. That is really no matter. What does seem important to me is that Hoffa does share with many other union leaders a common set of values and aspirations, based, naturally, on the predominant mores of American society.

"Don't give me that!" says Hoffa scornfully to me when I argue heatedly with him about the narrowness, in his perspective, of trade union purposes. "What do you think I am, the State Department? I don't want to get into world politics. I have enough trouble taking care of my own members."

"If I had a bunch of Detroit cops here, I'd clean out these joints in no time," he said disgustedly as we once strolled, loudly quarreling, along Grant Avenue, the Boulevard of the Beats, in San Francisco. "All these people need is a bath," he sneered scornfully as he looked at the habitués of the Co-existence Bagel Shop, thus expressing the most primitive reactions to anything out of the ordinary, anything disturbing the status quo; reactions more quietly shared by most other union leaders.

"I don't want to change the world," says Hoffa, and here again he only states openly what many other American union leaders actually believe, in spite of all the resolutions dutifully passed by them at all the conventions.

When Hoffa says he doesn't want to change the world, he is speaking for those union leaders who don't even want to change their own unions. Except for a few men, considered oddballs by their colleagues and, to a great extent, by their members, most American union officials are convinced that fundamentally the world in which they have achieved leadership is the best of all possible worlds and needs few changes, either externally or internally.

Indeed, I believe that if it had not been for the pressure exerted upon Meany by some of the old CIO leaders, coupled with the public attention given to the problems of corruption, the federation would not have expelled the Teamsters. Instead, it would have tried to maintain its traditional attitude of giving complete autonomy to international unions and distrusting any disturbance in the status quo, which is, after all, a good one, by and large, for most union leaders and members. It seems fairly clear, at this point, that the attempt within the federation to give the headquarters effective power over the affiliates, as in the old

CIO, is failing. On the ethical-practices level, the operating engineers and carpenters are still within the family; the NAACP complains bitterly that nothing has been done to take action against unions violating the civil rights provisions of the constitution; and jurisdictional battles go on, only slightly affected by decisions of either the umpire or council itself.

Let's now refer to the issue of democracy in the Teamsters, comparing Hoffa's union with others. During the CBS television show on the Teamsters, several shop stewards were interviewed and discussed the low attendance at union meetings. To outsiders, especially liberal outsiders, the fact that only a small percentage of union members attend meetings is somehow taken as an indication that undemocratic practices prevail. Yet the Teamster attendance record is probably neither better nor worse than that of any other union—throughout the unions attendance at normal meetings is poor. For many years, at union summer camps and training schools there have been dreary sessions devoted to increasing membership participation at local meetings. But attendance still remains the same—low. Suppose, however, it didn't. Suppose it went sharply up and there was none of the intimidation of members which may, in fact, exist in some Teamster locals. What problems would be solved? Does anyone seriously believe that Hoffa would not be overwhelmingly re-elected Teamster president even if every Teamster member voted in a secret ballot election? Would this fact make it right for Hoffa to be president?

Attempts to equate "democracy" in unions with membership participation conjure up sharp dilemmas within the Teamsters. At the moment, Hoffa is engaged in a struggle with a court-appointed board of monitors over his right to hold the presidency of the union. For months, Hoffa has been attempting to hold a union convention and have his right to the presidency reaffirmed by the convention delegates. The monitors, however, have thus far refused and instead are preparing court actions to have Hoffa removed from his office.

But Hoffa's desire for a convention and the monitors' refusal to permit it are obviously based on his and their belief that such a convention would certainly elect Hoffa president, even without his having to stuff ballot boxes, illegally elect delegates, or in any way attempt to influence improperly the choice of delegates to the convention.

In this situation the courts, through the monitors, are being asked to prevent the direct control of the union by its members —one form of that "union democracy" so glibly idealized by Congress and the press. I am not here suggesting that because Hoffa is the membership's choice therefore the membership is right; I am only trying to point out that "union democracy" in the sense of a free membership choice of a union president is not really wanted by many who plump loudly for it if the results are known, in advance, to be contrary to the generally accepted standards of public good or particular private interests. In this case, the generally accepted standards mean keeping Hoffa from the presidency, if possible, even though the membership may want him there.

One rather interesting element in this situation is that the remainder of the trade union leadership has been silent on this attempted intrusion by the monitors and courts into the Teamsters' internal life. If, as seems possible, Hoffa is prevented from holding an election and then deposed from the presidency, it could easily set a precedent for similar court action in other cases. Yet the possibility has not brought any public protest or comment from other union leaders in the AFL-CIO probably because, no matter what their feelings, it would be considered impolitic for any union leader publicly to identify himself with Hoffa in this situation. Similarly, even when the McClellan Committee attacked the teamsters incorrectly or for policies carried out by many other unions, there was deep silence from the AFL-CIO.

Yet there seems to be another consequence of the attempts of Congress and the monitors to remove Hoffa: sympathy with him appears to be building up within his own union and possibly among other union leaders. Just as the U.S. Government made a martyr out of Harry Bridges so Hoffa, in spite of all the Mc-

Clellan Committee's revelations about him, is beginning to take on the air of a man who is being harassed. When Hoffa addressed a recent meeting in San Francisco of the Western Conference of Teamsters, he shared the platform with and was applauded by the president of the very large California AFL-CIO and by its secretary-treasurer, the single most powerful labor leader in the state. Somehow, these officials feel more comfortable with Hoffa than with other, more ideological, leaders. Hoffa, more than Reuther, is their kind of a guy.

The sometimes public and more frequently private attitude of friendliness maintained by other union leaders toward Hoffa is also accounted for by simple economic self-interest. Strategically, the Teamsters are in an excellent position to assist or hurt other unions, and it is the recognition of this power, for example, that lies behind Hoffa's attempts, for three years, to bring about an alliance between the Teamsters and Harry Bridges' International Longshoremen and Warehousemen's Union.

Vis-à-vis their membership and the society at large, Bridges and Hoffa play startlingly similar roles. Both are outcasts or, more correctly, since it was not a voluntary act in either case, both are cast-outs from the main institutions of labor; organized opposition groups are as nonexistent in the ILWU as in the Teamsters; and both Bridges and Hoffa, oddly enough, have rather intellectual seconds-in-command—the Communist party-oriented Louis Goldblatt in the ILWU and the ex-Socialist Harold Gibbons in the Teamsters. Hoffa and Bridges are both tough, raw, and not especially cultivated. Nor are Hoffa's bad English (steadily improving) and Bridges' Australian accent with its cockney overtones handicaps to them, considering their membership.

Neither the Teamster nor ILWU membership appears disturbed about an alliance, although a merger would be far more difficult to sell to the ILWU ranks. In the case of the Teamster members, their expectations of Hoffa are of a simple order. Like most other union members, they are content, on the whole, with the wage increases he brings them and willing, indeed anxious, to abdicate to him all responsibility for making serious policy decisions. The great majority of them do not conceive of the union as either an instrument for the carrying out of any social ideals or as an arena in which they can seek leadership positions.

If a Teamster member does desire to be a union leader, he rarely pursues his goal through challenging the existing administration. Rather, he seeks to become part of the administration and attach himself to the leader in power. Here, too, there is a great similarity between the Teamsters and other unions. The special conditions of Teamster members, their lack of education, their isolated work, the character of the industry, etc., only define the particular ways in which the union operates but do not fundamentally differentiate the members from those in other unions.

Is it possible to raise the membership's expectations of Hoffa? Or must he be restrained from the outside? There are some who think neither of these alternatives is the answer but that the solution is in raising Hoffa's level of aspirations. I am dubious about this last possibility. Hoffa's only real interest is the economic role of the Teamsters Union and the power he derives from it. Never in any conversation has Hoffa displayed any concern except for the very narrowest of worlds. Within those worlds, he's enormously knowledgeable; outside them very ignorant, although obviously capable of learning quickly. But he evinces no real desire either to broaden his intellectual horizons or change many of his basic attitudes.

What does the future hold for Hoffa and the Teamsters? Predictions are always dangerous, but assuming that Hoffa retains his leadership of the union either overtly or covertly, the Teamsters should continue to grow faster than many other unions. The American industrial economy is changing rapidly. Automation is replacing large-scale worker production of goods while the work force in the service and distributive trades is increasing. Unions like the steel, auto, and rubber unions, dependent on mass production industries, will decline in membership while the Teamsters, organized more on the pattern of the English general union, has the opportunity of growth.

While I was in Detroit with the CBS television crew, I heard Hoffa speak to a group of city employees from Dearborn, Michigan, who were attempting to organize a Teamster local there. I sat in the rear of the room watching Hoffa assure them of his support and thinking how curious it was that a group of city employees, generally a conservative group, would come to Hoffa and the Teamsters in the face of the violent public attacks upon the union. Then I realized that these city employees were mad, damn mad, at their employer and I remembered, from my own experience as a union organizer, that when workers are angry enough voluntarily to organize themselves, at some risk to their jobs, what they seek in a union leader is, above all, the quality of toughness, so important in the American tradition. They want a union leader who, they believe, can solve their particular problems with their employer now, not one concerned with world affairs. It is precisely because Hoffa reflects the narrow but very sharp demands of American workers that his thundering against employers sounds like the rumbles of the class war. However, like a summer storm, far off in the distance, the sound is an illusion—to Hoffa, and his members, the class war is only a short engagement, occasionally violent, fought with no weapons barred, no quarter asked or given, but quickly ended by the signing of a new contract.

Thus workers come to Hoffa and they will probably continue coming to Hoffa, for Hoffa, without social concepts, is at least as much in the tradition of the successful American labor leader as is Reuther, with his deep concern for abstract ideas of justice.

INTRODUCTION

B Y 1962, Hoffa was no longer quite so much the figure of a crude racketeer that had emerged from the McClellan Committee hearings. The court-established monitorship over the Teamsters Union had ended and Hoffa had been elected the union president, as everyone expected him to be. His trials continued, though, both literally and figuratively, as Robert Kennedy, now Attorney General, continued the pursuit of Hoffa that had begun in 1957 but had still not come to a satisfactory conclusion, from Kennedy's viewpoint, with Hoffa in jail.

But the indictments, trials, appeals, reversals had lost much of their old interest. Perhaps there were too many of them, perhaps the public was getting bored with the continuous process. And Hoffa, too, was less flamboyant, more conscious that he was in the public view, and more interested in giving the public a better view of himself. Even when he got into a fist fight with one of his assistants, with whom his relationship had always been bad, the case died pretty quickly. And Hoffa continued to spend almost all of his time doing the only thing that seems to interest him—building his power in the union by moving continually all over the country to participate in contract negotiations and the settlement of disputes.

THE RESPECTABLE MR. HOFFA

(1962)   THE HUGE TRUCK pulled slowly
around the corner in San Francisco and jockeyed into position
alongside the curb, its long van docilely following the tractor
into place. The driver cut the noisy engine and wearily stretched
his arms inside the cab. Suddenly, a big car pulled up in front
of him. A short, stocky, hatless man walked back to the truck
cab and started speaking to the driver on the seat.

"I'm Hoffa," the man said. "What's your beef about the contract I'm trying to get?"

"Yeah, you're Hoffa," said the driver, "and I'm the King of
England. Now what do you really want, buddy?"

"No, I am Hoffa," the man answered patiently, "and I want
to know what your beef is. So start talking."

The driver took a close look at the powerful figure standing
next to the truck. "I'll be a son of a bitch. You really are Hoffa.
I'll be a son of a bitch. I've been a member of this union for ten
years and I never once saw a business agent out on the job, but
now the president of the union comes up to me on the street
and asks me my beef. I'll be a son of a bitch!"

"Who's your business agent?" a coldly furious Hoffa asked.
Given the name by the driver, Hoffa turned to one of his assistants who, like the driver's van, follows wherever he goes, and
said, "Fire that guy. I don't ever want to see him around again."

It doesn't actually matter, from Hoffa's viewpoint, whether
or not the business agent stays fired or gets transferred to another job some place. So far as that one truckdriver is concerned, and all the other drivers to whom he tells the story as

he sits drinking coffee in cafés from San Francisco to Denver, Jimmy Hoffa is the greatest union president in the world.

But that's not enough for Hoffa any more; for Jimmy Hoffa is trying hard to become respectable. And he might make it yet, too. These days, as he sits in his sumptuous Washington office overlooking the Capitol, it is only his still uninhibited language—"that guy belongs in a hatchhouse," "George Meany is a dopey, thickheaded Irishman," that, on the surface, at least, is a colorful and often profane reminder of the earlier Hoffa, that tough Detroit kid who stacked boxes in a grocery warehouse and grew up to be the hard-nosed president of the Teamsters Union, the largest union in the United States.

Even Hoffa's clothes reflect his shift in the direction of respectability. He no longer wears cheap, ill-fitting suits that look as if they had been put on right off the rack of a chain-store operation, nor ties that were slipped over his head, still knotted from the night before. Now, Hoffa is attired in well-tailored, custom-made suits, heavy white shirts, and matching silk ties. Even his socks have changed—the white cotton type he always used have given way to expensive colored ones, but only colored on the outside; on the inside, they are still lined with white cotton.

If Hoffa does achieve his goal of respectability, he will have completed a twentieth-century success saga in the old American tradition—from rags to riches, from disrepute to respectability, from snarling alley fights with his fists or a tire chain to decorous nationwide TV debates with the president of the United States Chamber of Commerce. And if Hoffa beats the latest legal charges against him in the Florida court where he is soon to be tried for using the mails to defraud, he'll just about have it made.

Clearly, one of the most amazing things about Hoffa is that he's still around at all and not sitting in some penitentiary cell. Five years ago, only a foolish man would have bet that Hoffa could escape jail, or at least enough public opprobrium to send him slinking off into some tiny corner of the United States to live out his life in hopeless obscurity. But instead he has not only survived but even thrived on a public attack by the President of the United States; a continual war waged against him by Congress and the Department of Justice; three arrests on charges for which it seemed absolutely certain he must be convicted; the official enmity of the AFL-CIO; a concerted attempt to use the courts to dump him from his presidency of the Teamsters Union, and a generally hostile press. As if this weren't enough, Hoffa has also had to escape the heavy burden he put and keeps on his own back when he spits in the public's face by openly flaunting his relationships with the underworld.

But even though the Teamsters Union treasury has provided Hoffa with a well equipped survival kit, and even though he has demonstrated great shrewdness and intelligence in using it, the real explanation for his success can only be found in the nature of American society. From that day of his first appearance in 1957 before the McClellan Committee, the tough, cocky union leader had a lot of things "going for him," as he would say, below the surface of American life. The distaste, even horror, with which he was viewed in the beginning gradually became mixed with a curious kind of admiration for a little guy who defied authority, wouldn't buckle under the relentless probing of Bobby Kennedy, wouldn't cringe under the pressures, wouldn't turn his back on old associates, even if they were very unsavory characters. Hoffa also managed to leave an impression, even if it wasn't the reality, of bluntly answering all the queries put to him. He is a Jimmy Cagney movie villain come to life and, like the original Cagney character, who pushed a grapefruit in his girl's face, he is also something of a hero-villain—a figure that has always been an important part of American culture.

In his fight to survive, Hoffa has also had another great asset: to the members of his union, whose support he must have, he is the man in charge of the cornucopia. And to workers in an industry not especially noted for its high ethical standards, the charge that Hoffa is getting rich illegally makes very little impression. "Sure, Jimmy might be taking some off the top for himself," the truckdrivers say, "but he's taking damned good care of us, too, so what do we care? All we know is that we're making a lot more dough and living a damned sight better out on the road. For our money, Jimmy's worth as much as he can get."

It's not important, in understanding Hoffa's power within the union, whether it's true that he is responsible for the great improvements in the lives of the truckdrivers; most members of the Teamsters Union believe it's so. They are convinced that Hoffa is doing a good job for them. He's continually on the move, appearing in all the important sets of negotiations, speaking at state and regional council meetings, and continually suggesting that the only reason he's being persecuted by the government is because of his work on their behalf; in their minds, he is very much one of them.

And because the Teamsters think he's one of them, they resent attempts from the outside to get at him. "Let the teamster fight the teamster," said one of Hoffa's most bitter opponents inside the union a few years ago, rejecting the idea that a battle against Hoffa should be financed from outside the union. The same kind of sentiments were expressed at last year's union convention by Hoffa's only opponent for the presidency after he was overwhelmingly defeated in his bid for Hoffa's job. "Maybe he's a son of a bitch, but, if he is, he's our son of a bitch," seems to pretty well sum up the attitude of Hoffa's union members toward the attempts of all the forces outside the Teamsters, including the government, who have been trying either to dump him from the presidency of the union, to put him in jail, or, preferably, both.

In Hoffa's present drive for respectability, he can count on some support from those of his former colleagues in the AFL-CIO who either need the support of the Teamsters on the picket line, or see in him an answer to the vacuum of power that will be left in the AFL-CIO when George Meany retires as president. Officially, Hoffa is an outlaw to the AFL-CIO, but there are many federation leaders who still maintain private relationships with the Teamster president, and even a few who do it openly, including three presidents of AFL-CIO unions who defied the federation's edict against Hoffa by addressing the last Teamster convention as official guests of the union.

As part of his attempt to regain leadership for the Teamsters in the AFL-CIO, Hoffa scheduled a meeting of the union's executive board in Miami at the same time as the federation's convention was held there in December, 1961. Some of his trusted lieutenants spent hours conferring on strategy with the AFL-CIO officials at the convention, and although they were unsuccessful, there is a good possibility that in a few more years the Teamsters will be readmitted, assuming, of course, that Hoffa stays out of jail during that time.

In Hoffa's attempt to be regarded as he thinks he should be —as a businessman, who happens to be in "the labor business" —there is the attitude of those other American businessmen with whom Hoffa deals. They are generally sympathetic to him. They not only don't draw back in horror from his sins, but many of them even share common aspirations with him and wish they could get their hands on some of those sins, too. To the owner of a fleet of trucks mostly interested in making a buck, Hoffa is a perfectly understandable guy, the kind of union leader all union leaders ought to be. His promise is good, he knows the problems of the industry, and they know that Hoffa won't open up a set of negotiations with a lot of talk about the social responsibility of the employers, the way Walter Reuther would do. When Senator Barry Goldwater told Jimmy Hoffa that he hoped Hoffa would win out over Reuther if the two had a fight, he was only publicly saying what many businessmen privately believe.

Hoffa, too, believes in the "American way," and, as he understands it, that "way" means that union leaders should limit their activities to getting as good a deal as they can for their union members in contract negotiations. As for what goes on in union leaders' private lives, well, here Hoffa shrugs and only complains cynically about the fact that while his private life is continually being made public through congressional interrogations, other "businessmen," who do far worse things, are left alone because, in Hoffa's view, they're corporation presidents instead of union leaders.

But if Hoffa manages to remain as Teamster president a few more years, he, too, will end up being accepted by society instead of hanging around its outside, still a marginal figure. Certainly, it will be a long step for him in that direction if he ever breaks that curious hold the demi-world has on him or the attraction he finds in it. But even if he doesn't cut himself off from some of the more sordid types who now hang around him, like sucker fish parasitically feeding on their host, he might still become respectable in most circles. After all, he won't be the first nor probably the last figure in American life to have kicked and clawed his way to the top and, exuding the smell of power, be crowned king of the hill.

Perhaps someday there will even be a Hoffa Foundation established and then Hoffa's sins will be forgotten as he achieves respectability like so many others before, even though their transgressions were equal to his.

INTRODUCTION

W H E N I S A W Hoffa during the spring of 1963, he was in San Francisco as an honored guest speaker at the International Longshoremen and Warehousemen's Union convention. We kibitzed a bit, as we always do, and then he told me that some of his "boys" were pretty angry with me about the last articles I had written about him. Hoffa wasn't sure just which articles were the offensive ones nor was he personally upset by them. Rather, he seemed to assume that he was going to be attacked in print by me and most writers, accepting such attacks as part of the natural order: after all, Hoffa's view of the world is one in which "give and take" refers to lumps on the head, not love.

But when Hoffa began talking about Bobby Kennedy, he grew angry and bitter. Hoffa is completely convinced that he is the object of a massive persecution effort in which all the giant resources of the government are being marshaled against him. He talks of telephone taps, of great numbers of Justice Department lawyers and special investigators whose sole job is trying to put him in jail. As an example of this persecution, he told me that people who had come to the Nashville, Tennessee, courtroom where his last trial had been held had been photographed and then questioned later about their reasons for coming to the trial.

That trial, Hoffa's fourth, had ended in late December, 1962, the same way as had his second one—in a hung jury. It is very uncertain whether he will be tried again on the same charge. Instead, the government moved against him on the allegations that he was involved in jury-tampering and in the misuse of union pension funds.

As must be obvious from what I have written about Hoffa, my feelings about him are very mixed. He is the complete antithesis of everything I believe a union leader should be, I think his relationships with men like Harold Gross and Joey Glimco offensive and dangerous, and I am appalled by the ruthlessness I see in him. But he is a very complex personality and in some important ways he is a good deal more open than some other union leaders who share his attitudes toward society but are far more hypocritical than he. Finally, I believe Hoffa's rights have been violated in a number of important ways, and I do not accept as justification for those violations any or all the defects in Hoffa of which I am very much aware.

EXTRACURRICULAR
ACTIVITIES
OF
THE
McCLELLAN
COMMITTEE

(1963) **R**OBERT KENNEDY'S first reaction to the government's most recent and fourth failure at obtaining a conviction of Jimmy Hoffa is not certain. But whatever it was, whether or not he clasped his head and moaned when he heard the jury was unable to reach a verdict, it is almost certain that, sometime soon, he will try again to put Hoffa in jail. And perhaps he will succeed, for it does not seem possible that Hoffa, even with the giant resources of the Teamsters Union at his command, can elude, forever, the gigantic effort being made by the Justice Department to jail him.

The bitter feud between Kennedy and Hoffa has been the subject of much discussion ever since it began in 1957. But the public discussion of it has tended, inevitably, to focus on the personalities of the two men who are involved, for they are each other's public and private *bête noire*. Because the dramatic interest in this personal conflict is intense, some larger issues have been obscured. One of these is the delineation of what limits should exist for the activities of a congressional committee *outside* its legislative and investigative role.

The empowering mandate of the Senate Select Committee on Improper Activities in the Labor or Management Field, more familiarly known as the McClellan Committee, was to conduct an investigation and study of the extent to which criminal and other improper practices or activities are, or have been, engaged in the field of labor-management relations or in groups or organizations of employees, and to determine whether any changes are required in the laws . . . in order to protect such interests against the occurrence of such practices or activities.

Did the committee overstep that mandate in both its conduct of the hearings and the involvement of its staff in extracurricular activities? During the hearings, for example, when Robert Kennedy was questioning a friendly witness about a wildcat strike in St. Louis that had occurred when some union members attempted to prevent the union from placing Negro drivers, he was quick to lead the witness away from revealing his own racial bias. On another occasion, the committee was raising a great row about the specter of an alliance between the Teamsters and the International Longshoremen and Warehousemen's Union under Harry Bridges. Louis Goldblatt, secretary-treasurer of Bridges' union, was confronted at the hearings with evidence of his Communist youth in 1934 and Hoffa was questioned at length about the alliance. To further cinch this case against Hoffa, Kennedy pointed out that the ILWU had been expelled from the CIO for following the Communist party line and that, in contrast to the Teamsters, the East Coast longshoremen had indignantly refused to be part of any deal with Bridges. However, Kennedy neglected, at the time, to also point out to the committee that the East Coast longshoremen he used as an example of political virtue had been expelled from the AFL-CIO for being dominated by racketeers at the very time they were expressing their righteous horror at the idea of being associated with Communists.

The committee was not above also using anti-union employers to discredit the Teamsters or capitalizing on a witness's recourse to the Fifth Amendment on some questions to ask other unrelated ones knowing that the Fifth Amendment would be used again in answer. And the committee charged, for example,

that a conspiracy existed between Teamster officials and underworld characters to open Portland, Oregon, for gambling and
prostitution. But when the final smoke was cleared from this
fiery allegation, the committee's own star witness had been convicted while the Teamster official and the mayor, two of the
committee's main targets, had been acquitted.

David Previant, a Teamster lawyer, has listed the kinds of
"guilt" the committee used against the union:

> We had guilt by association, guilt by marriage, guilt by
> eating in the same chop house, guilt by the general coun-
> sel's amazement, guilt by somebody else taking the Fifth
> Amendment, guilt by somebody else refusing to testify. But
> we think the "doozer" was the one that happened when
> the committee was taking testimony concerning a criminal
> case in which eight defendants were tried for eleven weeks;
> the jury was out only eight minutes and came in with the
> verdict of "not guilty." The police detective who helped
> prepare the case said the prosecution felt it was not a fair
> trial. The committee nodded in sympathy and agreement.
> This is guilt by acquittal.

The entire question of how congressional hearings should be
conducted in order to protect the rights of witnesses is, and has
been for some time, a subject of continuous discussion and litigation. But the standards for the extracurricular behavior of a
congressional committee staff have not been as well defined;
when a staff is as activist in its orientation as was that of the Mc-
Clellan Committee under Robert Kennedy, the question can assume great significance.

There can be no doubt, for example, that Robert Kennedy
and the staff of the McClellan Committee played a noninvestiga-
tive, extracurricular role (1) in the fight against Hoffa within
the Teamsters Union, and (2) in assisting the anti-Hoffa representatives on the court-appointed board of monitors in their
attempt to use the board as a vehicle for ousting Hoffa and in
trying to persuade workers to vote against the Teamsters in
a labor board election. Were these actions properly within the

function of a congressional committee staff?

The initial extracurricular activity of the McClellan Committee staff was focused around the lawsuit known as *Cunningham v. English,* which developed from an internal fight within the union.

The case was born in the summer of 1957. Prior to the filing of the lawsuit, the McClellan Committee had been investigating corruption and racketeering in unions, with particular attention being paid to the Teamsters. Robert Kennedy, who was then the committee counsel and especially interested in the affairs of Dave Beck and Jimmy Hoffa, had gathered around him a staff of investigators (many of them former FBI agents) whose naïveté about unions and ignorance of union procedures were outweighed by their personal devotion to Kennedy and their commitment to the task of rooting out evil from the unions.

As the committee began its hearings, there was a sensational new headline every day, revealing some sensational new iniquity. On television screens, millions saw the very substance leak out of Dave Beck through the hundreds of holes punched in him by the barbed questions of the relentless Bobby Kennedy. And, off in the wings, coldly watching Dave Beck collapse under the heavy weight of his Fifth Amendment responses, was Jimmy Hoffa, confident that Beck's downfall meant his own election as Teamster president at the union convention scheduled for the fall of 1957. During the early stages of the investigation, Hoffa had been tried in Federal court on charges of attempting to bribe an investigator for the committee, but he was acquitted—despite a movie taken by FBI agents showing him allegedly carrying out the bribery. This acquittal was just the first of the long series of frustrating setbacks Robert Kennedy has received in his campaign to jail Hoffa. (Before the bribery trial Kennedy had been so certain of Hoffa's conviction that he, Kennedy, announced that if Hoffa were not convicted he would jump from the Capitol. Hoffa has not allowed him to forget this unfulfilled promise.)

On the surface, Hoffa was completely cocky about his forthcoming appearances before the committee, despite being indicted again by a Federal grand jury in May, 1957, just as the hearings got under way. This time the charge was wiretapping. When Hoffa's turn to appear before the committee finally did come, not uncoincidentally in the week before the Teamster convention that seemed almost certain to elect him president, Hoffa was contemptuous of Robert Kennedy and defiant of the committee's attempt to pin him down with a confession of wrongdoing. By the time Hoffa had completed the first of his numerous appearances before the committee, millions of TV screens and newspaper photos had made him so notorious that even the crews on the planes he flew would leave the cockpit to stare at him, fascinated by the aura of evil strength that had been projected around him.

It was during this hectic preconvention period that thirteen members of the Teamsters Union, from locals in the New York and New Jersey area, joined in an attempt to legally prevent the convention from being held. Although none of the thirteen men had known each other before, there had been a loose coalescence of two or three groups that had talked vaguely for months of doing something to change the leadership of the union.

One of the self-described leaders who brought the thirteen together was a former Teamster member, John Patrick Kennedy, who had been expelled from the union. "Pat" Kennedy, as he's known, said:

[P]rior to the convention in 1957—as a matter of fact, for some years preceding that—guys, me and guys like me, were fighting in our local unions about different matters. In some instances, when we were successful, the International used to come in and intercede.

Finally, me and a couple of other guys got the idea we were shoveling shit against the tide by fighting on a local level, what we ought to do is see if we could do something on the International level.

To "do something on the International level," Pat Kennedy conferred in June, 1957, with Godfrey Schmidt, a New York attorney. A short time later, Pat Kennedy and the thirteen plaintiffs met with Schmidt, "and Mr. Schmidt agreed to start the action." Cunningham, in whose name the suit to enjoin the holding of the convention was filed, had been involved in a number of prior actions against the union. He had also attempted, unsuccessfully, to get his own local investigated by a number of government agencies and the McClellan Committee.

Schmidt, their lawyer, had come to public attention in New York in a strange combination of ways, first as labor advisor to Cardinal Spellman, when the Cardinal attempted to break a strike of gravediggers in Catholic cemeteries in New York, and then as president of an organization known as "AWARE," devoted to keeping allegedly pro-Communist actors and actresses from working. Schmidt's own professional affiliation with the theater world dated to the time he gave readings of children's poetry over the radio.

The suit against the union was based primarily on evidence drawn from the Senate committee hearings. Liaison was quickly established between Robert Kennedy, the committee staff, Godfrey Schmidt, and the plaintiffs; a liaison that was to be maintained during the entire period of the case. Before the suit was filed, Schmidt, Pat Kennedy, and some of the other plaintiffs met with and talked frequently on the phone to Robert Kennedy and members of the McClellan Committee staff; the two groups shared a mutual interest in preventing Hoffa from becoming president of the Teamsters.

"Kennedy had a lot of information which we didn't have," said Pat Kennedy, and so Robert Kennedy shared some of the information the committee had with the plaintiffs. Members of the committee staff showed the plaintiffs convention credentials which had been subpoenaed by the committee and even provided them with photostats of the credentials to be used in the lawsuit. The committee staff "helped us in a lot of ways" to prepare the lawsuit, said Pat Kennedy.

Ten days before the Teamster convention was scheduled to begin, Schmidt filed an action on behalf of his thirteen clients, asking Federal District Judge J. Dickinson Letts, an eighty-three-year-old jurist of the district court in Washington, D.C., to enjoin the convention from being held. Schmidt charged that the convention was rigged and that the union constitution had been violated. In addition to the request for an injunction, the thirty-page complaint also asked that the court appoint a "Board of Receivers or a Master in Equity or Masters" over the union.

Judge Letts issued the preliminary injunction on the day before the convention was due to open. The union appealed, that same day, to the Court of Appeals for the District of Columbia in the first of more than forty appeals made from the decisions of Judge Letts. The court of appeals stayed the decision of Letts, stating that his injunction against holding the convention went "beyond the necessities of the situation." The court of appeals decision was then upheld by Chief Justice Warren, sitting on circuit.

The attorney for the union during this period was Martin O'Donoghue of Washington, who for many years has represented the plumbers' union. (A year later, in the pattern that marked this entire case, Martin O'Donoghue shifted sides to become one of Hoffa's chief accusers.)

Because of O'Donoghue's successful fight against Schmidt, the union convention was held and Hoffa was elected president. At that time, he seemed to have triumphed over the combined efforts of the McClellan Committee, Robert Kennedy, the FBI, and all the other forces that were so clearly bent on keeping him from office. But Hoffa's triumph was a very short-lived one.

A few days after the convention ended, Schmidt once again applied successfully to Judge Letts for an injunction, this time to prevent Hoffa and his supporters from actually taking office. Once more, Martin O'Donoghue went to the court of appeals to seek a reversal. But this time the union lost, for, even though the court again said that the "findings and conclusions" of Judge Letts "go further than necessary," the injunction was, in substance, upheld. However, the judges of the court of appeals did call for a prompt trial and so, on December 2, 1957, the case began.

In the meantime, Hoffa also went to trial on the wire-tapping charge. The wire-tapping trial ended in a hung jury and was then rescheduled for early January. By this time, however, O'Donoghue had ended his representation of the union and was replaced by Edward Bennett Williams, who had successfully defended Hoffa against the bribery charge.

The earlier close relationship between the plaintiffs in the case and the McClellan Committee staff was maintained after the convention. According to Pat Kennedy, Robert Kennedy showed the plaintiffs copies of the questionnaire the committee had sent to all the Teamster locals, asking for data on the election of delegates to the convention.

While the case of *Cunningham v. English* was being tried before Judge Letts, Schmidt and Williams entered into private negotiations to settle the suit. After only a few meetings, Schmidt wrote George Meany (whom he claimed he knew although Meany denied this) a "personal and confidential" letter. In his letter, Schmidt said that Williams "made a 'confidential' proposal which I, of course, did not accept." The " 'confidential' proposal," immediately made nonconfidential by Schmidt, involved setting up a trusteeship for the union but permitting Hoffa to remain in office.

"Of course, I could not agree to this. . . ." Schmidt wrote Meany. "I shall not consent to any agreement under which Hoffa retains office," he continued. "Nor, indeed, shall I consent to any settlement without getting *your* full approval," he told Meany, who never responded to the letter.

Six weeks later, however, Schmidt signed a consent order on behalf of his clients, permitting Hoffa and the other union officers to take office "provisionally" and setting up a board of monitors to be paid by the union. According to the consent order, the district court retained jurisdiction over the monitors, who were subject to removal by the court. Further, the monitors were "subject as officers of the Court to supervision and direction of the Court in performing" their duties.

As the first experiment in setting up a new type of legal supervision over unions, the consent agreement could not have been much worse. It came into being only because Hoffa was desperate to get the necessary legal ratification of his authority as union president without giving up any real power and because Schmidt was desperate to get the suit settled without giving up the major task to which he had committed himself—to "keep Hoffa and his henchmen from office." And so a useless compromise was worked out—a compromise between the principle of business trusteeship wherein the trustees have authority to conduct the affairs of the business and the principle that union affairs are best conducted with a minimum of interference from the outside.

The agreement was more satisfactory to the lawyers than to their clients. Hoffa was not especially happy with being able to take office only "provisionally." But he was persuaded that, even if the union won the case, the decision would be appealed and the injunction against his taking office kept in force while the appeal made its long way through the higher courts. Hoffa had wanted the presidency of the union too long and too much to have it kept from him then. So, reluctantly, he approved the agreement.

Pat Kennedy, who along with Schmidt represented the plaintiffs in the negotiations that led to the consent decree, stated that the plaintiffs, too, were dissatisfied with the agreement because what they had

> started out to do here is to have a new election, and, according to the terms of this, the guys that were elected there are now going to be seated.
>
> Not only that—we were not satisfied with the terms of the consent decree, itself. In our opinion, it was too ambiguous. There was a lot of holes in it, and there was a lot of things we just didn't—we didn't hold still for it. It didn't embody what we started out to do.
>
> That was what our guys said, and Mr. Schmidt told us, in pretty plain English, that we would bloody well have to hold still for it because if we didn't hold still for this consent decree the only alternative was to go back to trial and Mr. Schmidt was not prepared to continue the trial.

As the board of monitors started to function, Schmidt and the plaintiffs chose himself as plaintiffs' monitor; the union picked one of its attorneys, Nat Wells; and both parties selected retired Judge Nathan Cayton, who was appointed chairman by Judge Letts. Meanwhile, Robert Kennedy and the staff of the McClellan Committee continued their active interest in the situation, meeting often with Schmidt and the plaintiffs to discuss strategy.

On the surface, the first few months of the monitorship were fairly smooth. But the honeymoon of the monitors' *ménage-à-trois* and Hoffa lasted only a few months. By the time that Judge Cayton, the first chairman, resigned in May, 1958, there were signs of grave troubles within the monitorship. As an instrumentality of the court, the consent agreement was obviously being interpreted quite differently by the parties to it and the judge who had approved it.

Hoffa believed that the monitorship was simply an expedient he had been forced to adopt in order to prevent a lengthy court suit that would keep him from office indefinitely. In his mind, the monitorship was going to last only one year, after which the union would hold another convention and he would again be elected president. Equally important to Hoffa was the principle that, during their year of service, the monitors were to have purely advisory functions; they were only to assist the union's executive board in carrying out its responsibilities.

Hoffa's attitude about the role of the monitors was shared, quite naturally, by the union's monitor, Nat Wells. Judge Cayton also seemed inclined to view the monitors in this same advisory capacity.

But not Godfrey Schmidt. In his mind, and certainly in that of his clients, the consent agreement under the court order gave the monitors far more authority than either Wells or Cayton believed they had. To Schmidt, "one of the primary means, one of the indispensable means" for the board to accomplish its mission was to oust Hoffa. This view of the monitorship was shared, evidently, by Robert Kennedy and his staff, who were continuing their investigation of Hoffa and their attacks upon him.

There were other differences, too, of not quite such a principled character, developing among the monitors, mostly over their fees and expenses. Indeed, before the monitorship ended and even afterward, a bewildering number of actions were instituted by Schmidt and other lawyers, asking for fees from the union. These suits ranged in scope from the $350,000 requested on February 13, 1958, by Schmidt and his two colleagues for six months' service as plaintiffs' counsel in *Cunningham v. English* to somewhat more modest requests by other attorneys.

In the middle of May, 1958, Judge Cayton suddenly resigned as chairman of the monitorship. In his letter of resignation to Judge Letts, Judge Cayton stated that the monitors had "made excellent progress toward achieving the objectives stated" in the consent order. "Our work is in such shape," wrote Judge Cayton, "that a new chairman can take over with little or no loss of continuity."

As a prophet, Judge Cayton was not very prescient. Whatever tensions had existed within the monitors and between the monitors and the union officers soon became the kind of strains which so weakened the structure of the monitorship that it soon degenerated almost completely into loud shouting, bickering, and disputing.

Two weeks later, over the vigorous objections initially of Godfrey Schmidt, Judge Letts appointed as impartial chairman of the monitors Martin O'Donoghue, who had represented the Teamsters against Schmidt in the original lawsuit. But, only a week later, Schmidt wrote Judge Letts to tell him that he had changed his mind about O'Donoghue, who had, Schmidt said, "already taken action that I regard as more prompt, more just and more efficient than has been the case with the board up to this time." Schmidt was particularly pleased, he informed Judge Letts, by O'Donoghue's "frank views on labor leaders who take the Fifth Amendment when questioned about their handling of union funds and stewardship." "Glory be to God," said O'Donoghue, "what is there to incriminate you by not testifying to an honest election?" Schmidt also wrote Judge Letts that O'Donoghue shared the view that the monitors "must not merely sit back and wait for complaints, but must take the initiative and follow the leads given to us by the McClellan Committee."

As allies, O'Donoghue and Schmidt constituted a majority of the monitors, and with the help of the McClellan Committee staff began actively moving against Hoffa. By the summer of 1958, O'Donoghue already was meeting with Robert Kennedy, utilizing the facilities and staff of the McClellan Committee. He had also moved his office as chief monitor out of the Teamster building and hired a staff of his own. Instead of making recommendations, O'Donoghue began issuing "Orders of Recommendation." Most of these actions were taken over the strenuous objections of the union monitor and the union but with the approval of Schmidt and of Judge Letts, whose decisions were consistently appealed and very often reversed or modified by the court of appeals.

At the end of only a few months, the war was on in earnest between Hoffa and O'Donoghue, who was supported by Schmidt and the McClellan committee staff. "We had a lot of things going back and forth," said O'Donoghue, discussing his relationship with the committee staff.

And while the raging disputes over the monitorship between Hoffa and O'Donoghue, flanked by Schmidt, were cluttering the dockets of the Federal courts, Robert Kennedy was continuously subjecting Hoffa to the pitiless glare of exposure. Moreover, the committee staff was not only actively cooperating with the anti-Hoffa monitors, but early in 1959, Carmine Bellino, the committee's chief accountant, advised members of an independent union not to affiliate with the Teamsters.

In June, 1959, the court of appeals held that there was a "conflict of interest" in Godfrey Schmidt's role as monitor because he also represented employers who dealt with the Teamsters. Schmidt resigned and as his replacement proposed Terence Mc-Shane, an FBI agent who had testified against Hoffa in the earlier wire-tapping case and who had been in virtually constant contact with Schmidt while Schmidt was a monitor. But the plaintiffs, who by this time were beginning to split among themselves and were becoming dissatisfied with Schmidt, rejected McShane and nominated instead Lawrence Smith, who had been an attorney in Schmidt's New York office.

Despite his resignation from the board of monitors, Schmidt still represented some plaintiffs and maintained contact with the board as did Robert Kennedy, despite his having resigned as counsel for the McClellan Committee in September, 1959, in order to run his brother's primary campaign.

One interesting example of the cooperation between the committee and the anti-Hoffa monitors during this period occurred when Walter Sheridan, a committee investigator, went to Joplin, Missouri, in December, 1959, to interview a prisoner, Carl Cates, in jail for parole violation. Previously, while out on parole, Cates had been a janitor for a Teamster local in Springfield, Missouri, some of whose records were allegedly missing. Under questioning, in the presence of his parole officer and the attorney for an anti-Hoffa group in the local union, the prisoner told Sheridan that he had seen some of the union officers taking boxes of union records from the hall and putting them in their cars. Cates said later he was not sure just who Sheridan ("Walt") was nor whom he represented. Despite this uncertainty, Cates signed an affidavit about what he had allegedly seen and the next day was released from prison.

A few months later, attorneys for the anti-Hoffa monitors who were checking into the disappearance of the same union records took an oral deposition from the ex-janitor in the presence of the attorneys for the union. But this time when Cates was questioned about whether he had seen the union officers take out the records, he denied it. The anti-Hoffa monitor lawyers, obviously shocked, produced the affidavit which Cates had given to Sheridan and which Sheridan had, in turn, turned over to them but not to Hoffa's lawyers nor the union-appointed monitor.

Why had Cates given Walter Sheridan the original affidavit that he later recanted? His explanation was that his parole officer had told him "that if I didn't try to help them that I couldn't expect any help myself." Cates identified the "them" as "Walt" and the "state officials" with him. The parole officer who had been with Sheridan at the jail and who was present also at the deposition declined to discuss the incident on the record. Within forty-eight hours after the ex-convict had reversed his story he was once more a convict, sent back this time again for parole violation.

Early in 1960, the running legal brawl into which the monitorship had degenerated by then erupted into an even more complicated situation. Lawrence Smith, Schmidt's successor as monitor, refused to sign an interim monitors' report that O'Donoghue, backed by Schmidt and Robert Kennedy, hoped to use as the basis for ousting Hoffa from the union. The report had been drawn up from material gathered by the McClellan Committee, but Smith believed it was "not designed to promote any policy which would implement the purposes of the Consent Decree." In fact, said Smith, he doubted whether O'Donoghue had any long-range policy except to "oust Hoffa as Provisional General President."

O'Donoghue also attempted during this period to hire Walter Sheridan and was prevented from doing so only by the court of appeals which stayed Judge Letts's informal order approving O'Donoghue's request.

At this time Robert Kennedy was actively at work on his brother's primary campaign. But on February 15, according to Godfrey Schmidt, Kennedy took time out from the campaign to call Schmidt, complaining that Lawrence Smith had refused to sign the report prepared by O'Donoghue's staff.

But despite the pressure exerted directly on him by Schmidt, and indirectly by Kennedy, through Schmidt, Smith refused to sign the report. The break between Smith and Schmidt, backed up by Kennedy, was characteristic of the Borgia-like atmosphere which flourished in this period, replete with plots and counterplots, proposals and propositions, secret meetings, and hurried phone calls. Schmidt was having confidential sessions with Edward Bennett Williams about ending the monitorship and promptly reporting to the FBI, Robert Kennedy, and Judge Letts. Lawrence Smith and Schmidt had become such bitter enemies that six of the original plaintiffs in the lawsuit attempted to break off their relationship with Schmidt, but Judge Letts refused to allow them to do so. At Schmidt's request, Judge Letts also removed Smith as monitor, putting McShane in his place. Smith, supported by the six anti-Schmidt plaintiffs, appealed Letts's decision to remove him; on May 12 and 13 the court of appeals stayed Judge Letts's order removing Smith from the board and decided that the six plaintiffs had a right to drop Godfrey Schmidt and retain new counsel. Five days later, two of the six plaintiffs were invited to attend a meeting in Robert Kennedy's New York apartment. Walter Sheridan, Terence McShane, Robert Kennedy, and one of the plaintiffs still loyal to Schmidt were also present at the meeting. The purpose of the session was to attempt to persuade the two plaintiffs who had broken with Godfrey Schmidt that they ought to go back to him and that they should accept McShane as their monitor nominee instead of Lawrence Smith. The two disgruntled plaintiffs refused both requests and angrily left Kennedy's apartment.

Quite apart from a dispute about what actually was said at the meeting (Did Robert Kennedy call one of the two plaintiffs a son of a bitch? Did he imply that when his brother was President help would be available?) there is a far more serious question involved here. As a private citizen, Robert Kennedy certainly has a right to be interested and concerned with the future of the Teamsters Union, but the fact is that, at the time, he was much more than just an *ordinary* private citizen. His initial involvement in the affairs of the Teamsters Union was as a congressional employee. His role vis-à-vis the monitors was derived from his position as counsel for that committee. His ability to possibly influence the decision of the six plaintiffs to return to the arms of Godfrey Schmidt and substitute McShane for Smith was due precisely to his special position. And what was true of Robert Kennedy was equally valid for Walter Sheridan.

Let me recapitulate the argument and attempt, simultaneously, to narrow it. From the start of Robert Kennedy's investigation of the Teamsters Union, he has been convinced that the union, under Hoffa's leadership, represents a "conspiracy of evil," and that the good of the country requires the jailing of Hoffa, if possible, and at least ousting him from the union presidency. Kennedy has been committed, openly and totally, to these two objectives.

To accomplish these ends, Kennedy was willing to use the legal power and the staff at his disposal as counsel for a congressional committee to assist the anti-Hoffa Teamsters in their private lawsuit to prevent the 1957 union convention from being held. Kennedy believed that the convention had been rigged for the purpose of electing Hoffa. This has been disputed by Solicitor General Archibald Cox, who said, in 1959, "Apparently there were widespread violations of the constitution and bylaws of the International Brotherhood of Teamsters in the choice of delegates for the 1957 convention, but many of them were technical and no one seriously believes that the majority of the members desired a different president."

When the attempt to enjoin the convention failed because, as Chief Justice Warren said, it called "for an extraordinary exercise of judicial power" and the court took over supervision of the union's affairs through the board of monitors, the congressional committee intervened actively and continuously in the affairs of the monitorship. During the life of the board, the committee, under the direction of Kennedy, lent its resources to the anti-Hoffa monitors in their attempt to use the board as an instrument for ousting Hoffa from the union presidency and to prevent a union convention from being held. Once again, these attempts were frustrated by the appellate courts. The Court of Appeals for the District of Columbia reversed fifteen of Judge Letts's decisions in favor of the anti-Hoffa monitors and reversed in part or substantially modified several others.

In this sense, it was the court of appeals that stood between Hoffa and those monitors, supported and sustained by the McClellan Committee staff, who were intent on using the monitorship as a device for ridding the union of Hoffa. As Justice Frankfurter said, the court of appeals "manifested an alert understanding of the gravity of the litigation, and has made manifest its sense of the high importance of assuring the most protective procedure on the part of the board of monitors. . . ."

At that point, frustrated by the court of appeals decision reversing the dismissal of monitor Lawrence Smith, Robert Kennedy attempted to accomplish the dismissal by a private meeting with two of the plaintiffs.

Jimmy Hoffa and the Teamsters Union are the antithesis of what I believe a union leader and a union ought to be. But my feelings about Hoffa are only important insofar as they affect what I write about him. Robert Kennedy's behavior toward Hoffa is of far greater significance, for Kennedy is not a private citizen—he is a public servant, and what he does about Hoffa involves not only himself but the very government itself. As staff counsel for the McClellan Committee and as Attorney General, he acts in a public capacity in the name of every citizen. For this reason he is open to judgment about *how* he exercises that responsibility.

The Kennedy-Hoffa feud has many political and moral dimensions which need examination, but it seems clear to me that the McClellan Committee's direct involvement in the *Cunningham v. English* lawsuit, and in the ensuing affairs of the board of monitors, went far beyond the committee's specific mandate and the general mandate of congressional committees. The evidence demonstrates to me that the committee and its staff, under Robert Kennedy's direction, trespassed heavily upon the rights of Hoffa and the union.

It is a cliché and a truism that the most important civil rights are those of our enemies—of the people with whom we disagree. And so, although I have nothing in common with Hoffa, the union leader, Hoffa, the citizen, is me. His rights are the same as mine and require the same protection.

INTRODUCTION

UNION LEADERS, like hairstyles, go in vogues. Once, Harry Bridges was a fashionable union leader, very much in style. From 1934, when he emerged as the head of the San Francisco general strike, to 1939, Bridges was in the mode. He conjured up the romantic image of the tough, militant, and honest union leader who had converted the West Coast waterfronts from jungles into reasonably decent places to work. Bridges's honesty and incorruptibility were widely admired. Then, in 1939, the Bridges fashion died down somewhat for he switched from his support of Roosevelt's collective security policy to the position that "The Yanks Are Not Coming" to the European war, which, to Bridges, had become an imperialist one after the signing of the Stalin-Hitler pact.

Bridges became very popular again after Hitler attacked the Soviet Union, for that surprise blow changed the nature of the conflict, in Bridges's opinion, to a "people's war." And Bridges remained popular all through World War II. But once again he fell victim to the vagaries of political change when the wartime romance between the U.S. and the U.S.S.R. soured, ending in the cold war. Because Bridges's view of the world in the immediate postwar period was much closer to the Soviet position than to the American one he went out of style once more as a union leader.

My relationship to Bridges was political, long before I had

any personal contact with him. All during the years of the Popular Front when Bridges and his union were staunch supporters of Roosevelt, I was a Trotskyite, committed to the working-class revolution. To the Trotskyites, Bridges was a potential sell-out artist who would betray his own union in the interests of Stalin's foreign policy. When Bridges switched sides in 1939, and began attacking Roosevelt, we continued our distrust of him, as a union leader, for we knew that the change took place only because of the Stalin-Hitler pact. And our distrust was verified as he took another 180-degree shift in position the moment Hitler turned on his temporary ally and attacked the Soviet Union.

All anti-Stalinist radicals were especially bitter about Bridges in that period for not only did he carry his support of the war effort to the point of strikebreaking, as in the Montgomery Ward strike during World War II when ILWU members went through another union's picket line, but he actively supported the government's prosecution of the Minneapolis Trotskyite group in the first application of the Smith Act. Even though I was no longer associated, politically or personally, with the Minneapolis group when this happened and had basic differences of opinion with them, I believed the role Bridges and his union played was that of finks, to use one of Bridges's own favorite words—supporters of the government in a manifestly unfair political trial.

I suspect that Bridges might agree today with some items in my bill of particulars against his past actions just as I would agree, today, that some of the charges he made against me and my political colleagues in the postwar period were also justified. When the cold war began, it was reflected in a vicious, internecine conflict within the CIO, which had a number of unions dominated by Communists. In that internal fight, the handful of "politicals" who were union officers played a peculiar role. We were completely familiar with the history of the Communist party and because some of us were experienced speakers and factionalists we were in the forefront of the fight with the Communists. And if, as ex-radicals, we were unhappy about the conservative politics of some of the allies we had during the battles, we swallowed our doubts in the interests of winning the larger war to rid the unions of the Communists. I suspect, too, that partially we were glad to get in some licks of our own after having been kicked around by the Communists for so long when they were in the drivers' seats.

Thus, week after week, I found myself denouncing Bridges, the ILWU, and other Communist-dominated unions at CIO council meetings in Los Angeles, amid roaring shouts of approval from the delegates who came to watch the show. Then, after the CIO had decided to hold trials of the unions suspected of being under Communist domination, I was asked to help prepare the case against the ILWU which had been postponed because of Bridges's trial in 1949 in a Federal court on a charge growing from his alleged membership in the Communist party. It was the CIO leaders' position that they wanted to keep their action completely apart from that of the government.

The CIO trial of the ILWU was held in May, 1950. I do not know whether it would have been possible to find impartial judges within the CIO but not much of an attempt to do so was made. The three-man trial committee was headed by O. A. Knight, president of the Oil Workers Union, my boss at the time. The other two members of the committee were comparative newcomers to the CIO and rather conservative in their politics. But it didn't really matter who they were, for Bridges and everyone else knew the verdict was decided before the trial was held. The committee's decision to recommend expulsion was so certain that I began to work on the writing of it while the trial was still in progress.

Later in this book there is a discussion of the general problem of whether or not the CIO's decision to expel the Communists was a wise one; now, I want only to raise the specific issue of whether or not the ILWU got a fair due-process shake from the CIO in 1950. I must admit, much as I hate to provide Bridges with ammunition to prove the assertions he made at the time, that there was very little due process in the trial that took place the three tense days of May 17, 18, and 19, 1950, in the boardroom of the old CIO headquarters on Jackson Place in Washington, D.C.

Five years later, in 1955, Bridges went on trial in a Federal court again but this time he was acquitted. "The Due Processing of Harry Bridges" was written about that trial, the last attempt made by the government to deport or jail Bridges.

There is a remarkable resemblance between the government's determined but unsuccessful efforts to win a case against Bridges and its current attempt to jail Hoffa. In both cases, too, although the government didn't accomplish its primary objective, the repeated legal forays did make a martyr of Bridges as they are making of Hoffa. Now, because the legal harassment has ceased, it is possible to criticize Bridges without his being able to charge that anyone who attacks his policies is, automatically, a government fink.

But there is not much criticism of Bridges in the ILWU. The amount of union militancy that can be found today on the West Coast waterfronts could be put in an eye without there even being the slightest sensation of a foreign body under the lid. The ILWU has been at peace with the waterfront employers for many years, and the mechanization agreement, signed in October, 1960, has become a symbol of amity between the now middle-class longshoremen and the employers. In exchange for the right to mechanize the docks, the employers set up a fund which provides the longshoremen with such a good retirement cushion that many of them are leaving the docks even before they are sixty-five. It is only in the resolutions adopted at the union's conventions that echoes of the militant voices of the past can be heard.

Interestingly, too, Bridges, who started his union career with a high degree of social consciousness and transmitted to the ILWU members his feelings that there was a larger world outside the union, now finds a close ally in Hoffa, who couldn't care less about world politics. The economic ties between long-shoremen and teamsters are obvious ones; the political alliance between the two unions reflects the fact that both unions are outsiders. At some point in the future, perhaps when Bridges retires, the ILWU may become part of the Teamsters and this will really mark the end of an era.

THE
DUE
PROCESSING
OF
HARRY
BRIDGES

(1956) "**I**T'S NOT an abuse of due process that I'm suffering from," Harry Bridges told one of his attorneys just before his most recent trial. "What I'm suffering from is an excess of due process! I've got due process coming out of my ears."

"Due process" for the leader of the West Coast's International Longshoremen's and Warehousemen's Union (ILWU) has included, since 1934, innumerable investigations conducted by the FBI, the Department of Labor, and the U. S. Immigration Service; two special congressional hearings; the introduction of two congressional bills, one of which passed, directed specifically at expediting his deportation; two lengthy administrative hearings before special examiners; one criminal trial before a jury; one civil trial before a judge alone; at least nine lower, circuit, and appellate courts' decisions; one Immigration Appeals Board review; one Attorney General's ruling; and two U. S. Supreme Court edicts.

A Bridges case has been before some court in fourteen of the nearly eighteen years since the first deportation warrant was issued against him. Twice, Federal agencies sought to deport Bridges as an alien (Bridges came to this country in 1920 from Australia). Then, after having granted him citizenship during the war, the government accused him of perjury and made two attempts to take that citizenship away. The first and fourth government cases were lost for lack of evidence, and the second and third because some violation of due process destroyed the government suits.

But maybe this almost interminable conflict between the United States government and Harry Renton Bridges has finally ended. The Attorney General failed to appeal, by last October 3, [1955] a July decision that acquitted Bridges, and thus tacitly acknowledged the government's latest failure.

The reason for this mountain of litigation is, of course, Bridges's relationship to the Communist party. From the beginning of his career as union leader on the docks in San Francisco in the early 1930's, Bridges has followed the party line through all its tortuous turnings. His support of Roosevelt during the period of the Popular Front changed overnight to the anti-Roosevelt, isolationist position adopted by the Communists after the Nazi-Soviet pact. Then he flipped back again when the Soviet Union was attacked by Germany. Literally overnight, Bridges shifted from statements like "No worker has anything to gain by the entrance of the U.S. into the war under any conditions" to urging, months before Pearl Harbor, that the labor movement pass resolutions asking a declaration of war against Hitler. When war came, Bridges, then CIO regional director, supported it so vigorously that he told one CIO group: "To put it bluntly, I mean your unions of today must become instruments of speed-up of the working people of America."

In 1943 he was booed off a San Pedro platform by members of his own union for urging that the sackloads of cement carried on the longshoremen's lift be doubled. Union members who protested the speed-up were denounced as "fifth columnists" or "Hitler's agents." A famous California civil-rights attorney, A. L. Wirin, who represented many CIO unions and councils, was described as an agent of Hirohito and was fired, with Bridges's knowledge and approval, because he opposed the evacuation of the Japanese from the West Coast when the

Communist party was supporting it.

But following the party line is not in itself a crime. In order to accomplish Bridges's deportation, the government, by its own admission, could not "point the evidence toward anything less than membership in the Communist Party." This has meant that the government has tried to prove that Bridges matched its own rather rigid image of a Communist party member—a dues-paying, card-carrying, totally committed, unquestioning agent of Moscow. Mere attendance at a party meeting or simply following the party line was not sufficient evidence of party membership to warrant deportation. The government had to show that he paid dues, was recorded as a member, and really was a committed servant of the party. In Bridges's case it wasn't that simple.

The relationship between Harry Bridges and the Communist party was not one in which the party gave orders and Bridges mechanically obeyed. Rather, the party generally found it necessary to "handle" Bridges, sometimes wheedling, sometimes cajoling, always feeding his ego. The arrangement between Bridges and the party was something undreamed of in the government's philosophy, a *quid pro quo* working alliance. Bridges had party members to help him organize, build, and control the ILWU; the party, with Bridges as CIO regional director, was in an excellent position to control state and local CIO councils. Bridges gave the front organizations a kind of status they would not otherwise have had. It has been a handy setup on both sides.

The government has proceeded in this unusual case in a routine and rather wooden way. First, in each trial it established that Communists were committed to the violent overthrow, etc., etc. Then it proceeded to examine the party's operation in the labor movement in a thoroughly unsophisticated manner.

It called some of its traveling panel of "expert" witnesses on Communism, and from their testimony one would get a picture of every Communist in the labor movement spending all his time loudly preaching armed revolution to his fellow union members. The government attorneys were usually satisfied with the simplest answers to the naïve questions directed at these "experts," and the variety and subtlety of Communist activity was never brought out.

Little explanation was ever given by government witnesses of the advantage the Communists in the labor movement took of legitimate grievances. There was little presentation of the Communists' skill in controlling a union for its name, its jobs, its influence in national labor circles, and its attractiveness to liberals. The fact that some party-dominated unions have concentrated much more on "pork-chop" issues than on political questions, especially on the local level, was largely ignored in the trials. Similarly forgotten in the last two trials was the war period when the needs of the Soviet Union required that the Communist party and its captive unions become the strongest supporters of American capitalism and the war effort. Instead, from the testimony of the government witnesses emerged a shadowy impression of totally dedicated Bolshevik longshoremen whose meetings were devoted solely to discussions of revolutionary tactics.

In one way the naïveté of the government's case is a cause for rejoicing, for it shows that we are not geared to the carrying out of political trials. Fortunately we lack some of the necessary accouterments of such trials, such as a trained staff of political prosecutors, skilled in exploring the byways of theoretical deviations.

But the government's unrelenting effort to press its primitive image of the Communist onto Bridges raises questions. There is the matter, for example, of how many times a man should be made to stand trial for the same offense. Since 1939, when Bridges was first acquitted of the charge that he was a Communist party member, he has been tried three more times on accusations that all revolved around the same central issue. Also, there is the question of the kind of witnesses the government was finally willing to use.

The government has always been forced to rely upon witnesses to try to prove that Bridges really did join the Communist party and pay his dues, and toward the end of the series it was scraping the bottom of the barrel. The obvious personal bias and animus of many anti-Bridges witnesses had destroyed much of their credibility. After Bridges was acquitted in his first hearing, none of the thirty-two witnesses was used again in the second hearing.

The verdict in the second hearing was based upon the testimony of only two of the government's thirty-three witnesses, and the two were cut to one by higher courts. An entirely new crew of witnesses was found for the 1949 trials. The new team itself was not perfectly satisfactory, in spite of the "guilty" verdict returned by the jury. One member admitted perjury during the trial itself, while two others were exposed as perjurers at a later date. By 1955, the perjury exposures and the public opprobrium attached to appearing in the trials cut the number of witnesses still further. The prosecution had a paucity of working materials.

No such problems existed when it was the CIO, instead of the government, that had Bridges on trial. For three days beginning May 17, 1950, in the board room of the CIO Building in Washington, D.C., the ILWU defended itself before a committee of CIO officials. The charge against Bridges's union was that its policies were "consistently directed toward the achievement of the program and the purposes of the Communist party rather than the objectives and policies set forth in the constitution of the CIO." The CIO trial concentrated first on documentary proof of the rather easily demonstrated fact that the ILWU, under Bridges's leadership, had followed "without deviation" the Communist party line. Then two witnesses, both high CIO officials, testified that they were present with Bridges at meetings where Communist party officials explained changes in the party line to union leaders. Another witness discussed the positions actually taken by Bridges within the CIO executive board, positions that never varied from those advocated by the party.

The testimony of these witnesses, together with an enormous number of documents submitted, resulted in the committee's recommendation that the ILWU be expelled from the CIO.

The question of Bridges's party membership, essential to the deportation proceedings, was never raised by the CIO and only came into the proceedings during Bridges's cross-examination of a CIO witness. After insistent questioning by Bridges, Hedley Stone, an ex-party member and official of the National Maritime Union, finally stated his belief that Bridges was a party member.

Today, as a result of his expulsion from the CIO, Bridges is isolated from most of the American labor movement. He finds his allies among the East Coast waterfront unions and the West Coast waterfront employers, who, in the interests of "expediency," have cooperated with Bridges since 1948.

But expelling a man from the CIO, a voluntary organization, is one thing, and deporting him from the United States is quite another. The CIO could look at the political record and, by convention vote, approve the expulsion. The government, necessarily, is more limited, and must deal not with political opinions but with the concrete fact of party membership. The prodigious effort to prove such membership in Bridges's case certainly increased his power by helping to make him a martyr.

To understand this, one must know the background of the San Francisco waterfront. Even though only a third or less of today's ILWU membership are longshoremen, the union and its leader are still identified with hard-bitten, rugged, and profane dock wallopers whose hand hooks hang down from the back pockets of their jeans as they descend into the cargo holds. And life on the 'front is still far from easy. The longshoremen get high pay, have good working conditions, and hire out by rotation from the union hall instead of by the corrupt shape-up, but they still get crushed in the 'tween-deck hold. Three-fingered hands are not at all uncommon, grasping heavy coffee mugs in the dockside cafés. In many ways, the character associated with today's ILWU was set by yesterday's waterfront conditions.

It was by his onslaught against those miserable conditions that Bridges first came into prominence in the San Francisco general strike of 1934. He gained much public sympathy for his successful efforts to erase corruption from the docks. During and following the 1934 strike, the employers' attempt to characterize Bridges as a Communist met with almost total disbelief in most of the community. The government's apparent joining of forces with the anti-union employers as it attempted to deport Bridges built up for him an accretion of support.

The attacks upon him by the employers—until 1948—and the continual government prosecutions have placed him in an almost sacrosanct postion within the ILWU and in some liberal circles outside the union. To attack Bridges is to run the risk of being linked with the employers and government in an effort to smash the union. Charges leveled, even by union members, against Bridges are described as "in reality against the union itself." Any attempts to build anti-Bridges caucuses are attacked as attempting to "split our union, divide our membership, create confusion, and eventually wreck our union and our hiring hall."

The name of Bridges is fully identified with that of the union. He and his supporters control the ILWU's staff, newspaper, and organizers, all three reflecting only the leadership's position. Since, as in every union, newly organized groups tend to give their allegiance to the people directly responsible for bettering their conditions, Bridges's greatest strength is not in the older ILWU locals but in recently organized groups.

Control is kept in the hands of a well-organized, articulate group of Bridges's supporters. Some results of that control are indicated by the fact that the ILWU conducts practically no internal educational program for its members, except for what a few locals may do on their own initiative, and by the fact that Bridges has tolerated an all-white longshore local in Portland. In this latter case, it seems clear that Bridges is more concerned with maintaining his organizational control than with tackling a question of principle that might result in a local union leaving the ILWU. But Bridges fully understands that there are limits beyond which he cannot manipulate his membership. These limits are more and more narrowly set by the increasing middle-class ideology of the members.

It is still possible for Bridges to call a one-day stoppage as a protest against a Red-hunting congressional committee, because the membership is convinced that such committees are covertly attempting to smash the ILWU. But it was not possible, and Bridges never attempted, to stop shipments of war materials to Korea. Bridges understands, better than does the government, that his membership can be bossed only up to a point.

Perhaps it's just as well that the government's long effort to deport him has finally been dropped. There is now a greater possibility that the assorted longshoremen, warehousemen, and pineapple workers of the ILWU will judge Bridges without any of the extra sympathy extended to one who is persecuted. At long last, Bridges will not be in any government courtroom, and will have to stand before his union membership solely on his record. But the government's citing of the United Electrical and the Mine, Mill, and Smelter Workers' unions as Communist-infiltrated organizations under the Communist Control Act of 1954 may presage a similar move against the ILWU. If so, another case involving Bridges will be added to the already huge heap of legal documents concerning him.

INTRODUCTION

A L H A Y E S, president of the International Association of Machinists, is as different, politically and personally, from Jimmy Hoffa and Harry Bridges as it's possible to be. And their unions are quite different, too. In Hayes's union, unlike Bridges's, there is a constitutional prohibition against Communists' holding membership and, unlike Jimmy Hoffa's Teamsters, the machinists' union is free of any influence that might even remotely be connected with the underworld.

But all three men share one characteristic: a distrust of opposition. And all three men are equally ruthless about limiting opposition to whatever extent is possible under their unions' constitutions and the law. So it was that Hayes, in 1959, expelled two members of a Chicago local who, to him, were vociferous factionalists disturbing the union's peace, and so it is that the machinists' union is now being sued by staff representatives who were fired by Hayes for supporting the unsuccessful election campaign of a union vice-president who ran for secretary-treasurer against a member of Hayes's slate.

However, Hayes's behavior toward opposition men or groups is not much different from that of most other union leaders. Most union leaders understand and sympathize with Hayes's attitude in not permitting active opposition to flourish inside the union. In that sense, Hayes's being chairman of the AFL-CIO Ethical Practices Committee is symbolically correct: to many union leaders there is very little connection between ethical practices and tolerance of opposition.

MR. HAYES
SETTLES
A LOCAL
DISTURBANCE

(1959) $\quad$ FOR TWO AND a half years now, the union local has been run by an administrator appointed by the international union's president. Recently all elections of officers to the local have been canceled and regular membership meetings have been suspended. The president of the international union has expelled two active members of the local and suspended a third from holding union office for a year—this after "rejecting and striking from the record" the report and recommendations of a trial committee which he himself had appointed to hear their cases.

Another sordid union scandal? No, not really; or at least not in the accepted sense of the term. The local involved is, as it happens, Tool and Die Makers Lodge 113, which belongs to the highly respected 900,000-member International Association of Machinists; and the president involved is the IAM's leader, A. J. Hayes, who is also chairman of the AFL-CIO Ethical Practices Committee.

The IAM is generally regarded as a good union. There has never been a serious accusation of corruption leveled against it. And Hayes is a good union leader—honest, blunt-speaking, and a righteous and aggressive defender of his union's interest as he sees them. High on the list of those interests is administrative efficiency; and when that efficiency is threatened, in Hayes's judgment, by "friction, division, and dissension" among the members, he is quick to take action.

Hayes, moreover, is particularly scornful of what he calls

present-day "disenchanted" liberals and "well-meaning but mis-directed" intellectuals who believe that the internal affairs of trade unions are something more than a trade-union problem. He is equally scornful of the kind of public review boards that have been established by the United Auto Workers and the Upholsterers to protect individual members' rights. How he runs his union, he implies, is no outsider's damned business.

President Hayes obviously must have cogent reasons, in his own mind, for the two-and-a-half year suspension of Lodge 113, in Chicago. Presumably, too, he had better reasons than the one he gave for ignoring the report and recommendations of the committee he himself had appointed to try the three members. (He actually said that since the text had not been given to the three accused, it was judicially nonexistent. Why he just didn't give it to them he didn't say.) But whatever Hayes's real reasons, he is most reluctant to share them with the public. He simply and summarily expelled Marion Ciepley and Irwin Rappaport from the union and suspended Leland Williams from holding union office for a year.

Ciepley and Rappaport are both members of the Socialist party; two of a disappearing breed—the self-educated, skilled radical workers who, with their insistent cries for industrial justice, were once the leavening agents of the labor movement. They are both aristocrats of their trade, Ciepley a tool-and-die maker who earns $3.30 an hour, Rappaport, a tool-room machinist who earns $3.25 an hour. They have both been at the trade for nearly twenty years. Rappaport has been a member of Lodge 113 since 1951, Ciepley since 1941 (although he transferred to an IAM lodge on the West Coast from 1943 to 1952). They are both active members of the local lodge, the kind who invariably come to union meetings, always speak their piece, and have no hesitation in embarrassing their union officials.

Hayes has repeatedly insisted, in the face of growing criticism, that the expulsions are not the business of outsiders or groups like the American Civil Liberties Union, which has taken an interest in the case and which met with a flat rebuff from Hayes when it requested information. In fact, one of the charges against Ciepley and Williams was precisely that they distributed a leaflet at an Illinois Federation of Labor convention calling for the labor movement to establish such public review boards of "outsiders"—boards that would have the authority to accept appeals from members who believe they have been done an injustice by union officials.

The three trials took place December 16, 17, and 18 of last year, in the Sunset Room of the Congress Hotel in Chicago. These trials were an outcome of events that stretched back several years. Lodge 113 had been the scene of internal conflict between a "reform" group—which included Ciepley, Rappaport, and Williams—and the incumbent union officials. Late in 1955, the "reform" faction had become suspicious that their financial affairs were not being properly directed by the local's paid officials. It charged that the officials had raised their own salaries without membership authorization, that the books of the lodge had not been properly audited, and that its funds were being mismanaged.

In June, 1956, after a good deal of battling within the lodge, by the reform group with the help of handbills and caucus meetings and by the officials through bringing charges—which were rejected by the membership—against some of the opposition leaders, an auditor was sent in to check the books by the Grand Lodge, as the IAM Washington headquarters is called. The auditor found, say the opposition leaders, that the dues stamps had been mishandled and that the lodge's funds had been kept in one of the paid officials' personal bank accounts. There were signs of other financial oddities too; and the auditor recommended that the financial officers be replaced unless they revised and corrected their procedures.

In October, 1956, under the pressure of an election they were almost sure to lose, the entire staff of business agents resigned. Almost all of them wound up later as management officials for various firms.

Lodge 113 was immediately suspended by Hayes, who assigned one of the union's vice-presidents as administrator of the lodge's affairs. The lodge's bylaws were set aside and the election of officers was indefinitely postponed.

The clue to Hayes's placing Lodge 113 under suspension undoubtedly is to be found in his general attitude, shared by many
union leaders, that dirty union linen must be washed only in
private. In this view, faction fights, malpractice charges, or accusations of financial irregularities bring union affairs into a
hostile public eye, a state of affairs to be avoided wherever
possible. As Hayes told the members of Lodge 113: "Grand
Lodge has made efforts over a considerable period of time to
assist the lodge in resolving the differences that existed. However, all indications are that all these efforts have failed to resolve or minimize the differences, the frictions, the division and
the dissension. . . ."

One of the administrator's first acts was to order the ending
of all partisan publications and caucus meetings. He also announced that he would prepare a new set of bylaws for the lodge
to replace the old ones.

At first the suspension was accepted by local union members
with good grace, and perhaps even some relief. But as time
passed, patience and tempers grew short. After the lodge had
been under suspension for some months, and when there was no
sign of autonomy being restored, the "reform" group began a
new campaign on the issue of having the local's suspension lifted
and giving it back its self-government.

In April, 1957, the administrator brought in the proposed
new bylaws to the lodge. They were first rejected by the membership and then finally accepted because, the opposition leaders claim, the administrator had promised that the suspension
would be lifted if the bylaws were adopted. These new bylaws
certainly put a damper on internal faction fights. They increased the term of office for business agents from one to four
years, and outlawed the right of members to circulate petitions
"related to union business" without prior approval of the IAM
executive board or the local lodge, except for petitions calling
for a special meeting or for recalling officers. The new bylaws
also stated that the "business handled in shop meetings shall
be confined to matters affecting the shop involved and shall

not include any item that properly is a lodge matter under the Grand Lodge Constitution."

Two bitterly contested elections were held during the period of suspension. In the first, conducted in May, 1957, the "reform" group elected one of its supporters as financial secretary-treasurer. The second took place in February, 1958, when the two opposing groups each put up full slates. The supporters of the administrator won eleven posts as against nine for the "reformers," but Ciepley was elected president of the local. The administrator then announced that a recount of the ballots showed Ciepley to have been defeated by a vote of 767 to 765. Ciepley appealed the administrator's decision to Hayes, claiming election irregularities, but Hayes turned down the appeal.

In May 1958, Hayes discussed the suspension of Lodge No. 113 before the Kennedy subcommittee of the Senate Labor, Education and Welfare Committee. He attributed the difficulties of the lodge "to the fact that most of the members were apathetic as to the conduct of the affairs of the local lodge." It is a curious kind of apathy that is evidenced by contested elections, publication of newsletters, and the holding of caucus meetings. And it would seem that prohibiting discussion of local lodge matters at shop meetings, as provided in the local's new bylaws, is hardly a device to encourage membership participation in union affairs. In fact, it seems clear from the position taken by Hayes that, while he may be interested in membership participation in the affairs of the IAM lodges, he is even more interested in seeing that such participation is not allowed to become a serious threat to union officialdom.

On October 21, 1958, regular membership meetings were canceled with this announcement by the lodge's administrator:

> Suspension of regular meetings of Lodge 113 will continue in full force and effect until there is concrete evidence the lodge membership is prepared to resume its responsibilities of directing its own affairs strictly in accordance with the laws and policies of the International

Association of Machinists, along with evidence of unity of purpose.

To establish unity of purpose and create an atmosphere that will lead to lifting the order of suspension, we must again request and direct that all unauthorized meetings of the membership, where union business or policy is discussed and all unauthorized distribution of literature be discontinued immediately.

A week later, on October 27, the deputy administrator wrote Rappaport that he was to "show cause, in writing," not later than November 3, why he should not be removed as the elected union steward at the Sunbeam plant and be prosecuted because he had called a shop meeting "for the purpose of discussing contract proposals and that prior to and during this meeting you did allow a petition to be circulated among the membership employed by the Sunbeam Corporation." Although Rappaport was given until November 3 to answer the charges and did so before the deadline, he was removed as steward by the deputy administrator on the morning of November 3 without any kind of hearing being held. The petition he had circulated was an appeal of the members to Hayes asking that local autonomy be restored.

The deputy administrator must have been busy on November 3, because he also, without explanation, removed Ciepley from his elected post as steward of the Hotpoint plant. That same day a new set of charges was filed against Ciepley, Rappaport, and Williams; on these charges they were eventually brought up on trial.

In the trials, the Grand Lodge did not follow the normal procedure of bringing the case before a committee of local union members, with this committee later reporting its findings and recommendations back to the local membership. Instead, Hayes exercised his right under the IAM constitution to appoint a special trial committee which could report directly to him, and whose verdict he could either accept or reject. His decision, in turn, could be appealed to the union's executive council, made up of IAM vice-presidents, and their decision might be finally appealed to an appeals committee of the Grand Lodge conventions, held once every four years. However, the convention appeals committee is appointed by the same executive council whose decisions it is supposed to review. Moreover, members appealing any decisions are not permitted to appear before the delegates in person.

Hayes appointed two vice-presidents and one Grand Lodge representative as the trial committee to hear the charges against Ciepley and Rappaport, as well as against Williams (who pleaded guilty). Eight charges had been leveled at Ciepley and Williams; four against Rappaport, one of which was withdrawn at the trial. All the charges ultimately arose from their having sponsored a resolution which they distributed to the delegates at the Illinois Federation of Labor convention on October 8, 1958. The resolution called upon the state convention to approve a program that included mobilizing "the rank and file as the main weapon in the struggle against corruption and unethical practices . . ." to "set up a committee of seven prominent and impartial citizens . . . to review grievances dealing with unethical practice and corruption within the labor unions," and to establish "a period not to exceed six months . . . for any such justifiable suspension, administratorship and supervision."

Toward the end of the trial, Ciepley was questioned about his opinion of public review boards.

Q.: And it is your position that clergy and professional people are better qualified to review questions involving the administration of union affairs than its elected officers?

A.: No, no, but I think it would be more democratic procedure to have an impartial committee take up grievances such as is being done in the UAW.

Q.: You think they would be better qualified to decide them than the elected officials of the union?

A.: Let us say they would be more democratic.

None of the defendants has yet found out how "democratic" the union officials who made up the trial committee were, since they have never been told what decision the committee reached. Instead, Hayes ordered Ciepley and Rappaport expelled, while Williams was prohibited from holding union office for a year.

The two defendants are now appealing Hayes's decision to the executive council. If they are turned down, as they almost certainly will be, they will have to wait until the 1960 convention. In the meantime, they are expelled from the IAM.

Rappaport is still working at Sunbeam, where he claims the support of most of the members; but Ciepley, who lost his steward's extra seniority when he was removed from that post, was caught in a layoff at his plant. Since then, he has worked in a number of other shops, harassed—he charges—by attempts of the deputy administrator to have him discharged. Even now, employed once again in a union shop at union wages, he asserts that his present employer was telephoned by the deputy administrator and advised to fire him.

This whole affair would appear to raise a great many serious questions about the internal functioning of trade unions in America today.

Unfortunately, in the case of the IAM as of so many other unions, when these questions are raised by any "outsiders," the immediate reaction of the union leadership is to become defensive about its own interests and frequently offensive about the intentions it ascribes to the outsiders. It is true that much of the union's attitude in these situations can be traced to the earlier history of the American labor movement. The preamble to the IAM constitution, calling for "organizations founded upon the class struggle," once had some real meaning; today, though the preamble remains unchanged, the position of the labor movement in our society is obviously far different. Mr. Hayes claims that liberals and intellectuals have become "disenchanted" with the labor movement because "they look nostalgically at the good old days of mass organization, sit-down strikes, and Memorial Day massacres, and conclude that, since such things are past, labor no longer has any cause, and that labor's prime concern now must be one of internal administration. . . ."

It is obvious that Mr. Hayes, both as IAM president and as chairman of the AFL-CIO Ethical Practices Committee, believes that "protecting the rights of members"—one of the functions assigned to his committee—is solely the concern of the trade unions. But in fact, since unions are recognized and protected by public law, some "rights of members" are indeed properly a matter of public concern.

DAVID DUBINSKY:
WHY HIS THRONE IS
WOBBLING

INTRODUCTION

JUST AS there is very little connection between "ethical practices" and the expulsion of dissidents, so, too, there can be a great contrast between the public reputation of a union and its internal spirit. For many years, the International Ladies' Garment Workers' Union and its president, David Dubinsky, have had the reputation, justly, of being one of America's most far-sighted and socially conscious unions. But, even in this union, the corrosive effects of institutionalized power have eaten away at the idealistic underpinnings which once marked it in a very special way.

This version of the article about David Dubinsky and the International Ladies' Garment Workers' Union has three paragraphs italicized which were not in italics in the original version when it appeared in *Harper's Magazine*. The italicizing has been done to call attention to the paragraphs, for they have become central to a controversy which is discussed in the commentary following the article rather than preceding it.

DAVID DUBINSKY: WHY HIS THRONE IS WOBBLING

(1962) **O**NCE OR TWICE a year I fumble through a small metal box in my dresser drawer, searching for those elusive plastic tabs that slip into the collar of my evening shirt. As I push aside broken tie clips and useless keys, my fingers usually roll around a small red-and-white lapel badge. Embossed on it, in tiny letters, is "International Ladies' Garment Workers' Union." I have saved it for more than twenty years from the days when, as an organizer for the ILGWU, I wore it very proudly.

To be a union organizer was one dream of many young liberals and radicals during the thirties and early forties; to be an ILGWU organizer, almost more than could have been hoped for in even their wildest fantasies. And for me, organizing shops owned by employers who had fled from New York to escape the union was even more than a mission; the status that went with being an ILGWU organizer meant a lot to me at a time when my life was bedraggled and miserable.

Almost too vividly, I can remember the details of sudden, brutal fights on picket lines and the mole on the chin of a strike-breaker whose head I was smashing against the side of a truck. I can still conjure up the sense of terror that flooded me the evening I walked slowly down a country lane, an insane farmer prodding me in the back with a loaded shotgun because I had tried to sign up his daughter in the union.

But there are scores of more pleasant memories too—the huge breakfasts we organizers ate after early wintry morning leaflet distributions, warmed as much by camaraderie and kibitzing as by the hot coffee we slurped up from heavy mugs; the lazy afternoons playing snooker in grimy pool halls before we started on our nightly round of visits to workers' homes; the weekend drives back to New York singing Socialist and revolutionary songs, all of us bound together by a sense of crusade.

Something else important is buried deep in my experience and, I think, in that of everyone who has worked for the ILGWU—the mark left by our relations, no matter how brief or peripheral, with David Dubinsky, the union's leader since 1932 and one of the most formidable and publicly admired labor leaders in the country.

By 1940, when I was working for the union, Dubinsky was already a legendary figure. All of us knew and talked about his quarrels with John L. Lewis over the use of Communists as CIO organizers and about his disputes with Sidney Hillman over the American Labor party. We knew, too, that he drank Canadian Club whiskey, that his daughter's name was Jean, that he worked ten or twelve hours a day, and that he had a formidable secretary. Very quickly we learned that it was "D.D.," as he likes to be called, who made most of the decisions in the ILG— ranging from where an organizing campaign should be started to how much of a car allowance, if any, should be granted. And it only took a few weeks to discover that all his colleagues were really his subordinates and that the awe in which they held him was mixed with fear.

In my imagination, Dubinsky was twenty feet tall, so it was a shock to me when I met him the first time at a birthday party given for him in the union's old headquarters, a small, rather shabby building on Sixteenth Street, just off Fifth Avenue. He walked into the room, accepting with a negligent wave the congratulations being offered him, and I saw that he was short and stocky, amost stubby.

"Hallo," he said to me when we were introduced, in a heavy Yiddish accent about which he is very self-conscious. He offered me a limp hand. But, despite his flabby grip, there was never a doubt in the mind of any staff member that D.D. was the supreme authority of our union.

Now, twenty years later, Dubinsky, once the source of the ILGWU's great vigor, has become the symbol of the union's internal weakness. For something important has gone awry inside the ILGWU; a sickness has turned the union's leadership rancid and mean. During the past eighteen months, the ILGWU, long idealized as a model of socially responsible and democratic unionism—one which President Kennedy said recently "deserves the heartiest commendations"—has been embroiled in two ugly quarrels which reveal deep dissatisfactions about the union.

The sickness of the ILGWU is not, however, a sudden one, even though its public symptoms are so recent. It has been developing for many years.

Normally, Dubinsky is a volatile man, quick to flare up into shouting anger, but his temper was even edgier than usual during the May, 1962, convention of the International Ladies' Garment Workers' Union. In a steady rage that seemed to last for the eight days of the convention, Dubinsky lashed out at those "enemies" of the union who, he shouted, wanted to "undermine us, degrade us," who used "sneaky ways" and "machinations" against the ILGWU. But it was not the employers, the garment manufacturers, at whom the seventy-year-old Dubinsky continually hurled his defiance; indeed, *they* were honored guests at the convention. No, the "traitors to our cause" were those members of the ILGWU staff, mostly business agents and organizers, who had organized a union of their own.

Why should the staff members of the ILGWU want to organize their own union? Their complaints are simple enough. Traditionally the union has paid them low salaries; they have to make demeaning personal appeals to their supervisors in order to get raises; often they must chisel on expense accounts to meet their legitimate needs. After years of grumbling, a small group of ILG organizers met secretly in the fall of 1959 to form a union to represent them, calling themselves the Federation of Union Representatives (FOUR). By December, 1959, the FOUR group believed they represented a majority of the organizers, business agents, and educational directors in the union. But when they sent a telegram to Dubinsky asking for recognition, they were flatly turned down.

"We look upon [an organization like FOUR] as a violation of the traditional spirit of our union," Dubinsky's executive board replied. "We are convinced that such an organization would be an instrument of internal dissension and strife, bound to undermine the standards and welfare of the ILGWU and its members." The board argued that it opposed unionization of the ILGWU business agents—who made up the bulk of FOUR's membership—because they have duties "directorial in nature" and are "spokesmen for the union."

With this, Dubinsky started using every legal, financial, and organizational resource of the ILGWU to smash FOUR, resisting all attempts by the National Labor Relations Board to give the new group a fair chance to establish itself as a union. When the NLRB ordered that an election be held to see how many staff members favored FOUR, the ILG unsuccessfully opposed the order. When it was determined that FOUR won the election, the ILGWU was ordered to bargain with it, but it has refused to do so and has been charged by the NLRB for refusal to bargain. Dubinsky has made it clear that he will drag FOUR through every court he can before recognizing it.

At the same time, he has conducted a massive campaign within the ILG itself. Members of FOUR have come under ugly pressures by their superiors to quit their union. A stream of editorials have denounced FOUR in *Justice,* the ILG's newspaper, and so have advertisements in the New York daily papers. Not long ago, one of the NLRB's most experienced examiners found the ILGWU guilty of unfair labor practices against FOUR, and the union was ordered to cease threatening staff members with reprisals for their activities on FOUR's behalf. Predictably, the ILGWU is appealing this verdict, just as it has the others.

There is nothing very surprising about the demand by the ILGWU staff to bargain with its employer. Many other unions have been faced with staff demands for some form of collective bargaining. Staff members of unions representing airline pilots, chemical workers, teachers, newspapermen, electrical workers, and the AFL-CIO itself have all negotiated agreements with their union leadership, although some were achieved in the face of considerable resistance. But no other union officials have reacted with the explosive violence of Dubinsky, who has made strident personal attacks on such men as Norman Thomas because they disagreed with him in the FOUR case.

The same choleric emotionalism displayed in Dubinsky's fight against FOUR has also been evident in the dispute between the ILGWU and the National Association for the Advancement of Colored People, which charges that "Negro and Puerto Rican members of the ILGWU are discriminated against both in terms of wages and other conditions of employment and in their status as members of the union."

This accusation reflects one of the fiercest dilemmas facing Dubinsky and his fellow leaders. They rose to power in the thirties when the ILGWU's strength was mainly drawn from Jewish and Italian immigrants. But now Negroes and Puerto Ricans make up one-quarter of the union's national membership of 400,000, and one-half of the membership in New York City. And it is particularly in New York where the NAACP claims that the Negroes and Puerto Ricans are getting a raw deal. In at least one case, the New York State Commission for Human Rights found "probable cause to credit the allegations [of discrimination]" which the NAACP had lodged against Dubinsky's own local of cutters in New York. (Only "probable" because, until recently, the local refused to supply the Commission with the information it requested.)

Last summer the charges of discrimination in the ILGWU became the subject of an inept congressional investigation sparked by Adam Clayton Powell, the Negro Congressman from Harlem who is chairman of the House Education and Labor Committee. Dubinsky has repeatedly denied all charges of discrimination and maintains that the committee investigation of the ILGWU is a "spite probe"—"based on malice, on blackmail." During Powell's absence, the subcommittee hearings were conducted by Representative Herbert Zelenko, who had been denied ILGWU support in the primary in New York this year; and Dubinsky points out that Herbert Hill, the national labor secretary of the NAACP, was serving the committee as a paid consultant.

There seems, then, to be some justice in Dubinsky's criticism of the impartiality of these confused hearings. But politics cannot account for all the savage bitterness with which he and his top leadership have reacted both to FOUR's request for a staff union and to the charges of the NAACP. Dubinsky is so convinced that his union is far better than any other that it is intolerable for him to witness public display of the ILGWU's alleged shortcomings or any real or imagined slights to his leadership.

For the union is Dubinsky's real family, his only real life. He is, as he told the House subcommittee, the "Poppa" of the ILGWU, to whom all the union's officials must account, the man who can "put the fear of God into their hearts." He believes the careers of the staff members are his to control as he wishes. One explanation of his vindictive response to FOUR is simply that he felt like a father whose children had turned on him. What he did not understand is that the badly paid staff felt they had to organize their own union precisely because Dubinsky views himself as the head of a family group for which he insists on making *all* decisions.

This paternalism encompasses not only the union but the garment industry itself. And although this is unfortunate, it becomes more understandable when one examines the bizarre world of clothes manufacturing which still centers around lower Seventh Avenue in New York City.

"For God's sake, Cohen, make some kind of an offer to the union," a state mediator once said to a dress manufacturer facing a strike by the ILGWU. "Offer the union a penny an hour if that's all you can afford—but offer *something* so they'll know you're bargaining in good faith."

Absolutely bewildered, the employer stared at the mediator. "It doesn't make any difference how much I offer," he explained patiently. "They *know* I'm not acting in food faith."

Indeed, good faith is a very rare quality in the garment industry, where some twelve thousand employers—most of them running very small shops—engage in notoriously ruthless competition. The capital investment is low; the profit from a dress or coat that "clicks" can be very high; and the employers search grimly for the slightest competitive edge. The average women's garment factory employs only thirty-six workers today—exactly one more than in 1900—and the annual death rate of garment firms is one of the highest in the country. Furthermore, about 80 percent of the workers are women, and they come and go so rapidly that the union has had to sign up 200,000 new members in the last three years merely to hold its level of membership.

In this concrete jungle, the ILGWU is far more than a conventional bargaining agent. It has become a major regulatory force. If it were not strong enough to dominate the rapacious animals of the jungle, they might eat one another up, devouring thousands of jobs in the process. Thus the ILGWU is not concerned simply with obtaining better wages and conditions for a highly fluid work force (a force increasingly composed of Negroes and Puerto Ricans with so little organizational experience that the union leaders, correctly or not, doubt their ability to solve their own problems). It is also concerned with keeping the frequently rickety firms it deals with in—or out—of business. And this peculiar situation is directly linked to the ILGWU's contention that its business agents—who deal directly with the employers—should be barred from joining FOUR because their duties are more "directorial" than those of business agents in other unions.

But for all the union's power, competition in the industry is so fierce and the profit margin so low that the garment workers receive relatively low wages—often not more than the federal minimum rate. In the past fifteen years, average wages in the printing, rubber, auto, and building industries—among many others—have all risen much more swiftly than those of the ILGWU members.

Nor do the average wage figures tell the whole story. A comparatively small elite of skilled garment cutters and pressers do in fact earn fairly high wages, while the far more numerous union members who work as floorworkers, finishers, examiners, and bundlers receive a great deal less. One of the NAACP's major charges is that Negroes and Puerto Ricans who do this low-paid work are barred from admission to the locals which control the more highly skilled jobs.

Whether or not discrimination is widespread, one thing is clear: little real communication exists between the growing colored membership of the union and the present leadership. No Negro or Puerto Rican holds any high office in the ILGWU. Under Dubinsky's hardened autocratic control, the union's aging leaders still reflect the patterns of an earlier era.

When David Dubinsky, a young, energetic, and ambitious Yiddish Socialist, emigrated to the U.S. from Poland in 1911, the garment trade was in a churning state of flux. The older Scotch-Irish and German-Jewish garment workers, who had made whole garments, were being replaced by the newer Jewish immigrants from Poland and Russia. These "greenhorns," unable to speak the language, were bound together by family ties, common European origin, and politics. Crowded together on the Lower East Side, they were forced to slave in ghastly sweatshops which sprang up throughout the slums. They worked for contractors and subcontractors who hired them to perform single operations on garments brought in bundles from the larger manufacturers—a single garment might travel by pushcart to three different factories before completion, just as it might today.

Many of the new immigrants who went into the needle trades were Socialists like Dubinsky who had been very active in the

Bund, the vigorous Jewish Socialist movement in Eastern Europe. At fourteen Dubinsky was already secretary of the bakers' union in Lodz, Poland, and helped run a strike that shut down all the Jewish bakeries in the city, including the one owned by his father.

Within a few weeks after Dubinsky arrived in the U.S at nineteen, he was actively participating in the vigorous Yiddish Socialist movements that had been transferred from Europe to the crowded East Side slums. Dubinsky throve in this atmosphere. In 1914 he married Emma Goldberg, a garment worker and Socialist from Lithuania, but the pattern of his life was basically unchanged, for his drives could only be fulfilled inside an organization.

"I remember Dubinsky when he was running a cooperative restaurant," recalls an ILGWU veteran, "and even then he was the manager while everybody else was just a waiter."

In New York, Dubinsky became a garment cutter instead of a baker. Then as now, the cutters were the aristocrats of the trade, for their skill in guiding a heavy cutting machine through many layers of cloth can mean the difference between profit and loss for the employer. The cutters' union was still a stronghold of the older garment workers, who were far more conservative than the young Socialists like Dubinsky.

Dubinsky had very little time to spare from Socialist party activity for union work during his first four or five years in this country, but when the younger cutters in his local organized a caucus to take over the leadership, he began to play an active role. Within five years he had become not only the general manager of the cutters' local but its secretary-treasurer as well—a pattern of control he was to follow in the years to come. But while Dubinsky was consolidating his position within the cutters' local, the national ILGWU was being torn apart by internal factional fights and badly run strikes. An active Communist group had been exploiting the dissension and trying to take over.

Dubinsky threw himself into the fight against the Communists and was a decisive force in defeating them. But this battle was so traumatic that he and many other ILGWU leaders developed a fear of factionalism which remains irrationally alive today, thirty years after the original cause has disappeared. The residue can still be found in the ILGWU's constitution, which prohibits the formation of internal union caucuses and factions, except for brief preconvention periods; and in Dubinsky's technique of presenting only one slate of officers for election. Incredibly enough, the old experience with the Communists has been used to justify the charges of "factionalism" which are being made against FOUR today. Dubinsky has even used Socialist support of FOUR as an excuse to conjure up a "Trotskyite" plot against the union.

By 1932 Dubinsky was in so strong a position that he was asked to become president of the international ILGWU on his own terms. These were that he be given the secretary-treasurer job as well—at least temporarily, until the splits within the national ILGWU were healed. When he took over the shattered union, it had only 40,000 members, almost all of them in New York, and it was more than $750,000 in debt. Two years later he was able to report to the cheering delegates at the 1934 convention that the membership had quintupled to 200,000 and that the treasury held a surplus of $500,000.

No doubt the election of Roosevelt and the spreading crisis of the Depression all contributed to this astonishing revival. But it was Dubinsky who ran the organizing campaigns and the strikes that brought thousands of garment workers all over the country flocking to the ILGWU. It was inevitable that he be formally elected president of the ILGWU at the 1934 convention. And after eliminating the new aspirants to the job of secretary-treasurer by preconvention deals, he was elected to that post too, "for a temporary period of two years." (In fact, he held on to the job until 1959, when he finally turned it over to his trusted follower Louis Stulberg, another member of the cutters' local.)

The 1930s were the most important years of the ILGWU's life. As the New Deal took hold, the old Socialist ideologies of the union's leaders became more and more diluted. If it wasn't possible to reorganize the world, the Wagner Act at least made it possible to organize more garment workers into union locals and clean up filthy sweatshops. But the leaders soon ran into trouble: they had to deal not only with the employers but with the industrial racketeering which had infiltrated their industry.

Originally, hoodlums and gangsters had been brought into the garment trade by some employers determined to keep out the unions. The racketeers quickly managed to gain effective control not only of some garment-manufacturing companies but of some union locals as well. It was at this time that Dubinsky began to demand signed but undated resignations from elected and appointed ILGWU officials—a practice that still prevails today. ("It's conducive to keep your union clean, very conducive," is Dubinsky's justification of the practice.)

No one will ever be able to write a history of the wars between the ILGWU and the mobs. Although the casualty list was long, the battles were fought in complete silence. Because the mobsters controlled so much of New York's political life, the unions couldn't count on the police. And so they were forced, sometimes, to be as unscrupulous as the enemy, allying themselves with their own strong-arm gangs against the racketeers, with both sides using the same arms—guns, acid, knives, and stink bombs. Honest union officials and dishonest hoodlums were trampled to death in vacant lofts in the same way. Tragically, the mode of conspiracy that the union was forced to adopt in those days has lingered on, inevitably affecting the way in which the union leaders conduct their fight against FOUR.

But this face of the union very rarely showed in public. Even if it had, no accurate sense of what the ILGWU was all about would have been gained by it. For despite Dubinsky's growing vanity and his increasing control over the union machinery, the organization under his leadership was still suffused with an élan that was unique to it then. If the leaders were no longer Socialists, they understood better than most union people that broad and unprecedented social possibilities were opening up in America.

Certainly the ILGWU's public programs were admirable. For

the members, a union-sponsored educational program was developed; health centers began to spring up; Unity House, the members' vacation resort in the Pocono Mountains of Pennsylvania, was expanded; and semi-independent political action started with the birth of the American Labor party in New York. Those were the years to which Dubinsky nostalgically returns today as the best years of his and the union's life; the years in which "Pins and Needles," the ILGWU's own musical revue (the first and last of its kind), ran for weeks in New York and even gave a performance for President Roosevelt at the White House. And the ILGWU could be counted on to support causes in which few other unions took any interest. Even though most of the union's leaders had emulated Dubinsky in leaving the Socialist party, the ILGWU was still a haven in those years for political nonconformists. Its devoted organizing and educational staffs included liberals and radicals from every section of the left except the Communists.

The salaries paid out to staff and officers in the thirties and early forties weren't especially important to them, for they were committed to the union as a social movement. As late as 1940 and 1941, when I was working for the ILG, an organizer's salary was still only around $40 per week—supplemented, if you worked outside of New York City, by a weekly expense allowance of $7.50. I can still remember having an expense account rejected because I had taken an upper berth. Coaches were good enough.

But, although we complained a little about our low pay and expense accounts, our biggest griping was reserved for Dubinsky's domination of the union and his demand for unquestioning allegiance.

"Everybody holler, 'Hurray for Dubinsky!' " Dubinsky would shout from the top of a table during summer parties at Unity House. And all the residents of "Vice Presidents' Row"—the cottages set aside for the union officers—dutifully shouted back, "Hurray for Dubinsky!" But neither the union officers who were dependent upon Dubinsky, nor those who felt they were part of a crusade in which he played a key role, would publicly complain about the internal management of the union. No member of the executive board revealed that Dubinsky enforced his demands upon them by threatening to resign if his policy wasn't adopted. No member of the staff even filed a public complaint about the donations they were pressured to make to causes Dubinsky favored. Those were family secrets to be kept from the outsiders.

So the public mystique of David Dubinsky and the ILGWU grew and flourished, aided considerably by a very skillful public-relations operation and a friendly press, especially in New York City, where Dubinsky was treated as a sacred figure. He was, after all, largely responsible for some excellent ILGWU policies: its publication of complete financial reports, long before the law required it; its public stand against racketeering in unions, taken long before the McClellan Committee revelations; its support of liberal causes; and its involvement in the creation of the CIO.

But now the family secrets are coming out. Some of the most significant disclosures have been made by the ILGWU officials themselves in NLRB hearings as they tried to argue that the union's business agents exercise such important authority that they must be considered as "representatives of management," ineligible to join a staff union like FOUR.

According to the ILGWU leaders, the business agent can deal with the employers in very different ways. He may use what is called a "hard" policy—if he feels that the employer does not "accept the union completely and wholeheartedly," he can exert pressure by invoking the union's contract at every opportunity. For example, he can bring every single discharge of a worker to arbitration, "even where the facts show that the case was with cause." On the other hand, the business agent may employ a "soft" policy—he may uphold the employer when a worker is discharged and "the worker's rights . . . end at that point." And he can accommodate the employer in other ways.

The same ambivalence applies outside the plant. As one ILGWU official testified at the hearings, local units of the union might support sit-in strikes by Negroes in some communities;

but "it's altogether conceivable that a business agent for a Southern local might participate in the deliberations of a White Citizens Council. . . ."

In such testimony, the ILGWU leaders reveal a dilemma they are unable to solve. Privately they believe they must maintain their disciplinary power over their business agents if they are to wield power effectively in the fragmented and risky garment industry, accommodating one employer with "soft" policy, disciplining another with "hard," warring aginst those gangsters who are still operating shops. But at the same time they tell their business agents that it would be improper for them to belong to FOUR because a business agent, as one leader put it, is in a category with a "priest or a rabbi or a minister." Dubinsky, in short, wants his staff to live and behave as if they were carrying out a crusading mission of the thirties. But the staff members know that in these days of finely calculated "hard" and "soft" policies, unions are no longer crusading organizations, except perhaps in the nostalgic memories of their leaders as their limousines cruise up the White House drive.

Nor does Dubinsky help matters by dismissing the FOUR sympathizers as "peanut politicians" who "feel that the president and vice-president live too long," as he did at the ILGWU convention. He was probably referring here to those FOUR members who were graduates of the union's own Training Institute, once described by the ILG as "labor's West Point." Amid great fanfare, the Institute was established in 1951 to train dedicated union members and outsiders for a career of service in the union. Today, less than 50 percent of the 308 graduates are still on the union's staff.

Some of FOUR's most active members were graduates of the Institute. This may be one of the reasons why the school closed down in 1961, ostensibly because there were no more jobs to be filled, and why Gus Tyler, the school's director—and once a bright star of political action in the Socialist and liberal movements—has single-mindedly applied his skills to the task of fighting FOUR.

Very little evidence has been produced to substantiate

charges that FOUR is really a faction trying to give itself the protections of a union, while directed by forces outside. But it's certainly possible that some ambitious FOUR members would like either to get power themselves or change the structure of the ILGWU—a structure in which family connections are a considerable aid to advancement. Shelley Appleton, Dubinsky's son-in-law, who became manager of a large ILGWU local after he married the union president's only child, was elevated to a vice-presidency at the last convention. And the fact that Appleton is extremely competent does little to erase the cynicism of other staff members not fortunate enough to have fathers-in-law who are ready to place them in what has become, in effect, a family business.

The tragedy of the ILGWU is that its leaders do not understand the membership of "their" union. A far deeper cultural empathy and common tradition exist today between the Jewish ILGWU leaders and the Jewish employers—many of them former garment workers themselves—than exist between the leaders and the members.

As much as anything else, the union's financial report for January, 1959—December, 1961 reflects the tight hold of the past. Of the $651,939.53 domestic donations made by either the ILGWU General Office or by a joint fund of ILGWU affiliates and the General Office, approximately $18,000 was given to Negro groups and $750 to a Puerto Rican group. The Congress of Racial Equality, one of the most active forces battling Negro segregation, received only $200, half the amount given to the New York Press Photographers Association. But the Yiddish and Jewish organizations to which the union's leadership is still bound received nearly eight times as much—more than $140,-000.

The union's overseas contributions of $462,000 made during the three-year period show an even greater disparity: almost $300,000 went to organizations in Israel or to Jewish groups operating overseas and $60,000 was given to Italian groups. One donation niftily combined both the Jewish and Italian interests in a grand public-relations gesture: $25,000 was

given to the Luigi Antonini Stadium in Haifa! (An additional
$25,000 had been donated earlier to the stadium, named for
an ILGWU vice-president.)

No one can reasonably object to the ILGWU's officers making contributions to what are, after all, very worthy causes. But
the large sums given to Jewish groups and the comparatively tiny
amounts given to Negro, Puerto Rican, and Mexican groups
illustrate the inability of Dubinsky to adjust to reality just as
much as does his fight against FOUR. The money belongs not
to Dubinsky but to the union members, most of them no longer
either Jewish or Italian, and the amounts expended to keep
alive the past are all out of proportion to the needs of the
present.

Through the use of ILGWU funds, Dubinsky is able to dominate whole areas of New York life. His control of the Liberal
party, the political action arm of the ILGWU, which was formed
after the American Labor party split on the Communist issue, is
another example of paternalistic ILG leadership. The Liberal
party has become, not the independent party it was originally
conceived to be, but instead the political organ of Dubinsky and
of Alex Rose of the hatters' union, used by them for the support
of the candidates they choose. It was power politics, not principle, that gave Robert Wagner a blank-check endorsement
for Mayor from the Liberal party before he had decided on
either his running mates or platform. And it is power politics,
not principle, that frequently determines whom the Liberal
party shall support for a judgeship. Dubinsky's choices are questioned as rarely in the Liberal party as they are in the ILGWU.

"Well, what do you want, Jacobs?" is a legitimate question.
"Haven't you changed, too, since those days when you were an
ILGWU organizer out on the picket lines?"

Yes, indeed, I've changed. The plastic tabs I go looking for
in the box with my ILGWU button fit into an evening shirt, and
it has been a very long time since I smashed anybody's head
against the side of a truck. But what is so deeply disturbing

about the American trade unions today is not that they have changed, but rather that they haven't.

What are unions doing to develop cadres of new leadership? To confront the baffling problems of fast technological change? To help disadvantaged groups learn new skills and gain a foothold in the economy? To assess the basic function of unions in the coming decades? Such questions are barely touched upon in the AFL-CIO today. And that is why the tragedy of David Dubinsky is not unique, even though his empire is ruptured in its own distinctive way. As with many another union leader, Dubinsky's success has led to his failure. The question now is where new leadership can come from to redeem the responsibilities that union officers ought to fulfill, but very rarely do.

POSTSCRIPT

NOT SURPRISINGLY, this article created a bitter and emotional row. For many years, Dubinsky and his union have been considered virtually sacred figures by the press and the community. A chorus of disapproval for the article arose from many people, including employers and management lawyers. But the response of the union concentrated on the italicized paragraphs.

The ILGWU maintains that my analysis of its financial contributions was "inaccurate" and that, in fact, "only $40,000 was given to Jewish organizations" in the U.S. instead of the $140,000 they claim I said was donated. In addition, the union also states I did not separate union funds from voluntary contributions, omitted the tremendous contributions for nonsectarian purposes made by the union, did not analyze or even mention funds representing an additional $3,750,000 distributed by the locals, and made no study of Puerto Rican contributions, including the sum of $25,000 earmarked for a Puerto Rican cultural center that to date has never been picked up.

In sum, the union's position is that I did not check its financial report carefully enough. Perhaps, if I had been allowed to do this with a responsible union official, I might have modified some details in what I wrote. I stress the phrase "if I had been allowed" for not only did the union never give me the oppor-

tunity to make the kind of analysis it later complained I should
have made but, on the contrary, it actively resisted my repeated
attempts to discuss the article with a responsible union officer.
When I began first to collect the material for the article, the
union attorney who was handling the case against FOUR refused
to discuss it with me and told me that he would not even give
me any of the official legal documents without permission from
his superiors. At that time, I did have a discussion about the situation with Gus Tyler, the union's political action and educational director, but at his insistence what he said to me was off-
the-record then and has remained so since. I asked for an
on-the-record interview with Dubinsky and was told that was
impossible. The only material the union provided me with was
its official convention reports, financial statements, and newspaper.

Later, during the preparation of the article, I wrote Tyler
twice asking his permission to quote from a letter he had sent
me about the union's fight with FOUR and complaining about
the lack of an interview with Dubinsky. I also wrote the union's
publicity director for explanations of some donations that were
unclear to me. To my complaint about being unable to see Dubinsky, Tyler offered sympathy but nothing more and my request
for permission to quote from his earlier letter was refused. Later,
when I wrote Tyler again, still attempting to get a statement
from the union, other than what they printed in their newspaper,
he refused me again. My request of the publicity director for an
explanation of donations that were unclear to me was simply
unanswered, although I did receive a reply to a query I made
concerning the union's executive board.

Now then, what is a writer to do in such a situation? Should
I have not written about Dubinsky because he refused to be
interviewed? Not written about the ILGWU's attitude toward
FOUR because I could get no statements other than press re-
leases from the union? Not discussed the donations because my
questions went unanswered? If these are the alternatives open,
nothing controversial would ever be written.

After the article appeared, Tyler wrote the following letter
which appeared in *Harper's*.

TO THE EDITORS:

Paul Jacobs' article, "David Dubinsky: Why His Throne Is Wobbling," is an artful caricature, but the features are so distorted as to reveal more about the artist than his subject. The piece adopts the new left posture: to assail the liberal "establishment." The ILGWU—for several decades a driving force in the "vital center"—has always been a natural target for snipers from left and right.

In the early twenties, the ILGWU was "red" because of Socialist leadership; in the late twenties, it was "social-fascist" because of its war on the Communists; in the early thirties, it was "bourgeois" because it backed FDR; in the mid thirties, it was "Communist" because it aided loyalist Spain; in the forties, it was a "red-baiting" outfit because it refused to go along with the fashionable fellow-traveling; in the early fifties, it was charged with "splitting" the labor vote because it fused with the Republicans in New York City to oppose Mayor William O'Dwyer. In the sixties, it was called plumb crazy for backing Robert F. Wagner's seemingly hopeless primary fight against Tammany.

Through all of this, the ILGWU grew: the average age of its leadership grew younger, thanks to the world's most extensive and expensive labor leadership training program; it continued to pioneer in bargaining for vacation benefits, medical care, retirement, and severance pay for its members. Its contributions to the community expanded through its program in housing, civil rights, counseling, and labor education.

Jacobs "reports" that the New York press always treated Dubinsky "as a sacred figure." This impression may be due to the fact that criticisms have been obliterated by the ILG's positive accomplishments. Recently, Dubinsky was asked how he managed to stay so young. "I do two things," replied D.D. "I take care of myself and I take care of my enemies."

Many years of abuse—whether in a tsarist prison, in Pegler's doghouse, in the GOP and Communist press, or at the violent hands of Joey Fay for opposing racketeering—have not made him soft. Jacobs is accurate only in describing him as a hard battler.

Not that the union (or unions) is without problems. In 1959 in an article in the *New York Times,* Dubinsky foresaw the need to develop young new leaders reflecting "the many ethnic, linguistic, geographic currents in our trade."

Dubinsky was addressing himself to basic problems and not to the sniping of FOUR (Federation of Union Representatives) and Herbert Hill, both facets of a factional flurry which Jacobs has blown up and distorted.

The ILGWU has been recognizing unions of union employees for decades. When the novel request to recognize a union of *officers* arrived, Dubinsky referred it to the general executive board. It offered to bargain with a union of *organizers,* but not with a union of *business agents,* who are in a position to name top officials and determine policies. Surely such officers are not typical employees, entitled to bargaining rights under the Labor Act. It is this question that the ILGWU wishes to test before the Supreme Court—in the same way it has contested other rulings of the NLRB in the courts—and won.

The FOUR faction was supported by Herbert Hill, who is not a member of the ILGWU. He has made charges of discrimination against Negroes in the ILG. Lester Granger, former director of the Urban League, countered that "the 'facts' presented in his [Hill's] report were so sleazy that any ILGWU spokesman could tear them apart with ease." These sleazy facts are the cornerstone of Jacobs' artful piece.

Have these "charges" had any impact on the rank and file of the ILGWU? Yes. Hundreds of ILGWU members—of whom a majority were Negroes and Puerto Ricans—threw themselves into a primary campaign to defeat the man who headed the Congressional investigation of Hill's charges. And they succeeded. A throne toppled, but it was not Dubinsky's.

In his most mischievous distortion, Jacobs belittles the ILG's contributions to Negro organizations in comparison with its gifts to Jewish causes. He does this by focusing on a report that accounts for only $1,113,000 out of a total of $5,240,000 in contributions. In this period ILGWU and its locals contributed more than $3,000 to CORE, not $200 as Jacobs claims. He labels as "Jewish" contributions to Brandeis University, City of Hope, and several nonsectarian hospitals, whose patients are mainly non-Jewish. He makes no mention of more than $400,-000 given to the Eleanor Roosevelt Cancer Fund and the March of Dimes, nor of the additional $3,750,000 contributed to other community and nonsectarian causes.

Jacobs correctly reports that "almost $300,000" goes to Israel and to the victims of Hitler. These contributions were voluntary, not taken out of the union treasury. Furthermore, the ILGWU believes that Israel is a bastion of democracy in the Near East. It also believes that $130,000 is not too large a contribution over three years to help the children of the six million Jews exterminated by Hitler. To do these things, the ILG believes, is *human* not *Jewish*.

GUS TYLER
Education Director
Inter. Ladies' Garment Workers' Union
New York, N.Y.

I do not agree with Tyler's analysis of his union's contributions, and after reading what he has written about it I still am convinced that the essence of my charge is true: the union's leadership is out of contact with its membership and the donations made by the union are one reflection of this disparity. I'm sorry if I was wrong about any specific detail. No writer wants to use incorrect data; but in this case the responsibility for any mistake rests very heavily on the union as well as on me, for if I had been allowed to discuss the situation more freely with the union officers such errors might have been avoided.

A few months after the publication of the original article and Tyler's reply, the National Labor Relations Board sustained the trial examiner's rulings that the ILGWU had coerced the members of FOUR, threatened them with reprisals for joining FOUR, failed to grant regularly due wage increases because of FOUR's request for recognition and refused to bargain with FOUR. Indeed, the board went even farther than had the examiner and ordered the ILGWU to give back pay to the staff members whose raises had been withheld. At the same time, the NLRB upheld the ILG's refusal to reinstate two FOUR leaders who claimed they were fired for union activity.

But the NLRB rulings brought little more than a moral victory to FOUR, since the ILGWU announced, as expected, that it would continue to resist the NLRB through all the courts available to it. There is every reason to assume, on the basis of precedent, that ultimately the ILGWU will lose the legal case, but it will succeed, nevertheless, in breaking its staff union for by the time the final decision is made, very little will be left of FOUR.

The war between the ILGWU and the NAACP, which I alluded to in the article, quieted down in early 1963 and an uneasy truce began. In late January 1963, the Negro who filed the charge of discrimination against Dubinsky's local was offered a job as cutter and in the middle of May, 1963, the State Commission for Human Rights complaint against the local was withdrawn by stipulation of the parties.

Of all the criticism directed against the article and against me for having written it, the most serious had nothing to do with specific details. Rather, it was that, no matter what my intent had been, the effect of the article, especially of the italicized passages, was anti-Semitic.

Every writer who tries, seriously, to deal with questions in which Jews are involved must at some point face this problem: assuming that what he says is the truth, does it still have the effect of reinforcing the anti-Semitic image of the Jews and therefore ought it not to be written? In view of the Jews' recent history, such questions are far more serious than is the criticism made of some union leader for smashing a union of representatives or running the union as if it were his private fief.

The question arises at a number of levels. While I was writing the Dubinsky article, I worried, for example, about mentioning Dubinsky's Yiddish accent, which happens to be a very thick one. What's the relevance of the accent, I asked myself; how does knowing that Dubinsky has an accent help the reader to understand him and how his union operates? I decided it did help because it aided in bringing Dubinsky to life, because it was just as valid a descriptive detail as the fact that he was short, was married, and that his daughter's name was Jean. Then, too, I answered my question by reminding myself that the query would never have occurred to me if Dubinsky had a Southern accent or a New England accent or damn near any other kind of accent except a Yiddish one.

Still, even after I had decided to leave in the reference, I was troubled, and I *was* attacked for having said it. For example, the *Forward*, a Yiddish right-wing social-democratic paper, intimately attached to Dubinsky and the union, ran an editorial denouncing me, in general and specific terms, for the article. One of the special points made in the editorial was that the reference to Dubinsky's accent was unnecessary and another proof that I was a Jewish anti-Semite.

But the *Forward* didn't bother me very much and in a way I was even delighted with the vitriolic tone taken by the paper. In a period when newspaper journalism is flat and pallid, at least the *Forward* is still around, not hesitating to denounce its enemies, in flaming print, instead of by gossip and innuendo.

The decision about whether or not to mention Dubinsky's Yiddish accent was a very minor one in comparison with the problem of discussing the empathy that I believe exists between the Jewish employers and Jewish union leaders or with writing about the contributions made by the union to Jewish causes in proportions that I believe do not reflect the makeup of the union's membership. There is no question to me that these phenomena exist in the ILGWU, but in writing the article I had to face the possibility that what I said about these matters might be used by anti-Semites. I decided that it had to be written anyway. Communists always justify their silence about Stalin's butchery on the ground that to have discussed such horrible events as the Moscow trials or the anti-Semitism in the Soviet Union would have aided the enemies of the working class.

I don't accept that rationalization for silence and therefore I was satisfied that it would have been wrong for me to eliminate the references to the Jewish aspect of the ILGWU's role.

Nevertheless, my belief in the intellectual correctness of what I wrote has given way to an emotional shock, for, after the Dubinsky article was published, I did receive some mail from anti-Semites, horrible mail congratulating me on having exposed the role of the Jews in running the unions and even inviting me to speak at meetings of one anti-Semitic group in South Carolina.

The injection of the anti-Semitic issue by Jews and anti-Semites into the post-publication discussion of the Dubinsky article shows how uneasy about Jews we still are in America— all of us, Jews and Christians alike. America is more polite about Jews than it is about Negroes but, still, it is a troubled politeness.

I do not intend to stop writing about Jews for, after all, that is what I am and part of what I know. I am disturbed because what I say will be misunderstood by some Jews and even worse, by some anti-Semites, but no alternative is open to me; one must either write his perception of the truth or not be a writer.

INTRODUCTION

THE NEWSPAPER strike in New York City, which began in December, 1962, and extended for 114 days, brought into
sharp focus a basic question about union democracy which chal-
lenges, directly, some implications found in the articles about
the machinists' and the garment workers' unions. The issues
over which the New York printers struck were complicated
ones, involving a fear of technological unemployment, but one
fact always remained clear and simple: the initial calling of
the strike and its protracted continuation were honest reflections
of the union members' wishes. Despite the loud caterwauling
about Bert Powers, the union president, it was the members
who wanted the strike.

The relationship between union democracy and the public
good is one of the most perplexing ones we must cope with in a
complicated society. It is not a simple one-to-one relationship:
in the short run, union democracy, in the sense that it is purely
participational, a kind of town hall society, may hurt the public good. The question that now must be studied carefully is
whether or not we can afford the *long-term* benefits that come
with union democracy. And in the answers given to that inquiry will be found some clues to the kind of society America
will be in the future.

UNION DEMOCRACY AND THE PUBLIC GOOD: DO THEY NECESSARILY COINCIDE?

(1958) Fㅤᴏ ʀ ᴛ ʜ ᴇ past ten years sociologists and political scientists have been making intensive studies of trade union organization, a subject formerly the exclusive preserve of radicals, labor historians, and civil libertarians. One of the most important studies in this field to have been published recently is *Union Democracy,* an analysis of the International Typographical Union, by S. M. Lipset, M. Trow, and J. Coleman, all sociologists. Their work is significant not only for the light it sheds on the ITU, but also because it raises a fundamental question about trade union democracy and the public good in the United States today.

After a thorough examination of the ITU, the authors suggest in their conclusion that the ITU "may well serve as a touchstone against which the internal political processes of other unions, and of other voluntary groups, such as the American Legion or the American Medical Association, may be appraised and criticized"—even though they believe that "the fundamental requirements for democracy cannot be met most of the time in most unions or other voluntary groups," with their "normal" pattern of organizational oligarchy and bureaucratization. Although *Union Democracy* thus casts the ITU as "a model of the trade union in a democratic society," its authors do not discuss this subject at any great length: their chief concern is with those internal factors which have sustained democratic processes in the union. In this article, I should like first to review the conditions making for democracy in the ITU, and then go on to discuss this larger question: Is a democratically run union like the ITU, whose leaders and rank and file believe their function is restricted to job protection, *necessarily* more useful socially than unions which are autocratically managed?

For more than a half century, the ITU, a union whose jurisdiction claims all the composing rooms in the United States, has evaded the "iron law of organizational oligarchy" described in 1912 by Robert Michels. It has a unique two-party system, not found in any other national union in the United States. Its officials are comparatively low-salaried and more or less directly controlled from below, through regularly contested elections marked by a high degree of membership participation; democratic control is also exercised by referenda, through which important policy decisions are arrived at. *Union Democracy* analyzes the history of this two-party system; the behavior of the union members in and out of the shop; the way in which union leaders are recruited; and the reasons why their power over the union is not absolute and why the members are sufficiently concerned about the government of their union to keep it democratic.

The origin of the ITU's two-party system goes back to a period of economic crisis in the middle of the nineteenth century, when a secret society arose within the union, composed of the most militant and loyal members, who banded together to resist employer attempts at blacklisting, to reinforce the union internally, and to compel the employers to accept union terms, working conditions, and wages. Even when the depression period of the 1870's had ended and the union's existence became fairly stable, the secret society continued to function, so as to prevent the union from falling into the hands of less militant members. Subsequently opposition to the secret society arose among union members outside the select group, who regarded it and its successors as political machines seeking to control the best-paying jobs in the trade for themselves. Eventually the secret societies were forced to dissolve; but it was out of the struggle to make them do so that the open two-party system finally emerged. Today the two parties are firmly established within the union, although the issues now dividing them are quite different.

In recent times these differences have rarely been of a principled character. The bitter election struggles between the "ins" and "outs" have been fought mainly over the most efficient ways of administering the union and of gaining concessions from the employers. Contests over political questions not directly concerned with immediate economic demands have been uncommon, although where a political issue was directly related to the economic position of the union, as in the case of the Taft-Hartley Law, it was fairly bitterly disputed. One party within the union, the "Progressives," opposed the law, believing that it "threatened the very existence of the ITU, for it outlawed many practices which had existed in the industry since the turn of the century." Reflecting the control of the union by the "Progressives" since 1946, the ITU in the last decade has insisted that employers agree informally to continue practices forbidden by the law, and have conducted a number of major strikes to enforce this demand. But as the strikes continued and their cost to the union grew, the opposition party, the "Independents," made a campaign issue of them, and at present appear to be gaining ground.

Since 1900, ITU members have voted in more than three hundred referenda on constitutional questions, major policy matters, assessments, convention dates, unemployment relief payments, the number of days a man may work, and a variety of other subjects. The authors of *Union Democracy* believe that close membership control over a union through referenda is impossible except where there is a two-party system. They argue:

In most organizations, union or non-union, it is assumed that the national convention of delegates elected by the members represents the wishes of the members. It is clear from the record of the conventions and the referenda in the ITU that this assumption need not be valid. A convention in fact usually represents the local leadership structure, and the local leaders who go to the . . . conventions may, and frequently do, have values and interests which are different from those whom they nominally represent. This gap is generally obscured by the absence of any means for the direct expression of the desires of the membership. Referenda provide such a means of expression, but *only when they operate within the context of an institutionalized party system*. Otherwise, as in plebiscitarian one-party states . . . they serve merely to legitimize the power and decisions of a ruling group. Although a large number of oligarchic unions have referenda, this has rarely resulted in the defeat of any administration proposal. In a context in which opposition and discussion of issues is not normal procedure, the average trade unionist can do little else but vote for the proposals of his permanent leaders.

In the ITU, the referendum-*cum*-two-party system has given the members great power over their officers. Thus the rank and file has been able to deny large salary increases to officials. "Since 1900, proposals for salary increases for international officers have been defeated 18 times out of 26." And further: "The ability of the members to limit the gap between their own salaries and that of their officers is probably a major factor sustaining the democratic system in the ITU, for it reduces the strain on ITU officers who return to the print shop following defeat."

I am inclined to think that Lipset and his co-authors go too far when they describe low salaries as "probably a major factor" in sustaining the democratic system in the ITU. Salaried officials, whatever their incomes, tend to perpetuate themselves as a group. In most unions the realistic alternative to defeat in office, understood by all contestants, is not "return to the shop," but a post with a national or state union federation, in government, or sometimes with management. Again, in most unions there are significant factors other than pay which cause officials to resist the return to the shop. Obviously social status is higher outside the shop than in it. Even on the lower levels of union hierarchy, the official has a good deal more status than the ordinary member. It is the union official, not the member, who sits on the Community Chest board, makes appeals for the Red Cross, and shares the platform with political leaders at campaign meetings. The authority given the official by virtue of his job is thus an important element in making him reluctant to return to the shop. He has power, often an adequate substitute for money. He is treated politely when he visits the employer, and to the workers in the shop he also represents power because he is one of the few with the professional knowledge necessary to deal with the workers' problems in a highly complex industrial society.

Above all, the union official has freedom from the routine drudgery of the shop. He comes and goes almost as he pleases. He is outside, physically outside, eating in restaurants when almost everybody else is inside, sitting near a machine or in a locker room and taking from a lunch box the bologna sandwiches, cup cakes, slightly mashed banana, and cork-flavored coffee from a thermos. I am inclined to think that most union officials would prefer to hold their jobs, no matter what their salaries, although this certainly doesn't prevent them from trying to get wage increases for themselves whenever possible. Such perquisites of union office as attending conventions and conferences (always on an expense account) are clearly desirable. Even if salary differentials are low, as they are in the ITU, why should the union official want to return to the shop? Most union leaders would deny that they represent a class movement, and they do not consciously seek to rise by bringing that class to power. Rather, by performing an important function for their followers, they seek to rise *through* their group to a level *above* it.

In the ITU, however, there is evidence that the printers have viewed themselves, and consequently their union, in a different light. It is this outlook that is important in the maintenance of democratic processes. The most striking feature of union life in the ITU is the fact that it revolves around a great number of communal activities. The authors point out that in most large printers' locals (such as those in New York, Chicago, and San Francisco), there are social clubs, lodges, sports clubs, veterans' groups, and many others. On the international level, there are three sports organizations, for baseball, golf, and bowling. These hold annual tournaments to which participants come from all parts of North America. The authors have this to say:

> The formal functions of most of the groups are primarily social. Some, at different times, have maintained regular headquarters, where men could gather to talk or play cards, chess, or checkers and get something to eat and drink. Some are primarily sports organizations, though they may run an occasional affair, such as dances. Still others, such as the typographical societies, link their social affairs to benevolent activities. Some have brought together printers who are members of the same ethnic or religious group, such as the Dublin Society or the Jewish Printers. Union Label Clubs have enabled printers living in the same neighborhoods to come together to further union objectives. Common past experiences have been the basis for groups such as war veterans or former employees of defunct newspapers. In this bewildering variety, trade and skill distinctions are another basis for grouping. Fraternal orders, such as the Masons, have also been the basis for printers organizations.
>
> Often within a large single printing plant, such as the large metropolitan newspapers, microscopic versions sprout up of the groups that exist in the occupation as a whole. Veterans' posts, lodges, social and athletic clubs composed of workers in the same plant are common. Some of the

smaller shops or shifts often constitute themselves extra vocational or social or recreational units.

Until fairly recently, regular weekly and bi-weekly
newspapers were published, devoted largely to reporting
the activities of the union and the various sub-groups. Like
the clubs, these newspapers (and there have been at least
three major ones) had no official relationship to the union and were published by private individuals. The most
recent of these in New York, the *Typographical Forum*
(1932 to 1943), reached a peak circulation of 3,500, or
more than one-third of the working members of the union. It ceased publication during the war, because overtime work did not leave enough free time to put out a newspaper.

Social clubs, organized leisure activities such as bowling
leagues and union newspapers are, of course, not unique
to the printers, although we know of no other occupation
which has as many and diverse forms of organized extra-
vocational activities as the ITU. What must be significant
about the printers occupational community is that it *developed without any formal connection* with the union.
The various benevolent organizations, newspapers, social
clubs, athletic teams, and lodges have for the most part
been organized by working printers in their spare time, by
men who felt the need to engage in such activities with
other printers.

The formal community of printers clubs is paralleled by
an informal one, that is, large numbers of printers spend a
considerable amount of their leisure time with other printers. In interviews, many printers reported that their best
friends are other printers, that they regularly visit the homes
of other printers, that they often meet in bars, go fishing together, or see each other in various places before and after
work.

It thus appears that printers comprise what *Union Democracy* describes as an "occupational community," in which the

union is only *one* of the elements giving cohesion to the community as a whole. Family relationships are another—many printers come from families of printers—while other factors heightening the sense of community are the comparatively high economic and craft status of the trade, as well as working conditions (much of printing is done at night) which encourage members to spend much of their leisure time together.

A somewhat weaker case is made by the authors for the structure of the printing industry serving as a factor to sustain democracy within the ITU. The industry is made up of small and medium-sized shops, with looser work discipline than is common in most enterprises. The on-the-job union organization is called the chapel, and its chairman is the counterpart of the union steward elsewhere. Because of the relative simplicity of ITU contracts, the chapel chairman has greater authority than is usual in most unions, and the chapel itself is a fairly autonomous body, both factors tending to hinder the development of a bureaucratic union administration outside the shop. Moreover, there are no wide differentials between either skills or wage rates in printing, and thus the ITU is more nearly a community of equals than other unions, with no special highly paid elite group of workers from whom its officers are drawn.

Yet there are other unions where conditions in this respect are somewhat similar, but which have developed in extremely undemocratic fashion. The explanation, according to Lipset, Trow, and Coleman, is that "the existence of democracy in the ITU is largely the result of the convergence of a set of events, each of which contributes to, or detracts from, the continuing stability of the system. If some one of them in the early history had turned the other way, then present-day democracy in the union would have been less likely. The existence of democracy at present may be likened to a series of successive outcomes of casting dice, dice which are with each favorable throw more heavily loaded toward a favorable outcome on the next throw."

Now if we accept the authors' view of the ITU as a model of union democracy, and their analysis of the factors which have produced and maintained democracy in the ITU, then the prospects for the labor movement as a whole are dim indeed. It is extremely unlikely that the factors which originally brought about and now sustain democracy in the ITU will ever be duplicated in other unions. No other union in America shows any signs of developing two parties, certainly a key element in the ITU system, and few unions can keep the salary costs of their officers at the level of the ITU, since so many must maintain large administrative staffs. Likewise few other trades have the sense of craft and occupational community characteristic of the printers. It is difficult to conceive of an auto worker wanting his sons to work in a Detroit plant. He is more likely to send them to college, if possible, and thus rescue them from the drudgery which he suffers.

Thus if the ITU is, as *Union Democracy* states, "deviant" from the normal pattern of U.S. labor organizations, we must examine realistic alternatives to its peculiar structure. To do this, we must first of all question the assertion that the "ITU stands as a model of the trade union in a democratic society."

What kind of union is a "model" in a democratic society? One like the ITU which has democratic forms and which in fact conducts its affairs democratically? May it not be that before we can characterize such a union as a "model," we must also examine it from the viewpoint of how it furthers the *values* of a democratic society? Even if we assume that the function of a union can be justifiably limited to raising wages and improving working conditions, we may still have difficulty in accepting the ITU as a model. It is worth remembering that, with practically no democracy of the ITU type, the Teamsters Union has brought about great improvements in working conditions and wages for its members. As an economic instrument it has probably been more efficient than the ITU. Indeed, in purely economic terms, the members of the ITU may well have paid too high a price for their independence.

Nor does lack of democracy necessarily relate to the question of corruption in unions, as witness the International Ladies' Garment Workers' Union. Here an autocratically led union is almost completely free from any large-scale financial corruption. Thus the protection of union treasuries, at least, appears not necessarily a function of democracy but one of proper methods of accounting.

Regarded from the viewpoint of society, the ITU presents a picture very different from that which it offers to its members. If we believe that the community should continually strive to realize the ideals of a democratic society, the ITU appears as a conservative, and sometimes even a reactionary group, indifferent to political ideals, generally isolated from the socially conscious elements of the labor movement, and tolerant of work practices as dubious economically and socially as, for example, "bogus."

"Bogus" is an apt name for a practice which the union contends was originated by the newspaper publishers but is now prescribed in ITU contracts. Whenever a newspaper receives and prints an advertisement already set up in plate or in a papier-mâché matrix form—the normal procedure when the same advertisement runs in more than one newspaper—it must be reset by hand or machine in the newspaper's own composing room. A proof is run off, checked for errors, and then destroyed, without ever having been printed, and the set type is then remelted. Some editorial matter supplied in matrix or plate form must also be reset in the same way. In New York and other cities, all bogus advertisements must be set within seven days after the original matrix has been printed. Though bogus is handled by regular employees at straight time rates, often extras must be hired to catch up on back bogus which has accumulated simply because no men were available who could be used to do it within the prescribed time limit.

Many ITU members refuse to do bogus work, even though the union insists on contract observance and attempts to enforce it. Some ITU officials privately agree that the practice is bad; yet the two-party democratic system of the ITU helps to keep bogus and other such archaic practices in existence. There is no doubt that if the leaders of one ITU party were seriously to call for the abolition of bogus, the opposition group would seize upon this as a campaign issue. Since there is no tradition of serious political debate within the union, neither party is willing to embark upon such a risky course. (Incidentally, it would be interesting to determine the effect upon printers—as craftsmen—of doing work which they know in advance is useless to society and will only be destroyed.)

To take another instance of its relation to the community at large: the ITU in New York City, together with the printing employers, until recently played an important role in preventing permanent political party registration from being enacted into law. In the absence of such permanent registration, all voters had to register anew each year, thus cutting down the size of the vote and lessening whatever influence labor might have had in the elections. The union's justification for its opposition to permanent registration was that printing new registration lists for each election provided its members with employment. (Needless to say, the printing employers were equally in favor of renewing their profits at each election.)

Thus we see that it is entirely possible for a democratic union to carry on practices which may seriously conflict with the interests of the community at large, or even the remainder of the labor movement. Like any other organization, the democratic union, if not restrained internally by a substantive commitment to democratic ideals, must often be curbed by conflicting or restraining forces outside it. In this context, the contrast between the ITU and the International Ladies' Garment Workers' Union becomes significant. No candid observer of the labor movement would describe the ILGWU as a democratic union. It is in fact totally dominated by its president and secretary-treasurer, David Dubinsky.* Yet no one thinks it odd that Dubinsky—always described as a modern labor statesman—should behave, procedurally, toward the ILGWU in somewhat the same way as the autocratic John L. Lewis behaves toward the miners or a building trades official toward his union. Labor

* A story (perhaps apocryphal) that causes ILGWU people to double up with laughter concerns the liberal-minded lady who attended her first ILGWU convention, at the conclusion of which she was introduced to the president. "Congratulations, Mr. Dubinsky," she said. "For what?" he asked puzzled. "Why," she replied, "upon your re-election, of course!"

journalists rarely analyze the dictatorial manner in which he runs the union. Newspaper accounts of ILGWU conventions dwell at length on details of speeches, pageants, and testimonials, but fail to give any discussion of the manner in which the officers are chosen. There are only dim memories of the days when there was an opposition candidate to the official slate. It is common knowledge that Dubinsky has already selected his own successor and made his choice known to the union hierarchy. It is thus obvious that although there is in substance great difference between the practices of the ILGWU and those of the Teamsters, the forms through which both organizations operate have much in common.

Yet Dubinsky *is* a labor statesman and the ILGWU, albeit internally undemocratic (at least on the international union level), is in many ways far superior to the ITU, to say nothing of the Teamsters. Viewed in the context of society as a whole, Dubinsky's policy decisions often appear motivated by considerations other than economic interests of the members; they are clearly based on a broader social philosophy. Obviously, then, there is a contradiction, or at least a confusion in terms, when the ITU is said to be a "model," unless it is also true that a union like the ILGWU can likewise be considered a model of a different kind. Presumably the authors would agree that the existence of union democracy by itself is not necessarily a guarantee that the union's role vis-à-vis the community, the labor movement, or even its own members, will be a healthy one. A union like the ITU—with its closed-off internal structure, not easily susceptible to pressures from the outside world—may very well end by perpetuating the standards of the group—not all of them equally desirable.

If one starts from the real condition of the American labor movement, rather than the idealized image which appears to affect the thinking of many observers, one must accept the probability that, for a variety of reasons, membership participation in the affairs of the union will in general continue to be extremely low—about an average of 3 percent—except during crisis periods. This is due to a number of factors. First, the

variable nature of American industry obviously affects participation. Workers who are scattered over a large area find it more
difficult to attend meetings than those concentrated in one lo-
cality. Again, nationwide contracts, effective as they are, limit
the members' areas of decision-making. The size of the industrial unit, whether a local union is composed of members from
one plant or a number of plants—all these and other factors
affect membership participation. In addition, one must also give
consideration to a factor generally characteristic of all American
unions: namely, that the members do not choose to take a more
active part because of their limited concept of the function of
their unions.

American unions have not on the whole developed as instruments of political expression for large groups in the community
as they did in Europe. Thus the commitment of most union
members to their organization tends to be narrow and shallow,
not much different in degree from that given to any one of the
vast number of organizations which vie for the loyalty and
support of Americans. In the eyes of its members, the purpose
of the union appears restricted to that of a service organization
—getting higher wages and better working conditions for its
members. The leaders of American unionism in general share this
view, even though it may not match the reality of the situation.
For, although it is *not* a political instrument, the average union
is also no longer merely an organization serving its members'
economic interests. In reality the unions have become part of
the machinery of American industrial life, sharing in important
areas of managerial decision-making. Labor-management relations and such matters as pension and seniority rights, which
have evolved through collective bargaining, now affect the life
conditions of both members and nonmembers. Thus we seem
to be confronted with a situation where most of the participants
in the labor movement, active or inactive, leaders and members alike, do not fully understand the nature of their own
work. They think it is one thing; it is actually another. And
this gap between understanding and actuality is probably one
of the reasons why the American labor movement has not been

able to develop a new outlook consonant with democratic values. In its early days, the American labor movement received an infusion of European Socialist ideology, but in the context of a generally expanding and socially mobile society, that element grew weaker. Utopianism was replaced by craft protectionism and craft rights were jealously fought over and guarded. With unions successfully raising economic standards, the American working class ceased to view itself as a whole and became fragmented into economic units often warring with each other for long periods of time. During the depression of the thirties, a kind of social ideology was provided for the unions by the New Deal, which expressed itself through the formation of the CIO. For a brief spell there was again an infusion of political awareness, but the rapid development of the war economy, coupled with the realization by the business community that it could recognize unions and still maintain high profits, weakened management's hitherto bitter opposition to unions, an opposition which if persisted in might have converted the union institution into a labor movement.

All that remains at present is the inevitable current moving the trade unions toward bureaucratization and oligarchy, a current accelerated by the desire of the government to maintain the kind of stable, responsible labor leadership which promotes harmony in labor-management relations. Unfortunately, stability and harmony often bring with them inertia and a loss of freedom. In the face of ever-growing corporate enterprise, matched by equally large unions, the problem of maintaining internal democracy in unions, without sacrificing their efficiency, is a formidable one. The development of a broader social outlook on the part of the unions is likewise a most serious matter. But the examination of questions such as these is clearly beyond the scope imposed upon their work by the authors of *Union Democracy*.

INTRODUCTION

THE STRUGGLE to bring together white America and black America has been one of the most tragic in the history of the U.S. Ever since slavery was introduced here, the country has been confronted with the dilemma that grows from a sharp contrast between stated ideals and actual practice.

One result of the contradiction between ideals and practice is that the white and black Americas are separate countries. True, they have something of a common language, they are physically located in the same land area and they both call themselves American but, in fact, they are widely separated worlds. Perhaps even worse, they are, to each other, unknown and therefore fearsome worlds, whose inhabitants are neither to be trusted nor wanted as friends. Many Negroes begin with the conviction that the institutions of the white world have the function, primarily, of keeping them in a condition of social, if not legal, inferiority; many whites are convinced, equally, that the Negroes are not yet equipped for social equality, even if they do possess the legal rights to it.

So the two nations go their separate ways, resenting each other, speaking the same tongue but a separate language. And, unfortunately, the unions, which might have played a major role in helping to solve this problem, have done only a little more than any other institution in society, and that for only a short period of time. In the field of race relations, unions have been leaders only rarely. Most of the time, unions have just accepted the mores of the world in which they exist, and so they too have become the object of Negro bitterness, viewed as instruments with which the white country protects its job territory just as ghettoization is the white man's weapon to protect his land. But slowly, inevitably, the patterns of job discrimination which developed, with union consent, are being broken under Negro pressure, and equality of membership is being opened to Negroes.

One consequence of the pressure has been that the weapons used by unions to achieve their purposes have been turned against them now by Negroes. As the Negro struggle for equality has grown sharper and sharper in the past five years, picket lines and boycotts were started, primarily from the impetus of the National Association for the Advancement of Colored People, to force unions into changing their exclusionary practices. These tactics, combined with continuous criticism and the growing strength of the Negro community finally are bringing about changes in union policies; changes union leaders said were impossible to achieve when this article was written in 1959.

THE
NEGRO
WORKER
ASSERTS
HIS
RIGHTS

(1959) "*W*hat's new?"

"*Same old story, white man's ahead, niggers bringing up the rear.*"

All over the United States there are Negroes who privately greet each other with some variation of this theme. But while once it was a bitter acknowledgment of the white world's habit of keeping Negroes in their place, today it is a call to arms. "Cap'n Charlie," the all-powerful white man, is still ahead, but the rear ranks are determined to catch up.

"We're tired of having to be taken care of by the good white folks," declared a Negro auto worker in Detroit, announcing his candidacy for union office. "From now on, we're going to take care of ourselves."

It is necessary "to remove the iron hand of reactionarism from the throat of Congress and give this nation real democracy, something it has never had," demanded a Negro newspaper, reflecting the increasing impatience of seventeen million American Negroes.

And in Daly City, California, a lower-middle-class suburb of San Francisco, a forty-year-old Negro, who says he mostly wants "peace of mind," has filed a complaint with the city Fair Employment Practices Commission against the Bartenders Union, charging that the union will not accept him into member-ship.

"Seems like the white folks just want you to be satisfied with a little and not get what you're supposed to have," says the bartender. "They tell you to be quiet, keep peaceful, but I'm tired of not getting decent pay for my work and not having any security on the job. Bartending isn't so great, but it's my trade and I'm good at it. And I think I should be allowed to get in the union just like anyone else."

These protests are typical of a new militancy among Ameri-can Negroes, a fundamental change that has surprised and even alarmed many white liberals who had complacently as-sumed that the struggle for Negro rights was their own special cause.

There are far fewer lynchings today than there were fifty years ago; and so, inevitably, when the murderers of Emmett Till and Matt Parker walk along Southern streets free and un-punished, there is far greater anger among Negroes. More ac-customed than their ancestors to believe that their persons are protected by law, Negroes are more likely now to respond to brutal unpunished lynchings as did that NAACP leader in North Carolina who called, in an unguarded but probably honest moment, for Negroes to resist violence with violence. Even though he was immediately censured and suspended by the national NAACP, there is no doubt that he voiced a senti-ment felt by many, many more NAACP members than its leaders would like to admit. It seems that when a minority group's aspirations are raised, the group becomes even more in-sistent on achieving the new level as quickly and as completely as possible.

Because more Negroes can now afford to move from their slum ghettos into better white neighborhoods, and some do, there is even greater resentment that most Negroes are de-nied the opportunity. "Thank the people of San Francisco for letting you buy this house," star Giant outfielder Willie Mays was urged after the resistance he had met in purchasing a home in a white neighborhood had been overcome. "What do I have to thank anybody for?" Mays is reported to have answered. "For letting me spend $40,000?"

Because Negroes are now determined to have the opportunities in reality that they have been told are open to them in theory, a new self-confidence and aggressiveness have been building up inside the Negro community. It is ironic, though not at all mysterious, that some of this should spill over into conflict with liberal organizations that have been traditionally benevolent toward the Negro's aspirations. The Negro is no longer satisfied with paternal assistance—he demands his equal rights. The recent ugly quarrel between the NAACP and the AFL-CIO is an important case in point.

At the founding convention of the AFL-CIO, in 1955, George Meany amiably described the NAACP as the organization that "brought to a successful conclusion twenty months ago a long campaign to end segregation in the public schools of America." Three years later, the NAACP lashed out at the Federation, publicly proclaiming that the AFL-CIO, in spite of its stated intentions and written constitution, had not ended "a variety of discriminatory racial practices" engaged in by not just a few but "many" unions. "All too often," charged Herbert Hill, NAACP labor secretary, "there is a significant disparity between the declared public policy of the national AFL-CIO and the day-to-day reality as experienced by Negro wage earners in the North as well as in the South."

That disparity is not new. What is new, in recent years, is the NAACP's attitude toward it. The struggle against racial discrimination in the American labor movement has been long and difficult. Furthermore it has not been pursued with any great vigor within the unions, except in some of the old CIO groups and a few outstanding AFL internationals. In 1891 Samuel Gompers, founder of the AFL, called for the forming of unions "which shall recognize no color line," but he had little success in persuading many of the unions that sought affiliation with the Federation to admit Negroes to membership. The Federation felt that it could not force its affiliates to accept conditions imposed from the top—a feeling with considerable basis in the reality of power distribution. When, therefore, it was faced with the choice of accepting a union that excluded Negroes or not granting affiliation because of racial discrimination, the "lily-white" group was invariably admitted.

For many years practically nothing was done within the Federation to solve this problem. Bored delegates to its conventions would walk about the hall and corridors, chatting with one another, while A. Philip Randolph, president of the Brotherhood of Sleeping Car Porters, made his annual impassioned speech appealing (in vain) to the convention for the opening of union doors to Negro workers. Then, very slowly— sometimes under pressure from government agencies, as during the wars, sometimes because of court rulings, sometimes because of competition from the CIO unions organizing the mass-production industries, and occasionally because of a decision to do the right thing—the AFL unions began to eliminate formal racial-exclusion clauses from their constitutions and to admit some Negroes into membership. According to the NAACP, however, many still keep Negroes out by a variety of covert screening devices, or, if they do allow Negroes to join, permit them to work only at the most menial jobs.

Today, only a few unions still exclude Negroes in their constitutions. One of these is the Brotherhood of Railroad Trainmen, whose bylaws provide that an applicant for membership "shall be white, male, sober, industrious, and of good moral character." Some of the NAACP's present bitterness toward the AFL-CIO stems from the fact that, when the BRT was admitted into the merged labor group in 1957, federation officials exacted a promise from the union, as a condition of admittance, that it would give thought to eliminating the racial-exclusion clause at its next scheduled convention, then set for 1958. That convention has since been postponed to 1962, and the exclusion of Negroes will certainly continue until then—at least.

At the time the merger convention took place, some of the old CIO chiefs probably expected that most union racial-exclusion practices would soon disappear. These expectations were also shared by Negro workers, who thought that since the Supreme Court had ordered integration in the highly sensitive and difficult area of public education, the unions would all the more readily and willingly follow suit. In 1956, the Negro president of a segregated Railway Clerks local in Tulsa asked for the elimination of his local and its merger with a white one in the same city, confident, he said, that "Since the schools of our city and state have integrated without incident, we are sure the same would happen between our Lodges." But by April, 1959, when nothing had yet been accomplished to bring about the integration of the two locals, the lodge president had so little confidence left that an NAACP attorney in Oklahoma filed suit against the Railway Clerks to force integration of the two locals. The fact that the president of the Railway Clerks is George Harrison, a respected member of the AFL-CIO Ethical Practices Committee who has been a U.S. delegate to the United Nations, does not lessen the bitterness among Negro workers.

During the first few years after the merger, the AFL-CIO was not able to pay much attention to the problem of abolishing discrimination. A Civil Rights Committee had been set up with James B. Carey, president of the International Union of Electrical, Radio, and Machine Workers, as chairman and Boris Shishkin, who held two other jobs as well, as executive director. The great internal stresses and strains of the new organization handicapped the committee's work, as Meany and other leaders wrestled with the difficulties inherent in bringing together a large group of ambitious, thin-skinned union officers who held widely differing philosophies and who still bore ancient jurisdictional grudges.

Almost as a physical symbol of the contradiction between the Federation's stated policy and its actual practice, Negro mechanics were not permitted to work on the construction of the new AFL-CIO headquarters in Washington because of the discriminatory rules of an Electrical Workers local and other building-trade unions.

But while the new AFL-CIO was trying to solve its internal

problems, a task not made any easier by the public ones posed for it by the McClellan investigations, the NAACP was solving some problems of its own. Before the postwar Supreme Court decisions on housing and schools, the organization was probably better known among whites than among Negroes. Founded by whites in 1909, the NAACP originally had only one Negro staff member and a predominantly white board. Today, the reverse is true; Negroes in the organization far outnumber the whites. (The traditional dominance of white leadership is memorialized in the practice of having the presidency held by a white man.) For many years, the NAACP was a headquarters operation, dominated by the personality of Secretary Walter White, with very little base in the general Negro community. Its membership was primarily upper-middle-class intellectuals and professionals, people to whom the legal-and-lobbying orientation of the organization had a natural appeal.

"The NAACP does not have a mass basis," wrote Ralph Bunche in 1940. "It has never assumed the proportions of a crusade, nor has it ever, in any single instance, attracted the masses of people to its banner. It has not impressed upon the mass consciousness, and it is a bald truth that the average Negro in the street has never heard of the Association nor of any of its leaders."

Walter White himself admitted, "There are weaknesses in our branch structure and we have not yet found the formula for selling to the public the nature, the extent, the details and the significance of the Association's program"; while Roy Wilkins, his successor, recognized "our lack of skill at mass appeal." But the lack of mass support among Negroes, the weak branches, and the limited professional staff, were not insuperable handicaps to the legal and legislative objectives. Thurgood Marshall and the NAACP legal staff were preparing themselves for their series of victories in the Supreme Court; and, under White, the NAACP did its lobbying and legislative work on behalf of Negro rights as part of the liberal-labor constellation.

But, after its Supreme Court victories, especially in the school case, thousands of Negroes began looking to the NAACP for leadership and guidance. It was its own legal victories that accelerated the NAACP's shift into other areas. Today, the NAACP membership has grown greatly, even in those Southern states where it is dangerous for a Negro to be known as a member. More and more Negro workers have joined it, and membership has become more and more of a prerequisite for leadership roles within the Negro community. And, as the Negro vote becomes increasingly important, the NAACP leaders and members have become aware of their political power and are beginning to exercise it.

The old NAACP is dead and nothing will bring it back to life. Now the NAACP is almost forced to lead Negroes in some directions it may not quite want to go, lest it end by merely following. This new militant NAACP is far more responsive to the economic and political aspirations of Negro workers than was the old middle-class organization.

The unemployment rate among Negro men is almost twice as high as that among whites. In any recession, Negroes are hit far harder than whites because so many Negroes work in manufacturing industries and have low seniority. In March, 1958, during the recession, more than 15 percent of male Negro workers were unemployed; and in November, 1958, when only 4.8 percent of the white males were still unemployed, the corresponding figure for Negroes was 11.4 percent.

Obviously, it is not just the unions that are to blame for Negro unemployment, since it is always the unskilled or semi-skilled workers who lose their jobs first in a recession. But the very fact that a high proportion of Negroes are still unskilled is partially the fault of the unions, particularly in the building trades and railroads, which refuse to admit them to membership.

Automation, too, is having a more severe impact on Negro employment than among whites, and here, too, the unions must bear some of the responsibility. When many unskilled jobs, held by Negroes, have been replaced by a smaller number requiring more skill, the white workers through their unions resist upgrading Negroes to the new jobs.

Theodore Pinkston of Cleveland is an electrician who learned his trade in the Army. Together with a few other Negroes, he applied for membership in Local 38 of the International Brotherhood of Electrical Workers. They were all refused. For eight years, the Negroes unsuccessfully attempted to gain admittance to the local. Both the Urban League and the NAACP were involved in the case, with NAACP labor secretary Herbert Hill making trips to Cleveland and attempting to work through the federation's machinery. Nothing availed until the Cleveland Community Relations Board took legal action against the local and forced it to admit the Negro electricians. Even then, Pinkston, who started the case, was twice rejected on the ground that he was not qualified.

The very fact that Hill attempted to operate within the framework of the federation made the NAACP subject to criticism within the Negro community. In Cleveland, the local Negro paper, reporting on the case, stated that "Hill was the major factor in the Cleveland branch [of the NAACP] decision to stall for time while long-winded conferences and appeals filtered through Hill to George Meany, boss of the AFL-CIO merger."

All over the country, according to the NAACP, there were similar cases about which the AFL-CIO was doing nothing. Carey had resigned from the chairmanship of the Civil Rights Committee and been replaced by Charles Zimmerman, a vice-president of the International Ladies' Garment Workers' Union and an old advocate of liberal causes. The pressures on the NAACP leaders were building up, and even the lobbying alliance between the AFL-CIO and the NAACP was beginning to show signs of strain. During the 1956 Congressional session, the NAACP supported Negro Representative Adam Clayton Powell's amendment to the school-construction bill—an amendment that prohibited the use of Federal funds to build segregated schools. The AFL-CIO lobbied against the Powell amendment, believing that even new segregated schools in the South were better than no schools at all. The school-construction bill failed to pass, and many union leaders felt that a major factor in its failure with the Southern Democrats' opposition to the Powell amendment. Charges of "irresponsible" leadership were privately made against the NAACP by labor lobbyists, and were responded to in kind.

The private quarrel became more and more public as the months went by. In the judgment of the NAACP leadership, very little was done by the AFL-CIO to solve or alleviate the problems of union discrimination against the Negroes. It was particularly rankling to the NAACP, already under pressure from within the Negro community for showing "little zest" to do battle with the trade unions, that even in New York City segregation in local unions still existed. On April 30, 1957, the New York State Commission Against Discrimination ordered Negroes admitted into the all-white George M. Harrison Lodge of the Railway Clerks and called for its merger with the all-Negro Friendship Lodge. But just as the union refused to integrate in Tulsa, so it refused in New York City.

In May, 1958, Hill, with complaints from NAACP members and branches piling up on him, met with Boris Shishkin to discuss what action would be taken to solve the specific cases he had called to the federation's attention.

By December, 1958, Hill, claiming that nothing had yet been done to clear up the complaints he had cited in May, sent a formal memorandum to Shishkin and Zimmerman summarizing the specific charges of discrimination made by NAACP members against unions. (The memo was not then made public, however.) Once again, the complaints of the NAACP included a number against Harrison's Railway Clerks.

The situation came to a head with a memorandum prepared last December by the NAACP for Barry Henderson of East St. Louis, Illinois, a member of Lodge 6115 of the Railway Clerks, in which Negro employees of the Wabash Railroad are segregated. According to the NAACP memorandum, "the system of segregated locals and segregated seniority rosters denies the Negro union members equal promotional rights and does serious harm to their economic status."

In this same memorandum, specific citations of discriminatory practices were made by NAACP members against a local of the Hod Carriers, charged with refusing to admit a Negro or to honor a traveling permit issued to him by another local of the same union; against a local of the Electrical Workers because it "has consistently refused to admit" a Negro into membership; against a local of the Plasterers that "maintains a rigid policy of excluding Negroes from membership"; and against a local of the Plumbers for limiting "membership to white persons exclusively." Charges of segregated seniority lists, "limiting Negro employment to laborer classifications and denying Negroes seniority and other rights," were made against locals of both the Paper Makers and the Pulp Workers. In the oil and chemical industry, according to the memorandum, similar complaints had been filed with the President's Committee on Government Contracts against local metal trades councils in Texas and Louisiana and locals of the Operating Engineers in Texas and Arkansas.

Even "In some industrial unions which generally maintain desirable civil rights policies, there is often found to be significant examples of discrimination and segregation at the work place," Hill charged, specifically calling Shishkin's attention to complaints against the Communications Workers of America for its contract with Western Electric in Greensboro, North Carolina, and against the Steelworkers for its contract with the Atlantic Steel Company in Atlanta.

"In addition to the Brotherhood of Firemen and Enginemen and the Brotherhood of Railroad Trainmen which exclude Negroes by constitutional provision many international unions affiliated to the AFL-CIO continue to exclude Negroes by tacit consent and other AFL-CIO unions limit Negro membership in most instances to segregated or 'auxiliary' locals," stated Hill's memorandum. The unions he listed as carrying out these practices included the Railroad Telegraphers, Plumbers, Maintenance of Way Employees, Painters, Railway Carmen, Boilermakers, Electrical Workers (not Carey's but the old AFL), Railway Clerks, Pulp Workers, Sheet Metal Workers, Carpenters, and Paper Makers.

In November, 1958, the Brotherhood of Locomotive Firemen and Enginemen had successfully defended in a Federal
court its right to exclude Negroes, without any public reproach
from the AFL-CIO. This further intensified the NAACP's
feeling that the federation was ignoring its charges. Hill's
memorandum to Shishkin was sent on to George Meany by
Roy Wilkins, who wrote Meany that "For the past three years,
the Association has cooperated diligently" with the AFL-CIO
Civil Rights Department and with international unions but that
"three years after the merger agreement there is clear evidence
that many unions continue discriminatory racial practices.

"I am sure you realize," continued Wilkins to Meany,
"that the NAACP is obligated to its own membership to press
vigorously for the elimination of discriminatory practices within
trade union organizations. In previous memoranda and in discussions with responsible AFL-CIO officials we have expressed
our conviction that the problem is of such magnitude that it
cannot be resolved by the present procedure of taking up
random individual complaints. We believe discrimination can
be eliminated only through a systematic program on the part of
the leadership of the AFL-CIO to enforce its basic policy of
non-discrimination throughout the organized labor movement."

Wilkins then informed Meany that the entire problem would
be presented to the NAACP's annual meeting on January 5,
1959, and might be "treated in a resolution" by the organization's board of directors that same day.

"We would be pleased to have any comment of yours which
could be cited with our January 5 report on the situation as
we see it," wrote Wilkins. The reply he received from Meany
was completely noncommittal.

Hill's report to the annual meeting was then released and
received widespread publicity. NAACP ACCUSES LABOR OF BIAS
LAG was the *New York Times* headline, and similar captions
appeared over stories or editorials in a variety of other newspapers and magazines. The Negro press all over the country
naturally featured the NAACP attack even more prominently.
Some sections of the Negro press even attacked Wilkins for

his "apologetic approach" to Meany and described his letter of protest as being "extremely weak." The bitter attitude of the Negro press was given even greater impetus when a Virginia local of the Textile Workers was revealed to have been involved in the activities of the White Citizens Council there.

Weak letter or not, the publicity attendant upon its publication undoubtedly helped bring about a meeting in March of Meany, Wilkins, A. Philip Randolph, and Hill at AFL-CIO headquarters. Following the meeting, a polite joint public statement was issued in which "The AFL-CIO assured the NAACP of its continuing determination to strive for elimination of discrimination in the American trade union movement. . . ."

The reaction of many Negroes to the meeting between the NAACP and the AFL-CIO was not quite so polite. "We'd like to know who's kidding whom in the tête-à-tête between NAACP Secretary Roy Wilkins and AFL-CIO President George Meany," said the New York *Amsterdam News,* an influential Negro paper. "What we need here is action on the part of the AFL-CIO to eliminate discrimination in its ranks against Negroes," continued the editorial, which concluded: "All of us know what is wrong. What we are asking is that the AFL-CIO do something about it. And it goes without saying that we expect the NAACP not to swallow Mr. Meany's platitudes hook, line, and sinker."

The problem of the federation, as the labor leaders see it, is that with the best will in the world there is very little that can be done, short of expulsion, to force an affiliated international union or a local union of an international to end its discriminatory practices. The Civil Rights Department has no authority to impose penalties or to enforce compliance with the federation constitution, which prohibits discrimination. All it can do is try to educate the leaders and members of the unions involved, a very slow process at best, and one that is made more complicated by some Negro local union leaders who also resist integration because of their own personal stake in segregated locals. The stubborn cases must be brought to the attention of the AFL-CIO executive board for possible action—

with the only real penalty, expulsion, not likely to be used on this issue.

Charles Zimmerman, chairman of the AFL-CIO Civil Rights Committee, angrily replied to Hill's charges by stating that people "seriously interested in combating discrimination recognize that the real need is not for demagogy and denunciation but for greater cooperation in the common cause." Zimmerman also stated that some of Hill's charges were discovered to be distorted upon investigation. The AFL-CIO's record in the fight for Federal and state civil-rights legislation, said Zimmerman, "is very considerably better than that of the Republican party or of the community as a whole."

As for the suggestion made in the Negro press that the case of the Textile Workers local in Virginia was "typical of what is happening in the AFL-CIO as a whole," Zimmerman fought back hard. "The fact is that the AFL-CIO has fought Virginia's 'massive resistance' policy. The fact is that the Virginia State AFL-CIO is integrated and has Negroes on its executive board. The fact is that the Textile Workers Union has taken a firm stand against segregation and the White Citizens Councils, even though it knew this invited serious difficulties for its organization throughout the South."

"It's very easy to expel unions," states Zimmerman, "but it's not the solution." Zimmerman defends the work done by his committee under difficult conditions and without great authority. "It's easy to be a hero," he says of Hill, "and get a lot of publicity with charges, but that doesn't solve any problems."

Zimmerman doesn't deny the existence of the situations pointed to by the NAACP but he replies: "The labor movement is part of the community. Union members don't become saints just because they take out union books. The influence of the community is stronger than that of the unions, especially in the South. We must change this outlook but it will take time. The very fact that there is a Civil Rights Committee is a recognition that the AFL-CIO knows there is a problem that must be solved. The big difficulty is in working out a solution."

Another big difficulty in the relations between the two groups lies in the fact that the unions *are* expected to behave differently from the rest of the community. They present themselves publicly as being motivated by social idealism. On this basis they requested aid, during the last election, from Negroes in beating off the attempt of employers to enact "right-to-work" legislation. But when any group asks for help or special status because it is a movement based on social ideals, it must be prepared to have demands made upon it to live up to those ideals. The fact that there are a few Negroes on union executive boards is no longer enough for either the Negroes or their organizations.

"The NAACP has always regarded the AFL-CIO as a friendly organization and still so regards it," says Roy Wilkins. "This does not mean that we regard it as being perfect or sacrosanct." Justifying his organization's charges against the federation, he went on: "Our business is the treatment of Negro Americans in all walks of life, and the opening and widening of opportunities for them as citizens. Our business is the removal of discrimination stemming from race, religion, or national origin. In past years we have received directly from Negro members of the AFL-CIO, who are also members of chapters of the NAACP, allegations of unfair treatment. For over three years, we have repeatedly presented these complaints to the AFL-CIO to little avail."

It's really not yet clear what the federation can do. The NAACP maintains that it is not advocating the expulsion of unions which discriminate but only the taking of specific steps by internationals to move toward the elimination of segregated locals in the North as well as in the South: the abolition of separate racial seniority rosters in contracts; the opening of membership to Negroes in those unions which exclude them, either constitutionally or tacitly; and the establishment of effective union liaison with state and municipal fair-employment-practice commissions.

All of these things *could* be done, maintains Hill, and "Very few of them are being carried out by the Civil Rights Committee, which seems to mainly have the function of a public-relations operation. The record clearly shows that the Civil Rights Committee is totally unable to effectively eliminate the discriminatory practices on an *ad hoc* basis."

Whatever steps the Civil Rights Committee does take to abolish discrimination—and there is no doubt that it has accomplished some things—it is handicapped by the old AFL tradition of international unions resisting any interference in their affairs from federation headquarters. Although this attitude is changing somewhat, primarily as a result of the expulsion of the Teamsters, the feeling still remains, especially in old AFL craft unions where Negroes suffer most, that each union ought to be free to conduct its own affairs with regard to its own locals. Even in some of the former CIO unions, like the Textile Workers, whose Virginia local was associated with the White Citizens Council there, cracking down on the local can raise serious difficulties, especially when—as in this case— the existence of the entire union is being threatened by Southern employers.

With the best will in the world the AFL-CIO would surely find it difficult to give the NAACP all of what it wants. It is highly unlikely that any union will be expelled for continuing discriminatory practices, especially now that the federation is faced with a shrinking rather than a growing membership. What is much more probable is that the uneasy alliance between the AFL-CIO and the NAACP will remain in effect, with the NAACP continuing to criticize and attack the federation. As more and more Negroes become union members, the internal pressure from them will get stronger until someday a new crop of national and local union leaders will emerge—independent Negroes elected by union votes, instead of, as now, Negroes with positions on international staffs, dependent upon the administrations for their jobs.

In Daly City, the bartender is acquiring more and more of an edge in his voice when he discusses the complaint he has filed with the Fair Employment Practices Commission: "I want to be allowed to join the Bartenders Union because I know that unions are good for the working man. I don't care any more about working in some fancy hotel in downtown San Francisco; I got over that dream a long time ago. I don't care where I work any more just as long as I get paid decent wages instead of having to work for five or six dollars a day less than the union scale. Now I have to work two jobs sometimes just to make ends meet. But most of all, I want some security. I'm forty years old and I've got a seven-year-old kid. I don't want to worry about losing my job because one night I take in $300 for the man and the next night only $285. I don't want to have to sweat about what happened to the other $15 worth of business and think maybe I'll get canned because I don't con people into drinking more.

"That's why I filed the case against the Bartenders. I just got to have some peace of mind."

THE FORGOTTEN PEOPLE
and
A MATTER OF SPIRIT

INTRODUCTION

JOB DISCRIMINATION against Negroes is ending because the combination of moral suasion and organizational pressures is a powerful one: the Negro groups can utilize their political power to force employers and unions to live up to the moral ideals of America. But migrant farm workers have no organizations with political power and so if they are no longer quite the forgotten people they were when these articles were published in January 1959, and October 1961, they are, nevertheless, still "The Excluded People." Cut off from a normal stable society, their poorly educated children are thrown out into the job market, ill equipped either physically or by training, to find a place in urban industrialized society. In most states, farm workers still do not receive coverage under workmen's compensation laws despite a high rate of accident, and hourly farm wages are still the lowest paid any workers in the United States.

But, still, there has been some slight improvement. The 5 percent of the farms which account for more than 70 percent of the farm wage expenditures are not as guilty as they were once of providing their workers with only the meagerest living quarters and inexpensive, bad food. Enforcement of the existing laws has been stricter and the Department of Labor raised the minimum hourly rates paid to Mexican contract laborers, although no such minimums yet exist for American farm workers. Senator

Harrison Williams of New Jersey has introduced a series of bills which he describes as "The Magna Carta of Mobile Serfs" which have served to call attention to the continued neglect of this segment of the population.

But it is not only Congress that neglects farm workers: other powerful forces of society are equally guilty. The AFL-CIO gave up its attempts to organize the farm workers as being too expensive for the number of migrants who joined the agricultural workers union; many urban state legislators are still willing to swap off the interests of the farm workers for what they believe to be more important gains, and the political pressures exerted by the large growers are still effective in keeping the whole question at a very subdued public level. But here, too, some change is taking place: even some of the growers now are convinced that conditions for farm workers must be improved.

The most bitter argument about the farm worker problem in the past ten years revolved around the use of Mexican contract laborers brought to this country under the provisions of Public Law 78. The growers insist that there are not enough domestic workers available to handle the crops while the organizations working on behalf of the farm workers maintain with equal insistence that if the growers paid decent wages, ample supplies of labor would be available. In some cases, too, growers contracted to bring in more workers than they needed with the result that the braceros had only a few days work in a week. To the surprise of very many people, the House refused to renew Public Law 78 in 1963, thus ending the bracero program. It will take a few years before the impact of this action shows up in the farm economy in any fixed way but it will certainly increase the rate of mechanization in harvesting.

This development may change the future of the farm worker: the Teamsters Union has decided to move into the field of organizing farm workers and if mechanization continues at its present rapid pace, the Teamsters may be in a position to exercise control over farm wages and working conditions.

THE
FORGOTTEN
PEOPLE

ITEM—*A picker was badly hurt in a collision while being transported in a truck. He was eleven years old, and had been working fifty-four hours a week.*

ITEM—*The cattle feeder was walking alongside a tractor when it suddenly backed up and crushed his foot beneath the tread. He was nine years old.*

ITEM—*He was shoveling grain into a moving auger and suddenly he slipped and his foot was caught in the auger. When they pulled him loose, his foot was completely mangled. He was fourteen years old.*

(1959) NONE of these children was "helping out" on the family farm. All three were illegally employed as farm workers during 1957 in California, as were 124 other persons under sixteen years who were injured. One-third of these children, some of whom were permanently disabled, were employed in violation of state labor laws. Many others were employed in violation of Federal child-labor laws and state school-attendance laws. But in 1957 only one California farmer was prosecuted for violating state labor laws.

California is the only state that compiles statistics on injuries to young farm workers, and so it is known there, at least, that from 1950 to 1957 more than a thousand children under sixteen years were seriously injured in farm accidents. Since no other state collects such statistics, it is impossible even to estimate how many children in the entire country suffer the same fate. All that is known is that the number of children illegally employed by farmers has been rising for the past few years. "Agriculture," says U. S. Secretary of Labor James P. Mitchell, "violates the child labor provision more than any other industry."

Except in a very few states, agricultural workers are still not even covered by workmen's compensation laws. This in spite of the fact that farming has the third highest fatality rate of any industry in the United States, exceeded only by mining and construction. Indeed, during one year, 1956, the total number of men and women killed in agriculture exceeded that of any other industry.

Neither are agricultural workers covered by Federal minimum wage or maximum hours legislation. At a time when the labor movement is attempting to raise the minimum wage from $1 to $1.25 an hour, the average farm worker's hourly pay is sixty-eight cents, as compared to $2.79 an hour for the construction industry or even $1.05 an hour in laundries, whose workers are one of the lowest-paid nonagricultural groups in the nation. All adult farm workers are now supposed, by law, to receive certain benefits of the Social Security system for which both they and their employers make payments. But it is common knowledge that a great many farm employers ignore the law— a state of affairs the Social Security Administration is well aware of but incapable of doing anything about.

But it is not just farm-labor laws or Social Security regulations that are violated by farmers. In Oregon there are farm-labor contractors who supplement their already large incomes by selling marijuana and supplying prostitutes to farm workers as well as by getting commissions from liquor and food sold at jacked-up prices. In New York, investigation of forty farm-labor camps revealed that only three kept the payroll records required by law.

In agriculture, the relations between workers and employers often seem to be a mean and ugly survival from an almost forgotten era. Employing at all times 700,000 workers and sometimes more than two million, agriculture has successfully resisted the social and economic progress achieved through legislation and unionization by other millions of workers in industry. For a variety of reasons, agriculture, even though it is a major segment of the American economy, is still given an almost blanket exemption from modes of conduct now considered essential to a civilized society. Economically and politically unorganized, farm workers can do little on their own to help themselves. They possess neither the economic power to wrest better conditions from their employers nor the political influence to exert pressure upon legislators. They are the unorganized debris of an organizational society. They are indeed the forgotten people—forgotten by the labor movement, by the urban liberals, by almost everybody except a small band of men and women who have devoted their lives and meager resources to fighting what must often seem a hopeless battle.

Even when a law is passed, usually over the opposition of the farmers, giving farm workers a few minimal protections, it is chronically and matter-of-factly violated by farm employers, usually with no penalty involved even when they are caught. Most state legislatures are still dominated politically by the agricultural interests, and these same interests have a disproportionate influence in Congress. There are, moreover, still some farmers and farm organizations that fight off any regulation of farm workers' conditions just as bitterly and almost in the identical language as they used in *The Grapes of Wrath*.

Investigating violations of the California state law dealing with illegal employment of minors is the responsibility of the state labor commissioner. Lacking an adequate staff, and with its main attention directed, almost inevitably, toward industrial workers, the commission has conducted such investigations haphazardly and indifferently. When questioned about an accident involving a fifteen-year-old boy whose toes were fractured in another auger accident, the labor commissioner's office stated:

"Inasmuch as this accident occurred at a location distant from any of the Division's offices, and for a considerable period of time there was no other Division business in the area, this matter was handled by sending the employer full information relative to child labor laws, together with a written warning."

There is not, in fact, very much the state labor commissioner can do, no matter how zealous he may be. "What jury of farmers will convict another farmer illegally employing minors when so many of them do it?" asks an official in the commissioner's office. "And, before we can get a conviction, we have to find a local district attorney who is willing to file a complaint. This is not easy either, in a farm area."

The hired farm work force in the United States is composed of three main groups: regular workers, seasonally employed workers, and the foreign farmhands, mostly Mexicans brought in under a special program approved by Congress. The 700,000 regular hired workers, those employed for more than 150 days a year by one employer, are almost all male; they take care of livestock, repair buildings, maintain equipment, drive tractors, and generally work without supervision. Frequently they live on or near the farm where they are employed. About half of this group are hired by the largest farms; 48 percent of them are working for farms of more than 1,900 acres.

The million seasonal farm workers normally work less than 150 days in a year, and they work for more than one employer. They do work that can be completed in a short time and are usually paid by the day, hour, or piece. They clear land, lay fertilizer, chop, weed, and do the harvest work—cutting, picking, packing, and toting. Forty-eight percent of all hired seasonal workers were employed on the two largest groups of cotton and fruit-and-nut farms in Texas, California, Arkansas, Mississippi, Louisiana, Tennessee, and North Carolina.

The seasonal farm workers split into two main groups: the larger group of local day-haul employees who may go out with a different farmer each day and are picked up by truck from a central employment point; and the much smaller number of migrants, mostly employed by labor contractors in the South and West and by crew leaders in the East. The contractors or crew leaders take the migrants from farm to farm along the migrant stream. They set a flat price with the farmer for the harvesting work, then paying the workers from their own pockets, or else they get a commission from the farmer for each worker supplied. The lush financial rewards open to an unscrupulous labor contractor are obviously tempting, and there has been a sharp increase in the number of people with criminal records who have applied for contractors' licenses in California.

There are six major streams of migratory workers:

1. The one on the Atlantic Coast is made up of about 60,000 workers, most of whom are Negro, supplemented by workers from Puerto Rico and Mexican-Americans.

2. The sugar-beet stream starts in Texas and goes up into the North Central and Mountain States. This group, too, consists of about 60,000 workers, almost all Mexican-Americans.

3. The wheat and small-grain harvest migrants also come up from Texas, generally as combine teams, and work north to Montana and North Dakota. About 30,000 men, also of Mexican descent, do this work.

4. About 80,000 workers of Mexican descent plus Negroes harvest cotton, starting out from Texas with one group moving off into the Mississippi Delta and a bigger one going westward into New Mexico, Arizona, and southern California.

5. From Oklahoma, Arkansas, and western Tennessee, about 30,000 people of early-American stock move north and west during the harvest season, picking fruit and tomatoes.

6. Finally, there are about 120,000 workers, of all backgrounds, working in the Western States, up and down the Pacific Coast.

In addition to the 380,000 American migrant workers, about half a million foreign farm laborers are brought into the United States each year. Most of these are the "braceros" from Mexico, who more and more are replacing the seasonal American workers, both local and migrant.

Seventy-five percent of the regular year-round farm workers and nearly 50 percent of all the seasonal workers were employed by only little more than one-tenth of all the farmers. Thus one-tenth of farmers cultivate nearly half the land, producing three-fifths of all the vegetables, nearly half of all the fruits and nuts, and two-fifths of all the cotton. Since 1940, the number of the nation's farms has declined from 6,350,000 to less than 5,000,000 in 1957. At the same time, the average farm increased from 174 acres in 1940 to more than 242 acres in 1954.

The average yearly income for all farm workers is only $1,250, including all nonfarm cash income and roughly $200 for perquisites. Farm workers, in fact, only receive twice as much pay now as they did in 1933, even though farm productivity has gone up nearly threefold since then. In some farm work, like the picking of cotton, the real value of the wages paid to the farm workers has actually declined since 1943.

It is because farm workers have such a low income level that so many of their children work alongside them in the fields. The money earned by the children is essential to keep the family on even a bare below-subsistence level. And so the children grow up badly educated because local schools are reluctant to take them as pupils, sickly because medical facilities are not easily available to them.

Why does this large group of people continue in farm work? Primarily because no other work is open to them. The minority groups among them find that much industrial employment is closed to them, while the white workers are generally unskilled and are ill adapted to urban life. The kind of lives they lead incapacitates them—and their children—for leading any other. And so they go on living as regular farmhands in shabby houses on the fringes of agricultural communities or on the farms, the migrants in tents, barracks, and occasionally decent camps.

These men, women, and children are utterly exhausted after working long hours in the field. Many of the children suffer from chronic diarrhea. They get horribly cramped, traveling long distances without sleep in broken-down trucks. And if some growers had their way, the trucks would never stop for rest. When the Interstate Commerce Commission held a hearing in May, 1957, to consider setting up safety regulations to govern interstate transportation of farm workers, it was informed by S. H. Butler of the Green Giant Company, Dayton, Wisconsin: "We feel that the requirement banning travel from 8 P.M. to 6 A.M. would work a hardship on the laborers being transported as well as upon employers. It has been our experience that these trucks can complete the trip from Texas to Washington in from fifty to sixty hours, with stops only for meals, gasoline, and general 'stretching.' The men seem to arrive in good physical condition and with a good mental attitude."

At the same 1957 ICC hearing, the Tri-State Packers Association, Inc., of Easton, Maryland, protested a proposal that trucks carrying farm workers be required to have seats. "The floors of the truck in which the persons are transported are normally covered with bedding or sacks of clothing which provide a more suitable resting place than would seats of the type suggested by the Commission—the requirement that seats be provided appears to be extremely undesirable. It is unsatisfactory as a safety measure for the reason that if seats are not provided, the transients will sit or lie on bedding or clothing and they would be in far less danger in the event of a sudden stop than would be true if they were sitting on wooden benches. In addition, these trucks are used to haul produce to the processor—it would be practically impossible to attach the seats securely and still use the vehicle to haul produce."

But a lack of seats did not act "as a safety measure" for the forty-one American men, women, and child farm workers jammed into the eight-by-fifteen-foot back of a dilapidated one-and-a-half-ton truck that pulled out from the side of a North Carolina highway on June 6, 1957, directly into the path of a ten-ton tractor-trailer. Seconds later, after a grinding crash, twenty broken and mutilated bodies were strewn over the highway. Of the forty-one who had been crammed together in that tiny space without seats, only five were unhurt. The North Carolina crash broke the record for this kind of accident—a record set previously in August, 1947, in Texas, when nineteen farm workers were killed.

Just as on the national level some powerful farm organizations bitterly—and usually successfully—resist any Federal regulation that affects them (except increased subsidies, of course), so too on the state level is the farm worker left unprotected. The prospects for including farm workers under the compensation acts are "bleak," writes Harold Katz, an authority on workmen's compensation law, "since farm organizations, which have traditionally opposed such coverage, exert considerable influence in our state legislatures."

The extent of the influence of farm organizations on state legislatures can easily be seen even in a state like California, where farm workers are somewhat better off than in many other states. A California state law provides that an illegally employed minor who suffers an accident while working shall receive an additional 50 percent increased payment in workmen's compensation, paid by the employer—unless the employer is a farmer. In that case, the penalty payment is not made.

Why this exception? State officials shrug. "It's the farm lobby in Sacramento," they say. "That lobby has lots of power."

There is no question that agricultural employers have a special difficulty in that they require large numbers of farm workers for short periods of time, lest an entire crop be lost. But if farm wages go up, will food prices necessarily follow? It is clear that the relation is not so simple as that: the labor cost is only one factor in the unstable price structure of those agricultural products that call for the use of migrant labor, and generally not the most important one. Even after a crop is harvested, especially if it be fruits and vegetables, the market price depends to an extraordinary extent upon factors over which the grower has had little control; the weather's effect upon the crop's quality, its size, its availability, and the fickle public taste. In Florida last winter, a freeze hit the orange crop. Thousands of farm workers, both local and migrant, faced such critical unemployment that the National Council of Churches appealed to President Eisenhower to establish a state of emergency. But their employers, the Florida growers, have made handsome profits because the freeze put oranges in short supply and the frost-bitten fruit could be marketed as "fair" frozen orange juice at a high price per can.

So too with other fruit and vegetable crops. Melon growers in California's Imperial Valley can make or lose fortunes overnight. But becoming a millionaire or a pauper does not depend on the wages paid the melon pickers; rather it depends on the quality of the melons and the time that they reach the market.

In the face of this enormously complicated problem, much of organized agriculture insists on keeping farm wages down. The farm employers' attitude was neatly summed up by a Texas congressman, himself a farmer: "I think the employers, everyone, would protest the twenty-cent minimum wage. Or a ten-cent minimum wage or any other minimum wage." As a matter of fact, Texas growers are accustomed to paying their farm workers sixteen cents an hour for a sixty-hour week.

The payment of substandard wages is justified by farm employers on the uncertainty of their profits. But while their employees are penalized in advance because of the growers' possible unknown financial loss, the farmers do not make any additional payments to their workers if the crop does bring in a large profit. The workers' wages remain the same—abysmally low—no matter what profit the farmer makes. No department-store owner expects to lower the pay of a saleswoman if a dress has to be marked down in price because it doesn't sell, but farmers successfully demand that *their* workers run all the risks of the market place without receiving any of its benefits.

So too with coverage of farm workers under state compensation laws. Farm organizations bitterly resist paying for such coverage, still relying on the fiction that all American farmers are "small," not able to afford insurance. Even if this were true—which it is not, since the great majority of farm workers are employed by the very largest and most profitable farms— what difference would it make? Small industrial employers must be covered by insurance as well as by wage and hour laws. Extending such coverage to small industrial operations was difficult, but it was done. No one would deny that protecting farm workers by law will also be difficult, but it too can be accomplished if farm organizations can somehow be convinced that arrogant refusals even to discuss the matter are not substitutes for social responsibility.

There is in particular one group of large farmers, associated with the American Farm Bureau Federation, that generally opposes any Federal or state regulations affecting employer-worker relationships, while at the same time it attempts to represent itself as speaking for the overwhelming majority of all farmers.

Attacking an official of the Farmers' Union, whose membership is made up of smaller farmers, for supporting regulations governing the transportation of migrant workers, J. Kenneth Robinson, president of the Agricultural Conference Board of Virginia and also representing the Frederick County Fruit Growers' Association, said: "The Farmers' Union representative this morning mentioned the fact that they stood 100 percent behind the regulations as proposed. I would point out their membership of 300,000 farm families is considerably less representative than the Farm Bureau's membership of 1,600,000 farm families."

In fact, however, the 1,600,000 Farm Bureau Federation membership includes not just farmers, but bankers, grocers, hardware merchants, filling-station operators, and a variety of other businessmen in rural communities, all of whom display their membership placards in store windows. And among the farmers, the Farm Bureau represents the half million biggest and richest who employ seven-tenths of the hired labor. It is these who are leading the fight against Federal regulation. "Minimum wages would result in limiting the employment of inefficient workers and would seriously limit the income of the average to superior workers," states one Farm Bureau official, while another demands that the Department of Labor "cease forcing users of Mexican national labor to furnish housing to Mexican national laborers that includes standards more rigorous than those usually provided domestic agricultural labor."

In 1957, the "users" of foreign labor employed nearly half a million foreign farm workers, mostly braceros, Mexicans legally brought into the United States first during the Second World War to meet the shortage of domestic labor, and in increasing numbers each year since then, under the terms of a treaty negotiated between the Mexican and American governments. The bracero program, the subject of much heated controversy, is administered by the Department of Labor. Before a farmer may employ braceros, the department must certify that his need for their services cannot be met by domestic labor.

Some twelve thousand British West Indians, one thousand Japanese, sixty-five hundred Canadians, several hundred Filipinos, and groups of Bahamians were also brought into the United States, but on temporary entry cards, under the control of the Immigration Service. Some Mexicans also come into the country this way, including one group brought to Oregon, where the farmers then took away their permits to make it impossible for them to leave the farms, while keeping them living in unspeakably bad conditions.

In attacking the Department of Labor for imposing regulations governing the living conditions of the braceros, the Farm Bureau people are frequently joined by another group, the contracting associations set up by growers to bring the Mexican workers into the United States, house them, and then supply them to the association members as they are needed. E. S. McSweeney, secretary of the Arizona Cotton Growers' Association, one such group, complained to a congressional subcommittee in 1958 that "we as farmers or farm organizations" have "become quite bitter about this constant regulation down to the minimum detail." One of the camps operated by Mr. McSweeney's association was described by a Labor Department official on a 1956 inspection tour of camps in California and Arizona as "by far the worst. . . . Each unit is about ten by twelve. Four men and a kerosene stove are squeezed into each hut. . . . The door to some of the huts can't be closed from the inside. As a result chickens invade and leave their droppings on the floor. Crushed woolly worms are also very much in evidence inside the huts. The garbage is infrequently collected. The shower floor is covered with filth and smells like an outhouse."

In fact, Department of Labor regulation has been neither constant nor consistent. Lacking an adequate compliance staff, the department has been under pressures from the inception of the bracero program—pressures exerted by the growers and expressed through their organizations and their congressmen. Such pressure is focused mainly around three problems: the standards by which the department assesses the growers' needs for employing braceros, the department's establishment of minimum wage rates for the braceros, and the housing requirements specified by the department.

Under the terms of Public Law 78, which governs the importation and employment of Mexican nationals, no braceros may be employed if domestic labor is available to do the work at the prevailing rate of pay. The state employment services, often susceptible to grower influence, are charged with the responsibility of determining whether there is enough domestic labor available and, if not, certifying the need for braceros to the Labor Department.

During the spring recession of 1958, a group of growers in Texas claimed that they needed braceros for harvesting. On March 31 they communicated this need, by letter, to Maurice Acers, commissioner of the Texas Employment Commission, who replied: "You know I understand the problem. Count on me to do everything humanly possible." But on April 15, an attorney for one growers' association reported to his clients on a meeting with the Texas Employment Commission that "apparently because of the alleged recession back in the East, pressure had been brought to bear upon the Department of Labor causing them to shut down the bracero program. They further stated that the Department of Labor was constantly and continuously making things tougher to allow braceros to come into this country and making more and more requirements for them to meet."

The attorney then reported that the Department of Labor had wired the Texas Employment Commission, insisting that the Texas farmers attempt to fill their need for tractor drivers in Oklahoma and Missouri, where single workers were available at a dollar an hour, as a prior condition to the use of braceros. The attorney wrote that "The above quoted telegram caused quite a stir at this meeting, because, as stated by the Texas Employment Commission, this was the first time the U. S. Department of Labor had ever attempted to require the farmers of Texas to go outside the state of Texas to locate potential employees and recruit them there, and also the first time that they had ever attempted to set a definite wage rate."

One reason given by the attorney for the growers' unwillingness to recruit tractor drivers "outside the state" in Missouri and Oklahoma while they were willing to recruit "outside the state" in Mexico was: "The farmers did not have any housing facilities to take care of a family type of migratory workers. That since the bracero had come into play in this area, a few of the farmers had been able to construct good bachelor quarters for the braceros, but the married domestic was unwilling to live in such quarters and do the job required. . . . Where a man now is able to house ten unmarried or bachelor farm laborers, he would only be able to put one family unit or one worker."

Another objection raised by the association to the procedure of going "outside the state" was that "a tractor driver in this area does more than just drive a tractor. He will be required to drive a tractor as his principal job, but at the same time will also be required to irrigate, move tubes, fill in ditches, and dig in the mud. In addition to this, he will not have an eight-hour day but will be required to work from twelve to sixteen hours a day. Experience has taught us that very few domestic laborers . . . are willing to do this type of work for that many hours for the pay scale that can be paid."

The cost of making trips to Oklahoma and Missouri, which they would have had to bear, was also an issue to the Texas growers, perhaps especially since under the bracero program the U. S. government, not the growers, bears the cost of feeding the workers at the assembly stations in Mexico and the cost of transporting them to the American reception centers and feeding them en route as well as there.

Quite apart from the question of wages and housing, however, the way in which the bracero program is conducted depends upon how well the treaty between the United States and Mexico is enforced. Here, even with the best good will in the world, the Labor Department is handicapped by a lack of compliance officers, and by the few opportunities for training those it does have. The department's field offices in Arkansas and Texas had only thirty-five men to serve more than a hundred thousand braceros in those two states during 1957. Even this was an improvement over 1951, when only fourteen compliance officers served the same area. A similar shortage of compliance officers has existed in other areas. Although there are more now, there were only seven officers in 1956 to cover the entire southern California and Arizona area. One of them was given the responsibility of inspecting approximately two hundred camps.

The compliance officers frequently exchange their low civil-service salaries for the higher financial rewards of the contracting associations. One of the camps described in 1956 by Department of Labor investigators as being "over-crowded and filthy" was operated by an association whose manager was a former compliance officer; and Mr. McSweeney of the Arizona Cotton Growers' Association stated that the two government compliance officers in his area prefer now to be called "employers' service representatives."

The Mexican consuls in the United States are supposed to help enforce the agreement. The Reverend John F. Godfrey, a Catholic priest of Chesterfield, Missouri, has described in some detail what happens when a bracero complains to him about a contract violation. Father Godfrey lives close to St. Louis, where there is a Mexican consul, while "the field representative from the Department of Labor is situated in Kansas City, 250 miles away. The Mexican bracero is advised to present his complaint to the Mexican Consul. I explain to him that I will call the Mexican Consul on the telephone and then he can explain his difficulty in Spanish to the Mexican Consul. The usual reaction of the bracero is 'No, Padrecito, the Mexican Consul is not my friend, he is the friend of the patron.' If I think the matter is serious and ought to be presented for consideration, I will say, 'If you do not present it, I will present it to him.' Then, in the presence of the bracero, I call the Mexican Consul and explain to him the difficulties the Mexican has presented to me. Usually I get a lot of double talk from the Consul. He explains to me that the contract should be interpreted this way or that way; often he interprets it more in favor of the employer than he does of the bracero. However, once in a while I just lay it on the line for him and he does something for me, but all in all the dealing with the Mexican Consul is a very unsatisfactory experience."

Complaints about the behavior of Mexican consuls toward the braceros come from other sources than priests. Abe F. Levy, a union attorney in Los Angeles, states that in one case when he began a workmen's compensation action for a bracero who had been hurt while working but did not know he was entitled to compensation, the Mexican Consul first attempted to get Levy out of the case, then attempted to have the bracero shipped back to Mexico before final disposition of the case. Levy charges that many bracero compensation cases are deliberately stalled by the insurance companies until the bracero has left the country and then are settled for perhaps 25 percent of normal compensation. When such a bracero has left the country, or when death benefits are paid for a bracero who has been killed, the payments are made to the Mexican consuls. They in turn, it is assumed, send the money on to Mexico.

The insurance company that writes some of the workmen's compensation and all nonoccupational disability and life insurance for the braceros coming into California also benefits from the consuls' failure to protect the braceros' interests. Because of the low number of claims made, this company gives a high refund to the employers who pay for the workmen's compensation insurance; and the company maintains an extremely profitable retention rate for itself on the nonoccupational disability and life-insurance policy which is paid for by the bracero. The surprisingly low number of claims is probably the result of either the braceros' ignorance of their rights or the fact that a bracero is out of the country before his claim can be processed. In California at least, when the braceros pass through the reception center they are not informed of the benefits to which they are entitled under the policies, although a Mexican consul is at the reception center.

These insurance policies also figured in an investigation initiated by Governor "Pat" Brown, when he was attorney general, into charges that at least one growers' association in the Imperial Valley deducted premium payments from braceros' pay checks but did not remit them to the insurance company. Discovering this, the company subsequently collected the premiums from the association—and kept them, even though the braceros from whom the money had been taken had long since returned to Mexico.

Many serious charges that the bracero program was being badly administered were made in a study written in 1956 by Dr. Ernesto Galarza and published by the Joint United States-Mexico Trade Union Committee. Galarza, one of the devoted band attempting to improve the lot of farm workers, made his charges on the basis of an investigation he conducted in California. His accusations were hotly denied by the growers' associations and also by Secretary of Labor Mitchell, who wrote in September, 1956, that the study "contains some very serious inaccurate statements and misleading allegations concerning the conditions under which Mexican workers are employed in agriculture in this country." But a few months later a report of an investigation by Department of Labor officials stated that although Galarza's arguments were "specious" many of the unsavory conditions he described did exist.

However, Secretary Mitchell seems more genuinely concerned with attempting to solve the bracero problem than any of his predecessors were. There are signs of recognition within the department that the bracero program has become a national disgrace, requiring action to protect the standards of both braceros and Americans.

One of the factors complicating the Labor Department's ability to perform this role, and possibly accounting for its somewhat cautious attitude, is the continuing effort being made by the growers and some congressmen to take supervision of the foreign-labor program away from the Labor Department and put it, instead, under the jurisdiction of the Immigration Service. Some Labor Department officials believe that if they antagonize the growers too much, the effort to swing the program to the Immigration Service might become more determined and successful. The Immigration Service permits the growers to make their arrangements directly with the foreign workers through their own governments, and leaves supervision over wages or working conditions to those governments. It was under just such an arrangement that Bahamians were imported to work as apple pickers by Virginia growers, ending up in labor camps (including one operated by Senator Byrd) under ghastly conditions.

An official of the Joint United States-Mexico Trade Union Committee charged that, under a similar agreement with the Japanese government, the Japanese workers pay their own round-trip transportation and subsistence between Japan and the United States, have no voice in setting their wages or in selecting their own representatives, may be used as strikebreakers, pay 5 percent of their wages to welfare funds in which they have no voice, and must contribute 50 percent of their earnings to a special fund. If the worker returns to Japan after finishing his contract, his earnings are then returned to him; but if he fails to return or dies in America, the money goes to the Japanese government.

Puerto Rican farm workers, who are brought here under the protection of the Puerto Rican government, are treated a great deal better. According to a Puerto Rican official, the conditions demanded by Puerto Rico for wage guarantees, workmen's compensation, adequate housing, and other safeguards "sounded strange to many employers." The official went on to say that "This attitude has also changed, partly because there is a clause in the agreement which provides that representatives of the Puerto Rico Department of Labor must be allowed access to the men, the housing, and the payrolls."

But in spite of the Labor Department's staff problem, in spite of the continuing resistance of growers—supported by farm congressmen—to regulation, in spite of all the loopholes and the violations, Public Law 78 does provide some minimal Federal protections to the Mexican farm worker. Such Federal protection and supervision are almost completely denied the American farm worker.

A migrant's children may either have to work in the fields or stay unattended in a filthy camp. Not many communities have adequate child-care centers for the children of migrant farm workers. "There are very few facilities available to migrant mothers for day-care of their children," states a report of the Florida State Board of Health. "Much publicity is given to those maintained by church groups, but in all fairness it must be said that they are too few and too expensive to be available to many migrants."

For the nonmigrant seasonal farm workers, life is not very much better. They too frequently work for contractors on a day-haul basis. In a typical Florida farm household, the eleven-year-old daughter of the family was absent from school forty-one days out of eighty-five because the mother had to work and could not afford to pay a day-care center's fees for her three children under six. A Board of Health report of her activities for one week reads as follows:

"Sunday: picked six baskets of beans, earned $3.60. Monday: no work available in Belle Glade; paid $.50 for her transportation by truck to 'the coast,' where the crop was poor. Picked three baskets, earned $1.80. Tuesday: rained, no work. Wednesday: picked four baskets of beans, earned $2.40. No more work available that day. Thursday: picked five baskets of beans, earned $3.00; transportation cost $.50. Friday: picked eight baskets of beans (in eleven hours in the field), earned $4.80. Saturday: 'chopped' peppers in the field for twelve hours, earned $6.00.

"The total earnings for the week (less transportation costs) with which to support herself and her four children were $20.60."

Children of school age were involved somewhat differently in a revealing incident that occurred in September, 1955, when there was a shortage of prune pickers in the Santa Clara County, California, area because, stated the California Department of Employment, there was a "loss of students, housewives leaving to enter children in schools, and men drafted to fight forest fires." According to state law, children cannot be employed during school hours. The opening dates for schools throughout the county were therefore postponed a week, "at the request of ranchers in the area," according to one of the local newspapers. As a result of this postponement, approximately 34,000 school children went to school a week late because the ranchers in the area needed, again according to the employment department report, 250 prune pickers.

There are some signs of hope in this hitherto grim situation. For too many years, the farm-labor problem has been almost solely the concern of a few groups like the National Council on Agricultural Life and Labor and the National Sharecroppers Fund, whose yearly money-raising appeals are wearily opened and rather indifferently put aside. For too many years, the priests, nuns, and laymen associated with the Catholic Council for the Spanish Speaking and the National Catholic Rural Life Conference have shouldered their great burden without much help. For too many years, the representatives of the American Friends Service Committee have had to appear alone before state and national legislative committees. For too many years, union leaders, with a few exceptions, have either ignored farm workers or considered them political and economic pawns, useful only as sacrifices for larger stakes. But recently there has been a widening public interest in the problem. The governors of some states, among them Pennsylvania and Oregon, have set up special committees of farm groups and prominent farmers. Early in February, the National Advisory Committee on Farm Labor, a new group of respected and distinguished citizens, will hold public hearings in Washington on the farm-labor problem. There seems to be a revival of the instincts for social compassion and indignation—qualities recently absent from our society, perhaps because it is so difficult for the prosperous majority to identify itself with a destitute minority.

A
MATTER
OF
SPIRIT

(1961) A<small>LL SUMMER LONG</small>, the wet fog hung over the Monterey Peninsula of California and the patio furniture dripped with sweat on the lawns of the elegant homes in Carmel and Pebble Beach. "It must be very hot over in the valleys," said the fashionable people of the peninsula, sleepily looking out their picture windows on Sunday morning and slowly coming alive for a lazy breakfast with the newspapers.

They were right about the valleys. It was hot in all of them— the Salinas, Sacramento, San Joaquin and Imperial Valleys— the four rich basins that run lengthwise through the state. There was no escape down there from the hot sun that burned in the bright blue sky, from the heat waves that shimmered across the highway, from the hot winds that nauseated.

Alongside the roads in the valleys, trucks were certain to be parked even on Sundays during the summer, and hunkered down alongside them, squeezed together in the little shade thrown by the truck bodies, were the farm workers, come in from the fields for a hasty midday dinner. They dripped with sweat, too, the drops running down their faces and dissolving into the lumpy mass of beans thrown on their plates. Sunday was a work day for them, like any other day; the crops must be harvested and so the farm workers stayed bent over in the fields from early morning until late at night, picking.

Sometimes the groups next to the trucks were all men, instantly identifiable by their straw sombreros, their dark brown weathered skin and the way they squat on their heels while they eat, staring incuriously at the autos racing by them on the highways. They were braceros—Mexican contract laborers brought north under Public Law 78 for the harvesting season. If they were Americans, old jalopies were parked on the road and the women were out in the fields picking too, while their children played in the ditches.

These are the farm workers, the "stoop labor," whom the AFL-CIO tried for two years to organize in a campaign directed by Norman Smith, a veteran of the CIO wars. Unconsciously evoking the past, the farm organizing group was called the AWOC, the Agricultural Workers' Organizing Committee, and its dedicated group of organizers literally labored in the vineyards under conditions very reminiscent of an earlier time in labor history.

The organizers' efforts, failures, and successes were eloquently described in May by Franz Daniel, AFL-CIO assistant director of organization, to a meeting of the Industrial Relations Research Association. Daniel, another CIO warhorse, told of the handicaps to union organization created by the migrant workers' lack of self-confidence, the growers' use of the braceros, the collusion between the police and the farmers. The bitter resistance of the Western Growers' Association surely must have stirred the audience as Daniel read part of its call to anti-union arms: "Proponents of panty-waist public relations, people with revolving cheeks and sensitive souls who shrink from using heat to cure the union blight should file quietly from the hall at this point. Low purposes spawn at low levels and cannot be met successfully with an invitation to tea in the upper parlor."

Organization work among the farm workers had been extremely difficult, Daniel reported. "The union had to fight each inch of the way." But despite all the considerable handicaps, including a very bitter strike in the Imperial Valley, the union had made some "actual accomplishments." Wage increases of more than $11 million could be traced with some justice to its work, the number of braceros had been cut down, and more efficient harvesting methods had been developed. To do this, the AFL-CIO invested approximately $500,000 in the AWOC.

Daniel's description of the AWOC's work ended with his calling upon the American labor movement to use the organization of farm workers as the AFL-CIO's "opportunity to renew its youth and to reassert its claim to the idealism of man's duty to his brother and to society."

But Daniel's call was either unheard or unheeded. Six weeks later, at a meeting of the AFL-CIO executive board held in Unity House, the International Ladies' Garment Workers' lovely and cool summer resort high in the Pocono Mountains, George Meany announced the ending of the farm workers organization drive and the dissolution of the AWOC. The AFL-CIO president's action was not totally unexpected. At the executive board meeting held in February, 1961, Norman Smith had asked for a $500,000 organizing fund but had been given only $250,000. The drive might even have ended in February, except for the pressure exerted upon Meany by John Livingston, AFL-CIO organization director, backed up by a few union presidents.

But in May, no one at Unity House protested Meany's announcement. Indeed, no one even spoke publicly about it. The matter was raised and disposed of within the span of a minute or two.

So now, up in Stockton, California, the operations of the AWOC have been sharply curtailed. Smith is still on the AFL-CIO payroll, but there are other staff members who have been dropped and the AWOC is trying to raise funds from outside sources and unions in the area.

Naturally, the California growers, the corporate farmers, are gleeful about the way in which their enemies have been forced, by orders from the top, to retreat from the battleground. Neverless, they were frightened. And as they sit in their favorite restaurants in El Centro and San Francisco, or walk in their dusty but very soft leather boots across the thousands of acres they own, these remnants of the feudal age, California's agri-industrialists, are thinking hard of what they can do to make sure no union ever tries to organize farm workers again. For, despite their victory over the AFL-CIO leadership, the shadow of the Teamsters can be seen on their land: Jimmy Hoffa is giving serious consideration to moving into the vacuum left by the cessation of the AWOC activity.

The AFL-CIO will make no further attempt to organize the farm-workers. "More important than material things is the need of spirit," said Franz Daniel of what was required to organize farm workers. Sadly, one must conclude that the AFL-CIO has very little spirit left for dealing with problems which are not easily soluble in the old ways.

For a long time to come, in the valleys of California, the trucks and jalopies will still be parked alongside the highways, the men and women will still be in the fields, their wages and working conditions still far below those of industrial workers. Perhaps only a few of them understand the real significance of the AFL-CIO decision, but for those few there is only bitterness left as they look back at the effort they made to help themselves in the past two years.

It is a very long way, much more than the actual three thousand miles, from the AFL-CIO's air-conditioned marble palace in Washington to the hot, dusty valleys of California. Measured in other, less tangible units, the distance is nearly infinite. Meany was angry, for example, that the AWOC moved part of its organizing operation from Stockton, its headquarters in the north, five hundred miles south to Imperial Valley, where the growers fought back viciously, causing a bitter strike. But Meany's anger was the result of his not understanding that the agricultural workers are used by the growers as a highly mobile labor force that is shifted from one part of the state to another by trucks in a matter of hours.

Perhaps someday the AFL-CIO leaders will come to California, not merely to attend a convention or a meeting in one of the state's two big cities, but to walk in the hot, dusty valleys and talk with the "stoop labor." Then they may understand that organizing these people is, as Franz Daniel said, a matter of "spirit." If not, if the union leaders stay inside the cool comfort of their air-conditioned autos and only look out the windows, the workers in the fields will simply stare back incuriously. To them, all the big cars that whoosh past look alike, and all the people who ride in them are alike.

INTRODUCTION

THE SINGLE most important domestic problem this country faces in the next decade is unemployment. The fear of unemployment was one of the basic motivations behind the New York printers' strike as it was one of the basic motivations in the resistance of the railroad unions to the industry's desire to cut back thousands of jobs which the railroad companies insist are unnecessary.

In all the editorial fulminations against featherbedding that have filled our eyes and ears for the past few years, very little is ever said about the function of featherbedding in providing employment. In England, for example, long after the Blue Water missile had been canceled, workers continued to produce carefully inspected fins for the missile. If they had not been employed at this useless task, they would have been unemployed. Which is worse?

"Dead Horse and the Featherbird" tries to answer that question and although it deals specifically with airlines and newspapers the issues it discusses apply generally to all industries.

DEAD
HORSE
AND
THE
FEATHERBIRD

(1962) THE COMPOSING ROOM of the newspaper is comparatively quiet; no linotype machines chatter harshly, nor does the floor quiver from the running of the presses in the basement. It is the lobster shift—those off-hours when the printers set type without the pressure of a deadline. The men stand at their long composing tables adjusting metal rules, checking type against the copy for the advertisement at their elbow, and occasionally talking with each other.

The foreman walks over to a hook on the wall, a spike festooned with printed copies of advertisements that appeared in the newspaper days before. He takes one off the hook and carries it to a printer who has just finished tying up the type and metal for an ad that will run in tomorrow's paper.

"Here," the foreman tells the printer, offering him the printed ad. "We're falling behind on reset. Get this one."

The printer looks up sullenly. "What do you think I am—a lousy amateur? I don't want to set that stuff. I'm no blacksmith. Give me some live copy, not that goddamn dead horse."

The foreman does not argue. He calmly puts the advertisement down on the table and walks away, saying over his shoulder, "Get started before I call the chapel chairman over."

The printer begins to set the type for an advertisement that had already been run some months earlier. The copy announces an Easter sale in a department store, and it is now the end of summer. Mumbling to himself, the disgruntled printer starts work on the ad, knowing the foreman has authority to demand that the work be done and that the chapel chairman of the shop (the union's chief steward) would back up that authority.

The compositor slaps together whatever type he can find which fits that of the ad, encloses the type in a metal form, and walks over to a table where he slams it down beside a dozen similar forms of ads that have also appeared earlier in the paper. Soon, another printer will pick up these forms from the table and take them over to a proof press where a proof copy will be made of each one. Then, the proof copy will be checked for errors and the necessary corrections made in the type. Finally, another proof of the ad will be pulled and the printer's work will be ready for its final destiny: to be destroyed without being used —melted down in the "hell box," where used type becomes hot lead once again.

This is the process by which printers do "unwork"; work that is actually performed and paid for but goes unused. It is called "reproduction," "reset," "bogus," or "dead horse."

The jet airplane seems prepared to hang in the air forever until that moment when its wheels touch the concrete runway and it is instantly transformed from a graceful creature of the air into a screaming, speeding, metal monster, ungainly and awkward out of its natural element. With a frantic roar, the jet engines are reversed and the plane protestingly slows down. It taxies up to the landing area and in moments a horde of attendants are swarming over it, chocking its wheels, moving up the passenger ramps, unloading baggage, and readying the ship for its next voyage.

Finally, the last passenger walks down the ramp, speeded on his way by the fixed smile of the stewardess at the door, mechanically repeating the airline farewell: "Goodbye now. Come back and fly with us again." Their work finished, the crew members walk down the ramp with the captain-pilot first, followed by co-pilot and flight engineer—American culture heroes in their natty uniforms, each carrying one bag of luggage and one black valise stuffed with the maps, charts, and manuals that are the paraphernalia of their craft. They walk across the oil-stained concrete ramp to the flight operations office.

Inside the office they are met by a crew from another airline who will cajole the same jet into the skies for the next leg of the journey. They talk a bit of the new traffic pattern at the Los Angeles airport, of the near-miss one of their group had with an Air Force jet, and always of the weather. But this second group of fliers has an additional man in it, for the company that flies the next segment of the trip in the very same plane does it with four crew members instead of three.

That fourth flier is a "featherbird" airman. When he arrives back at his home base, he will walk into the flight operations office there and ask the superintendent, "Any chance of getting back to flying yet? I'm a pilot, not a damned chairwarmer." The superintendent may shake his head sympathetically. "Negative, there's nothing open for you on pistons."

Thirty thousand feet of vertical space separate the newspaper compositor setting type that will never be used from the airman squeezed into a seat with no instruments in front of him. But "unwork" is a common link between them. The industries in which they perform their "unwork" are widely separated, too— by different histories, structures, economic patterns, and by contrasting relationships to government: newspaper publishing is relatively free of state regulation while commercial aviation is subject to rigid supervision by a number of governmental bodies. There is a difference also in costs. The setting of not-to-be-used type is not a heavy economic burden upon most publishers; the presence of a fourth crew member represents an airline expenditure of millions of dollars.

But, despite the differences between these two industries, setting "dead horse" and flying as a "featherbird" have much in common. They derive from the same source, could not exist without management collusion, and have the same demeaning consequences for the men who are paid to perform "unwork." Even more, the common source of "unwork" that links together pilots and printers affects millions of other workers, all of them sharing a fear of unemployment and a consequent loss of identity. Thus, they can be viewed as two examples from a catalogue of meaningless work and fruitless effort carried on in America today. Current apprehension about unemployment related to our technological advance, to automation and "cybernation," make the "unwork" of these two industries symbolic of a major issue in the 1960's—how to maintain a full and free economy without a fully employed work force.

I

The compositor who despises setting type for an ad that will end in the hell box has an ancient lineage. Imprinters, men who put symbols or letters on bricks, were found in ancient Babylonia. Roman coins had letters on them; nobles used a form of printing when they pressed their seals into wax; and the Chinese had paper money printed from wood blocks before the tenth century. Typography was known in China as far back as 1041. In 1314 a Chinese printer used sixty thousand separate wooden characters to publish a book on agriculture. But books in the Christian world were laboriously copied out by hand; only the Church and the richest men could afford them. In the Middle Ages, books were chained to the lectern in the monastery or college fortunate enough to possess them. Charles V of France had a huge collection for the fourteenth century—910 volumes.

In the middle of the fifteenth century, Johann Gutenberg's invention for the cutting and casting of metal type created an enormous demand for books throughout Europe and England. To meet the new demand, printers were needed. In an age when most of the population was illiterate, a journeyman printer not only had to know how to read, spell, and write, but also had to possess an artistic sense, a flair for selecting the appropriate type and setting it in an attractive manner. Complicated measurements requiring a knowledge of mathematics were necessary to set up his forms. In addition, he had to be a skilled mechanic, capable not only of maintaining his equipment but of building new equipment.

How were these early craftsmen paid for their work? The first printers were paid in accordance with the amount of type they either set or produced. But as new type faces and sizes were introduced, more and more skill was required of the printer. Typography was becoming an art, and it was soon clear that the system of paying printers merely for the type they actually set would have to be changed.

How, for example, was a printer to be paid if some of the work he normally did in the shop was done outside and then brought into his work place? How was he to make a living if an unlimited number of impressions could be made from the type he had set? And if the journeyman printer could not earn a living from one master, he might wander off to the next town in the hope that there would be more work for him there. A good printer was hard to find in those days; an employer, a master printer, had a big stake in keeping his skilled workers available even when work fell off. And so, in order to protect themselves, the master printers, not the journeymen workers, began developing restrictions on how many copies could be made from any one form of type.

During the sixteenth century, most English printing journeymen and masters lived in London, where there were printing presses, each licensed and rigidly controlled under the tight guild system. Except for a press at Oxford and another at Cambridge, the London presses were the only ones in England. By 1557 the master printers of London had banded together as the London Stationers' Company and carried on their trade under a charter from the Crown. The Company, controlled by twenty-odd master printers, was among the most rigidly operated of guilds. By 1587, the work rules of the Company provided that type, once having been set and used, could not be used again without first being broken up and put back in the type box. Rule 1 decreed: "Ffyrst that no formes of letters be

kept standinge to the prejudice of Woorkemen at any time."
Rule 2 imposed a limit ranging from 1,250 to 1,500 on the number of impressions that might be made from any one form of
type, except for "Grammars Accidences Prymers and Cate-
chisms" when "3000 at the moste" were permitted. There were
a few additional exemptions—"the statutes and proclamacons
with all other bookes belonging to ye office of her maiesties
printer which by reason of her maiesties affayres are to be limited to no numbers," "all Calendars printed Red and black,"
and, finally, "all Almanaches and prognostications."

By 1635, the Stationers' Company had issued a new set of
rules governing the operations of print shops and presses. An increase was granted in the number of impressions that might be
drawn from a single form and the old rule that "no formes of
letters be kept standinge" was modified to permit the use of the
standing form, provided that if a compositor in the shop wanted
work, he would be paid for the form that was used just as if
he had composed it himself.

The most important of the new rules was Number 15, which
prohibited the exchange or interchange of type material by journeymen. The rule, originally adopted for the benefit of the masters, "That noe work man lend Letter type without consent first
obteyned of the Master on paine to loose the benefit of Holly-
dais and Copies," was the forerunner of the present law of the
printers' union on "reproduction."

In the course of many years, another rule emerged: the
printers in a shop or newspaper had a right to set all the type in
that shop or be paid for any type or drawing that was actually
used even if the master printer had borrowed it or purchased it
already set up from another shop. There seemed to be no other
way to handle the interchange of type and other materials, and
the rule was accepted by both journeymen and masters.

"It may be safely presumed that America inherited its methods
of working and trade customs from London, upon which it was
always to some degree dependent on men, ideas and equip-

ment," Benjamin Franklin wrote in 1754.

Like sailors, printers were internationalists, taking their craft with them all over the world. By 1638, there was a press established in colonial America—Stephen Day's at Cambridge, operated under the English practices brought to America from across the sea. But since most of the print shops of colonial America were one- or two-man operations, the labor customs common to England were unnecessary in colonial America. It was not until the middle of the eighteenth century that American printers began to worry about their own employment difficulties.

As early as 1815, the New York printers' union was issuing traveling cards to its members. Without such a card, the printer had a hard time finding work and a harder time keeping it. Lacking such a card, he was viewed suspiciously by other printers, who were fearful that he would work at wages less than those demanded by the union men. During the last years of the eighteenth century and the first part of the nineteenth, printers in New York, Albany, Boston, New Orleans, Washington, Philadelphia, and Baltimore made attempts to form unions or associations in their local communities to deal with employers. By 1831, the printers felt strong enough to demand a closed shop from their New York employers. Two years later they were insisting that any dispute between a printer and his employer would be finally resolved by the union members who were working at the place of employment, a practice still in effect today. In 1850, the scattered local unions of printers banded together to form the Journeymen Printers of the United States, the first national union of printers. It later became the International Typographical Union.

But up to the Civil War, in spite of their skills and the protection given them by their unions, American printers often lived as close to poverty as had their sixteenth-century English cousins. They still set type by hand and worked under the old piecework system without any guaranteed minimum weekly wage. When a printer reported for work in one of the early newspaper offices, he never knew if there was to be any work for him and, if there was, how long it would last. If it was a slow day for news, he might set type for an hour; if war had broken out someplace, he might work steadily for fifteen hours. Sometimes, the printer arrived at the newspaper office to find an edition being printed from type that had been used earlier that day or even the day before.

Those were years of bitter rivalry between newspapers, and so there was very little interchange of type between them. Each paper had its own column width, which presented a formidable mechanical obstacle to the exchanging of type. Type out on loan was also unavailable for the publishers' own use. And there was an additional hazard—the type characters were made of heavy metal, not easily transportable through the crowded streets. Thus, in the formative years of the printers' union, the exchange of type between employers was no great problem for the union's scattered locals. Instead, they concentrated on getting and maintaining the closed shop, enforcing the seniority rules by which men were hired and fired, trying to limit the number of low-paid apprentices, and setting piecework rates. By 1871, however, the exchange of type between publishers was becoming general enough to provoke a discussion at the union's convention. A newspaper publisher from New Albany, Indiana, appeared before the convention delegates to appeal a ruling against him made by the printers in his own plant.

Most American cities of the time had at least two daily newspapers, and the larger ones often more than a dozen. There were no nation-wide newspaper chains, all printing the same kind of paper throughout the country; instead, most papers were separately owned and competed bitterly with each other in circulation and advertising wars. That was how the papers in New Albany operated, too, until one of them began to borrow type, already set, from one of the newspapers in Louisville, just across the river. The printers' union in New Albany decided that the publisher there would have to pay for setting the borrowed type if he wanted to use it. The local union's reasons were simple: the practice, if permitted, would have eliminated the jobs of the compositors who otherwise would have set the type that had been borrowed. But the union had another good reason to prohibit the practice—it had to protect the other publishers in the area. The use of borrowed type by one paper gave it an unfair competitive advantage over the other newspapers in New Albany because it could sell more pages without having had to pay the cost of producing them. Thus, the union was forced to use its economic power to police the industry, a policy since then often urged on it by employers anxious to reduce their competitors' economic advantage.

The New Albany publisher appealed the local union's decision to the national convention of the International Typographical Union, and lost. On June 7, 1872, the union, as part of its law, binding upon both members and employers, established "that the transfer of matter from one firm to another is detrimental to both proprietor and printer and should not be allowed."

For the next several years the "loaning and borrowing of matter" kept coming up at union conventions, until the prohibition extended to include even morning and evening newspapers printed in "separate and distinct establishments" by the same publisher. As yet, no union member was being paid to set type that had already been set and printed; rather, the union law was only that the type could not be used over again after it had been used once.

Meanwhile, technology was catching up with the printers. From the Civil War until 1890, the publishing industry in the United States was revolutionized by a series of inventions: the stereotype process, photoengraving, the web press, and, finally, the one the printers believed threatened them most, the linotype machine.

When Otto Mergenthaler patented his linotype machine in 1885, type was still being set laboriously by hand. Two years later, fifty-five of the machines were manufactured. By 1891, the national union leaders had become convinced that the linotype represented a grave problem for their members. A committee investigated the machine's operations in New York and reported its findings to the union members. Linotype operators were doing three times the work of the hand compositors, the committee said, and seemed capable of increasing that amount to four times. The committee recommended that linotype operators be paid on a time basis instead of by the old piecework system and that the hours of work be cut. The union convention, held that same year, adopted both these principles, calling for a cut in the work day to a maximum of eight hours.

Linotypes were quickly put into use by newspapers all over the country. In 1894, 890 of them were produced; in 1895, more than a thousand; and by 1904, 7,500 linotype machines were in operation in the United States and Canada. The displacement of hand compositors by linotype operators grew as more and more of the machines were installed. Some of the younger men were able to learn the new skill; many of the older compositors became permanently unemployed.

But the introduction of the linotype did not have the long-run catastrophic consequences on their employment that the printers had feared. Instead, the standardized, inexpensive papier-mâché stereotype mats and the photo-engraving process permitted manufacturers to advertise their products nationally, without the great difficulties and expense involved in sending copy for advertisements to many different newspapers, all with different kinds of type and column sizes. Papers got bigger as the amount of advertising increased; there was more work for the printing trades. Because the linotype meant that printing could be done more cheaply, more printing was done; newspaper editors took to changing stories in later editions as changes in the news developed, since the cost of such changes was now a good deal less.

The eyes of the printers, however, were not focused on long-range, future developments. Even though the calamity they had been expecting did not take place, the immediate effect of the linotype was to disemploy the older hand compositors. In 1895, the secretary of the New York Typographical Union reported to the labor commissioner on the relationship between the linotype machine and printers' employment: 293 machines had displaced 544 hand compositors—just less than two men to each machine. The older compositors who were now reduced to loitering around the union office or doing odd jobs of substitute work were a constant reminder to employed printers that perhaps their own future was just as dismal.

The depression of that period reinforced these fears. Many members of the ITU roamed the streets. And so "unwork" in newspaper publishing was created from a constellation of circumstances: the difficulty of devising equitable standards for printers' pay, the desire of employers to have printers constantly available for work, the fears of publishers that their competitors might gain "unfair" economic advantages through new technological advances, the printers' apprehensions about being unemployed. In 1901, the national convention of the printers' union changed the flat prohibition against "loaning and borrowing matter" that had been enforced against the New Albany, Indiana, publisher. The union decided to allow the "interchanging, borrowing, lending or buying of matter previously used, either in the form of type, matrices or photo-engraved plates" but under one condition—that it all be done over again. In the years since then, the original blanket insistence that *all* such "matter" be reproduced has been modified to cover only the advertisements inserted by local companies.

Thus it is that an ITU member can find himself sullenly and sloppily setting type, in August, for an ad that had run in the paper the previous Easter. The sullenness and sloppiness are the direct consequences of men who are tied to "unwork," which they despise. But without the "unwork," they fear, they might face permanent unemployment. And the fact that there is no unemployment in their industry at present does little to allay their apprehensions.

Typographical Terrace, until very recently the national headquarters of the printers' union, is a sprawling, old-fashioned brownstone mansion, surrounded by a wide lawn, on North Meridian Avenue in Indianapolis. The union's clerical staff always seemed a little uncomfortable there with such modern devices as typewriters and switchboards, as if they would be more at home dipping scratchy pens into inkwells and cranking phones by hand. Even the union's officers were jammed together in small, crowded rooms in sharp contrast to the marble, air-conditioned AFL-CIO headquarters building in Washington, D.C. The dedicated national officers and representatives of the printers' union are among the lowest-paid group of union officials in the country, sometimes earning even less than they would if working at their trade, but there is nothing fusty about the conscientious manner in which the ITU conducts its operations.

Local ITU contracts with publishers vary greatly all over the country, but, whatever other differences there may be among them, they all have one clause in common—that governing reproduction. No local union is permitted to sign a contract with a publisher, and the international union is constitutionally forbidden to approve such a contract, unless it includes the standard reproduction clause. However, more and more in recent years, the officers have had good reason to suspect that a great many of the locals have been ignoring the reproduction clause in their practices. There were rumors that a paper in Cleveland, Ohio, had fallen behind nine years in doing bogus, with the tacit approval of the local union, while another in St. Louis was allegedly backed up two years, again with the knowledge of the local union. Undone reproduction was evidently being exchanged for a variety of other benefits to the workers. To get around the national constitution, occasionally a local would submit a contract to the International for approval that contained the standard reproduction clause but also included a provision specifying the continuation of "present practices"—a euphemism for not doing reproduction.

Under the ITU national constitution an unemployed printer can walk into the composing room of any newspaper in the country and check the reproduction hook. If there is copy hanging on it, he has the right to demand that he be allowed to work. But the union "law" is often broken by the union members. Obviously, if bogus can be exchanged later in collective bargaining for other benefits to the regularly employed union members at the paper, they have a stake in allowing it to stack up on the hook. And, although the ITU law does not require that accumulated reproduction must be set by the regular printers, sometimes when there is a shortage of substitutes available to do the work the permanent employees do it at overtime rates. So the unemployed printer, for whose benefit the reproduction clause allegedly exists, often finds the atmosphere in a strange composing room so chilly that he is quickly frozen out.

Thus, there is a great gap between the national union law and its enforcement in the shops. Until recently, neither the union members nor the newspaper publishers knew precisely how much reproduction was actually being done. One good reason for the ignorance of the publishers and of the officials of their trade organization, the American Newspaper Publishers' Association, is that when a publisher has some kind of private deal going on with his own employees he rarely tells his competitors about it. He is more likely to keep quiet, be vague about the amount of reproduction his paper actually does, or deliberately exaggerate the amount. It is to the publisher's advantage, in collective bargaining, to let the union representatives believe that reproduction costs the paper more than it actually does, for then he can more successfully plead his inability to give higher wages or other benefits as long as he must continue paying for unused, useless reproduction.

In the same way, the officers of local unions are not going to tell the national officers when they have been violating the union's constitution. Instead, many members and officers of local unions publicly declare their fealty to the reproduction clause while privately ignoring it. In the past, too, the contradiction between the private actions of some ITU leaders and their public statements about it has been covered up by the political operations of the union's unique two-party system, the only one functioning in any American union.

The ITU's Independent and Progressive parties compete vigorously for the votes of the members, and if a union officer does not want to become a wall trophy of the opposition party, he tends to take positions he thinks are popular with the members.

Like the politicians in the South who believe that the segregation issue is the decisive one determining votes, many ITU politicians have been convinced that defeat in office was the price they might easily have to pay for opposing reproduction.

Elmer Brown, the current national president of the union, a gray-haired, quiet, soft-spoken Southerner who was once president of the powerful New York local, has taken a dim view of reproduction for some time. From his own experience as a vice-president of the ITU, he knew there was a discrepancy between what the contracts called for and the actual practice. "No one likes to do useless work," he says as one explanation for the discrepancy. He realized also that as new techniques of photo-printing began to develop reproduction might someday simply disappear without the union getting any benefits in return. But before Brown could make any move to bring the issue out into the open, he needed the facts. In 1960, therefore, the ITU Executive Council, the overwhelming majority of whom are Brown supporters, mailed a questionnaire to the 782 locals of the ITU asking them about their reproduction practices. At the same time, Brown assigned a special representative of the ITU, Joseph Baird, of San Francisco, to make a personal survey of the reproduction situation. Baird visited fifty-nine locals in twenty-five states, the District of Columbia, and three Canadian provinces.

Baird never announced in advance to anyone where he was going. He would arrive at the newspaper plant, introduce himself, talk with the union officials and sometimes with the publisher. Once a union member in the composing room of a paper showed him a letter from the local to the publisher, illegally exempting the paper from doing reproduction. Later, when Baird questioned the local union president about the letter, the president's only concern was to find out which union member had spoken to Baird.

Baird's report to Brown and the other national officers of the union confirmed them in their belief that the reproduction clause in the union constitution ought to be changed. Baird estimated that only about 2 to 5 percent of the locals he had visited were actually doing reproduction and that group was restricted to the larger cities. "Reproduction was being used by some locals for everything and anything except what it was originally intended for," he said, citing the informal exchange of it for such things as coffee breaks, time off, sick leave, or overtime.

For example, Baird discovered that one local, which had contracts with two papers, was up-to-date on its reproduction for one of the papers and six years behind schedule for the other. The local was reluctant "to make an issue of it for fear that the paper that was up-to-date would find out what the other paper was doing."

"Many locals," reported Baird, "keeping accurate records on reproduction and in negotiations use it as a weapon to reach a settlement, and as part of the settlement each year they cancel out the past year's reproduction. One local wanted to sell several years' backlog and could not understand why the ITU would not allow it, even though the president of the local stated he thought reproduction was one of the most important clauses in the contract."

Another local Baird visited "has faithfully been clipping and saving reproduction and has up to eight years' backlog. This local is making no effort to put reproduction into production, feeling that they have the publisher in a bind. When they have an opportunity to work on reproduction they go home early, take coffee breaks, and do anything to avoid working on it."

At another local, a large one, the officers admitted to Baird that they refused to enforce the reproduction clause against one paper because it "was such a nice place to work."

In the eyes of the international union, even worse than the failure of the local unions to enforce the reproduction clause are the strikes that take place over the issue. Baird cited one case where a strike was called ten years ago for the sole purpose of securing a reproduction clause in the contract. At great expense, the strike was won, the men returned, and since then "not one line of reproduction has been set."

The reponse of the local unions to the questionnaire the international union officers sent to them was revealing. Of the 782 locals who received the forms, 558 returned them. Of these, 361 admitted they were doing nothing about reproduction, 86 stated they were putting the ads on the hook but not setting them during the month the questionnaire was received, and only 110 said they were actually doing it. However, the international union officers have doubts about those 110 locals because they made no reference "to exemptions and practices that are followed locally. . . ." With good reason, President Brown believes that Baird's report "conclusively proved that a large majority of our chapels do no reproduction and in other chapels some gesture is made, but it is evident the reproduction provisions in contracts are not fully enforced."

Another serious dilemma has developed for the responsible union leaders with the application of reproduction to papers in the large decentralized suburban areas that have grown up in recent years. These suburbs sprout daily or weekly papers. But there is a shortage of printers in the United States because so few apprentices were taken into the trade between 1932 and 1946, the years covering the depression and the war. As a result, the suburban papers now operate right up to their productive capacity with neither more men nor more plant space available to do reproduction.

The union thus faces the problem of either forcing the employer to expand his operation in order to do reproduction or having him accumulate it for years. If expansion is forced, the employer might go out of business and his printers become unemployed; if the reproduction is saved and the employer ultimately made to do it, its cost could easily be more than the worth of the paper.

However, when Brown finally brought the issue of reproduction before the 1960 convention, urging the delegates to amend the union constitution and allow local unions the option of exchanging the reproduction clause for a national pension plan or some other benefit, he met with a storm of opposition. Of the eighty-one delegates who spoke on the question, fifty-one opposed Brown, often vehemently.

The speeches of the delegates reflected their memories of the depression of the thirties and fear of unemployment. "Sometimes it means eating or not eating. Things have boomed over the last few years, perhaps for the last decade, perhaps for the last fifteen years," said one delegate, "but I don't think we should live in a fool's paradise. Many of you are reminiscing about the hungry thirties and the old-timers in my local tell me emphatically that had it not been for reproduction their bellies would have been touching their backbones on many occasions."

Again and again the delegates voiced the recurrent fear of workers that they might lose their jobs. "In prosperous business years, one might consider reproduction as irrelevant but in bad business years it is a deterrent to unemployment for our members," said one member. "Reproduction has always, in my thirty years' membership, been a life-saver to many members," stated still another. "Should we choose the pension plan in lieu of reproduction, we would lose twenty situations," one delegate from Salt Lake City pointed out. A printer from Toronto worried that if the three papers there "start trading their mat-ads I venture to say there will be two hundred men put out of work." One from Washington, D.C., said that at his paper "reproduction represents 12 percent or $300,000 a year of the paper's total composing room wages."

No doubt the members exaggerate the amount of work gained through reproduction, but their fear of possible future unemployment keeps it as part of the union law. Even if doing "dead horse" conflicts with his pride as a craftsman, or even if his local union never does it, the printer still wants it in the contract because sometime in the future he may need it. When the issue went to the union membership in a referendum a few months after the convention, the officers' proposal was defeated. Despite all of Brown's urging, the support he got from the other union officers, and Baird's report to the members on the actual situation in effect throughout the country, nearly forty-two thousand union members voted against Brown in the referendum, defeating his proposal by some eleven thousand votes. Brown has said reproduction is clearly a subject upon which many union members "have a private view and a public view."

*   *   *

The stubborn insistence of the printers on retaining "reproduction" at all costs has had curious and sometimes expensive
consequences. The union has not insisted, for example, that
"national" advertising on mats be reproduced since it was clear
that these ads meant new additional work for the printers, while
the ads of local stores in the same mat form do replace work the
printers might normally have performed. But there have been
endless quarrels, and sometimes bitter disputes, between publishers and locals over what determines a "local" ad, just how
much of it must be reset, and how the resetting is to be done before it is destroyed.

The variations on the arguments over reproduction are, in
fact, almost infinite. Is an ad national or local if the name,
phone number, and hours of business of a local merchant are
added to an ad for a nationally distributed refrigerator or automobile? What about the ads of a nationally owned and operated
chain like the Federated Department Stores, whose local outlet
in New York is Bloomingdale's but whose stores have forty
other names in other metropolitan areas? If an ad has some
hand-lettering in it, must such lettering be reproduced even if
it was never set in type but takes up room where type might
have been? Answering questions like these has provided attorneys and arbitrators all over the country with an adequate
substitute for a full employment act.

Squabbles over bogus also break out within the local unions.
At a Philadelphia paper in 1954 the local complained that the
paper had permitted unemployed substitutes "to walk" even
though there was a substantial amount of bogus hung on the
hook. The union claimed that the men who hadn't found work
should be paid for the bogus they might have been able to set.
The publisher retorted that the only reason for the accumulation
was the refusal of the regular printers to work the shifts when
reproduction was normally done. The case finally went to arbitration, with the decision made against the union.

Reproduction has had less harsh treatment from legislators

and courts than from arbitrators. It was not specifically included under the featherbedding provisions of the Taft-Hartley Act, which made it an unlawful practice for a union to demand payment for "services not performed or not to be performed." Then, in 1948, the American Newspaper Publishers' Association failed in an attempt to have the National Labor Relations Board declare it an unfair labor practice under the anti-featherbedding provisions of the Taft-Hartley Act.

"It is not our function, of course, to pass upon the social or economic desirability of the practices," said the board, upholding reproduction as legal. The board's decision was based on their belief that reproduction was not an "exaction" from the employer for work not done, this being the definition of featherbedding used by Senator Taft in the legislative discussion of the Taft-Hartley Act. ANPA appealed the board's decision to the Seventh Circuit Federal Court, which upheld the board, and this decision, in turn, was taken to the United States Supreme Court.

The Supreme Court split 6-3 against the publishers. The majority opinion, written by Justice Burton, concentrated solely on whether Congress had made the setting of bogus an unfair labor practice. Basing the decision on the lack of discussion about reproduction during the legislative debate on the Taft-Hartley bill, the Court took the absence of debate to mean that Congress exempted reproduction from being outlawed as featherbedding.

The three dissenters were vigorous in their attack upon the majority. Justices Vinson and Clark, in a joint dissent, charged that the majority opinion "twists the law by the tail" and described as a "Sisyphean journey" the process of setting type, proofreading it, resetting it for corrections, and then consigning it to the hell box for melting into "pigs" so that the same process can be repeated again.

Justice Douglas was even more outspoken in his dissenting opinion. He described reproduction as "not only unwanted, it is totally useless. It does not add directly or indirectly to the publication of the newspaper nor to its contents. . . . No matter how time-honored the practice, it should be struck down if it is not a service performed for an employer."

Unsuccessful in the courts, some publishers have tried to rid themselves of reproduction in other ways: unsuccessfully in contract negotiations, more successfully by arbitrating how much of it is required and how it is to be done. And the government has continued its traditional policy of not intervening in the relations between the ITU and the newspaper industry.

But the publishers do not entirely fit the picture of a highly principled group being forced against their will to submit to the outrageous demands of a rapacious union. "It has ever been the burden of the union to police the industry, to whatever extent possible, against unfair practices of unethical employers and employees," Woodruff Randolph, then president of the union, told a congressional committee in 1953.

Frequently, it is the employers, not the employees, who seek the application of the reproduction rule as a way of stabilizing costs in the industry. In New York City, the publisher of a Spanish-language paper demanded of the union that another publisher be forced to do reproduction on those pages of his New York paper which he was flying in mat form from Puerto Rico, where he owned another paper. The first publisher claimed that his competitor was taking unfair economic advantage of him by using type twice that had been set and paid for only once.

So, too, the union is under continuing pressure from some owners of daily papers to force reproduction payments from the publishers of weekly suburban papers or advertising throwaways. With the development of new photo-printing techniques, it is easy for a small publisher to cut up the ad of a supermarket that has appeared in a daily paper and paste it up in a somewhat different way. In this way the weekly paper is able to use the ad without having to pay for typesetting and is able to sell its advertising space at a far lower rate than the daily paper.

Similar difficulties develop among the daily newspapers. Frequently, a company that wants to place an ad in all the dailies in a city will have the original advertisement set at one paper and mats made of the ad for the other papers. Obviously a paper that gets an ad in mat form has lower typesetting costs than the one that sets the type originally, and so publishers often insist that the union enforce the reproduction clause against competitors of this sort.

An amazingly intricate employer-union relationship has grown from reproduction. Officially and publicly, the publishers' association denounces it, in bitter language, as "an illegal and exorbitant demand that can only be characterized as extortion." Even though the attempts of some publishers to use reproduction for bettering their own economic interests weaken the charge, their case against reproduction is a strong one. Nevertheless, if reproduction *had* been made optional by the union referendum, how would the industry be policed? When no other force exists to maintain stability in an industry, there is always great pressure on the union to fill the role. To protect the jobs of its members, a union frequently must protect employers from each other, as the ITU does by enforcing its reproduction clause.

The irony of reproduction is that printers, men with a deep sense of pride in their craft, should so demean themselves because of their fear of unemployment. Perhaps it is even tragic, for it reveals that the nightmare of joblessness is persistent even in an affluent society and that proud men still feel the economic need to do useless work that they detest.

II

The Aviator—the Superman of Now . . . The world has its eyes on the flying man. Flying is the greatest sport of red-blooded, virile manhood. Make your vacation the greatest you ever had by joining the Wright Flying School. Live in the open—in the aviators' tent city. Convenient hotels for the fastidious.
　　—Advertisement in first issue of *Aviation,* August 1, 1916

There is little resemblance between the commercial airline pilots of today and the World War I aviators who in story, film, and maybe even sometimes in actual life bravely saluted each other as they went down in flames over the trenches, their white scarves whipping in the wind, their goggles smeared with oil thrown back from the burning engines. Today, though in small boys' imaginations "Smiling Jack" pilots are still pictured as romantic figures, the aviator is far more concerned with questions of job security than with becoming a "superman." Many years have passed since the glamour of flying was considered an adequate substitute for steady work at high wages.

Technology has made possible ever faster and larger aircraft —two characteristics that, in turn, have created for pilots economic and social problems curiously similar to those faced by the printers. "The whole story of air transportation . . . has been the fear of the flight crew that . . . the machine is somehow going to displace the people," said a president of the airline pilots' union, accurately summing up the attitude of members toward aviation technology.

The first American fliers after World War I were gypsy pilots who hopped from cow pastures to circuses in their tiny war-surplus planes. They earned a precarious living by carrying daring passengers at a penny a pound in slow circles over little villages, or by keeping the plane steady as a daredevil, helmeted, wing-walker edged her way out from the cockpit to thrill the crowds in the circus ground below. In those days, a pilot could correctly say, as did veteran Dick Depew, that "the greatest hazard in flying is the risk of starving to death."

Until November, 1920, when the Aeromarine West Indies Airways Service began flying between Key West, Florida, and Havana, Cuba, there were no regularly scheduled passenger airline operations in the United States. The Aeromarine planes were two-engine converted war-surplus flying boats accommodating eleven passengers in seats that had been built into the hulls. The passengers on the first flight were "agreeably surprised," according to a news story of the time, "to find all the comforts a private yacht or a high-class limousine offers." Two pilots sat in an open cockpit with a mechanic behind them in Aeromarine's first planes, romantically named *Santa Maria* and *Pinta*. The Key West–Havana flights were made only during the winter months; in the summers, Aeromarine moved its planes north to fly wealthy passengers between New York City and the then fashionable summer resort of Atlantic City. But only a few could afford to use the service regularly, and, lacking the government mail subsidy that later became essential to airline operations, in four years the line went out of business. Despite its financial failure, Aeromarine did demonstrate that passengers could be carried on schedule and safely.

All through the 1920's, airline services rapidly expanded throughout the world. In 1925 the Kelly Air Mail Bill, which authorized the Postmaster General to contract for the carrying of mail by air, gave a big push to American commercial aviation. Airlines established for mail service were soon able to expand into the passenger business. By the end of the twenties, coast-to-coast combined air-rail service was being offered by two different groups. It was during these early years of commercial development that aviation came under Federal regulation. In 1926, Congress passed the Air Commerce Act, placing responsibility for the regulation of air commerce upon the Secretary of Commerce.

In the depression, airline operations, like most businesses, fell off sharply. One way the airline operators attempted to ease their economic difficulties was to try to cut the pilots' pay and simultaneously to increase the number of hours they flew. The response of the pilots to this threat was to form a union.

"The idea of the airline pilots organizing was first conceived in 1930," according to Dave Behncke, the founding president of the pilots' union, who began as a barnstorming flier and then went to work for what later became United Airlines. "They were not referred to in those days as airline pilots because they had very little of anything and not even a proper name. They were totally unrepresented and unprotected. The first organization meeting of regularly scheduled airline pilots was held in 1930 at the Troy Lane Hotel in Chicago, Illinois. There were six pilots present at this first meeting, and this was the spark that kindled the flame which resulted in the establishment of the Air Line Pilots' Association. . . ."

No one is certain how much airline pilots got paid before 1931, nor how many hours they worked, but the first pilots, later known as captains in a terminology borrowed from the sea, probably received somewhere around $350 a month, and co-pilots, if they were lucky, about $90. In fact, some airlines even charged their co-pilots on the theory that they were being taught how to fly. The number of flight hours—time actually spent in the air—ran about 120 hours a month for pilots, and even more for co-pilots. In February, 1932, one airline tried to cut the pilots' pay by $100 a month and the members "withdrew from work," as the pilots describe their strikes. This first "withdrawal" was successful, and the struck airline was forced to sell out to another company.

Between 1931 and 1933, the airlines, in response to technological advances in the industry, changed their methods for computing pilot pay and thereby created a problem that has plagued the industry, the pilots, and the public ever since. Before 1931, pilots had been paid a modest, fixed monthly wage, plus additional pay for whatever mileage they flew. Later, as faster and larger planes began coming into service, the pilots still received the small monthly rate but no additional pay for mileage flown; instead, additional pay was computed only for the number of hours they flew.

The airlines' reason for making the change was clear. Mileage pay was comparable to piecework, and because it was certain that the planes would continue to get speedier, there seemed to be no limit to a pilot's potential earnings. Of course, from the pilots' point of view, payment based on time was unfair, for they were flying a greater number of passengers for longer distances at the same rates of pay. An airplane's productivity is measured by the number of passengers it carries, and obviously its productivity increases the more passengers it can carry at higher speeds in less time. What was unresolved, then as now, was how the continuing increases in an airplane's productivity should be distributed between the airlines and their pilots.

The pilots' fears about their future were expressed late in 1933 when their union threatened to "withdraw from work" over issues of increasing wages and shortening hours. "My fellows made a big fight for reduction of flight hours in 1933," recalls Clarence Sayen, who succeeded Behncke as the president of ALPA, "saying that machines coming in then were going to put all pilots out of work." At the last moment, the strike was averted by the National Labor Board, which appointed a fact-finding commission to investigate the situation. In May, 1934, the board issued its famous Decision 83, based on the commission's recommendations. Decision 83 was the first of an endless series of governmental orders or recommendations relating to labor conditions on airlines.

The decision was also the first of many compromises between the positions taken by the companies and those by the pilots. The airlines believed that 140 hours a month should be established as the flying limit for captains and 160 for co-pilots (or first officers, as the co-pilots were beginning to be called). But Decision 83 set a limit of eighty-five hours per month for all pilots (a limit still in effect on domestic airline routes). Because the board believed that "the industry is on the threshold of technological improvement which will greatly accelerate the speed of airplane travel and which may result in some technological unemployment," Decision 83 combined the pilots' request for a wage scale based wholly on the number of miles they flew and the companies' request for a wage scale based on hourly rate only. The result was a complicated formula using both hourly and mileage pay scales in addition to the fixed monthly base rates and automatic yearly increases. The circular slide rule that every pilot carries for making rough computations of speeds and distances flown found another use as a computer of pay earned.

Under Decision 83, a pilot's hourly rate was first divided into day and night rates, which varied according to the average speed of the aircraft being flown. Average speeds were assigned to all aircraft, those in actual commercial operation and those contemplated, and were to serve as the standard for computing pay, even though in actual operation the planes might be flown at faster or slower speeds. Pilots flying planes with higher speed capacity got higher day and night rates than those who piloted aircraft lumbering along at slower speeds. The mileage formula was equally complicated: the more miles a pilot flew, the less he was paid per mile. On the theory that all co-pilots eventually became captains, Decision 83 provided no hourly or mileage pay for co-pilots; instead, they were given a fixed monthly wage, to increase with each year of service.

Since the pilots' union had no contracts with any airlines, they lobbied instead to get Decision 83's limitation of eighty-five flying hours incorporated into the nation's aviation law. They were successful. The provision was included first in the Airmail Act of 1934 and subsequently in all legislation regulating civil aviation. Today, although the restriction has become part of all pilot union contracts, it has also remained in the over-all Federal aviation regulations.

In December, 1935, the Douglas DC-3, perhaps the sturdiest of its class, went into airline service and was soon adopted for use by almost every company. These twin-engined "workhorses of the air" carried twenty-one passengers, flew easily at 170 mph with great stability in the air, and were easily maintained. A "forgiving" airplane, the DC-3 seemed to have a built-in compensation factor for pilot error. But despite the pilots' personal delight in the flying capabilities of the DC-3, its increased speed and passenger-carrying capacity posed, again, the problem of job security.

From 1935 until April, 1940, when General George C. Marshall headed a party of guests in Pan American's first official flight of its brand-new Boeing 307 Stratoliner, no new aircraft went into operation on any large scale in American skies. The 307 was the first four-engined aircraft with a pressurized passenger cabin. Comfortably carrying thirty-three passengers, the 307 could fly more miles per hour and at far higher altitudes than the unpressurized DC-3. A few months later, TWA began using the 307 in coast-to-coast service with a three-man crew—two pilots plus a flight engineer to operate the pressurization system and assist the pilots in other ways. The average speed assigned to the Stratoliner was 180 mph, which, according to Decision 83, would automatically increase the Stratoliner pilots' pay by $80 per month. But the pilots stated that "Decision 83 did not adequately compensate the pilot for productivity increases due to flying the newer, faster and heavier equipment."

The dispute over Stratoliner pay rates was finally resolved in 1941 by an arbitration award. The arbitrators revoked the separate rates for day and night flying established by Decision 83, substituting a composite rate that took both day and night flying into account. Then the pilots were given $1 an hour more for flying the 307 than they would have received under the provisions of Decision 83, and co-pilots were given $20 more per month. This meant a $152 per month increase for pilots flying the 307.

Although the pilots' position—that increases in the productivity of a plane could be measured in units of increased speed and passenger capacity—was implicitly accepted in the arbitration award, nothing in the award allayed the pilots' fear of possible future unemployment or of being forced to return to co-pilot status at greatly reduced pay if layoffs should take place. No one knew then whether the capability of the airlines to fly more passengers at greater speeds would pay off in increasing the total number of passengers using the service. If such an increase did not take place, fewer pilots would be needed; if it occurred slowly, layoffs would be made.

World War II put a temporary end to the employment worries of the pilots. Not only did they get a pay increase when their maximum monthly flying time was raised from eighty-five to a hundred hours, but Air Force pilots became the glamour boys of the military forces. In their crushed hats and snappy uniforms, the fliers and their feats of daring always made good copy for the newspapers. Getting up into the wild, blue yonder became the dream of every American boy, a dream encouraged by the smart publicity men of the Air Force.

But the end of the war brought back the old problems. As

new airplanes were introduced into commercial aviation, the pilots' union and the companies continued the argument that had begun when the 307 went into service before the war. The union's position was that at any time new equipment was introduced a new contract had to be negotiated; the airlines maintained as adamantly that the wage schedules set by Decision 83 were adequate to handle any situation. The dispute between the pilots and the airlines continued from 1945 through 1947, finally causing a strike. It was settled by another arbitration award that settled very little, and all the earlier fears of the pilots about the effect that new equipment had on their jobs were intensified when companies began using four-engined aircraft like the DC-4 and the Constellations on domestic flights.

In 1947, another problem began to engross everyone—the question of air safety. In that year, 247 people were killed in twelve airline crashes and the Federal Civil Aeronautics Board was projected into the middle of a controversy, ostensibly over safety but in reality over economics as well.

The Civil Aeronautics Board had two great handicaps in trying to carry out its responsibilities for air safety: it had only a small staff, and its members were political appointees, not necessarily familiar with the technical problems of the industry. As a result, the board was badly lamed as it tried to keep pace with the tragic events of January 12, 1947, when an Eastern DC-3 crashed, killing eighteen of its passengers and crew; of April 23, when a mid-air crash between a small plane carrying officials of Delta Airlines and a converted Army trainer killed nine people; and of May 12, when a TWA Constellation carrying out a training flight exploded over the middle of Delaware Bay, killing its crew of four.

Then, on the evening of May 29, a United DC-4 scheduled for a non-stop flight from La Guardia to Cleveland, was held up by crowded air traffic and bad weather. Finally, at 8 P.M., the control tower gave clearance and the DC-4 lumbered out to the end of the runway. As the plane quivered and shook, the pilot gave the engines a final run-up and the ship moved slowly down the runway gathering speed for the moment of take-off. The men in the control tower watched the plane shoot past the point of normal take-off, scream across the highway at the end of the field, and hurtle into a marshy ditch where its engines burst into flame. Seconds later, the plane was a blazing crematorium. Thirty-eight people were burned to death in the crash and four others died later from injuries. Only the pilot and one stewardess survived the accident—the worst until then in American aviation history.

The record lasted less than twenty-four hours. At 6:45 P.M. the next day, an Eastern Airlines DC-4 flying over Maryland at between 1,000 and 1,500 feet suddenly flipped over in mid-air, flew acrobatically upside down for a few moments, and then plunged straight into the ground. All forty-nine passengers and the crew of four were killed. The pilot was a veteran flier, one of the company's most experienced men, and a satisfactory reason for the crash was never determined. Two weeks later, on June 14, another DC-4, operated by Pennsylvania Central Airlines, rammed into a West Virginia mountain, wiping out fifty lives.

Air safety, economics, and politics have all been combined in commercial aviation since the Decision 83 limitation on flying hours became part of Federal aviation regulations. Such a volatile mixture can flare up at any time, and it did when the pilots' union tried to persuade Federal aviation authorities that carrying a third crew man in the cockpit of all four-engined planes was essential to safety. The argument involved not only the two-man DC-4, the plane most involved in crashes, but also the DC-6, which was then going into commercial use and had also been certified as safe with a two-man crew. The Boeing 377, in its final production stages, was being built for flying with either a two- or three-man crew, depending on the airline's decision. Only the Lockheed Constellation was specifically designed to be flown by three men—two pilots and a flight engineer. Redesigning the cockpits of the other planes, or converting them to a three-man operation, would have cost a great sum of money and the pilots' union naturally met with strong resistance from the airlines and the manufacturers.

And there was still no let-up in the crashes. In the middle of

July of 1947, a chartered war surplus DC-3 from New York to San Juan went down in Florida, killing twenty-one of its thirty-six passengers and crew, with all survivors badly hurt. The airlines, already suffering from loss of public confidence, were also worried about reports coming from pilots of fires and smoke on the DC-6.

By September, 1947, a Civil Aeronautics Board report was ready, and it recommended a change in the minimum crew requirements of the DC-6 from two to three men. The report described the original DC-6 certification for two men as having been made on a "marginal basis." Later experience had shown, according to the report, "that the operational complexities of the DC-6 airplane were more than could be normally and safely handled by any two average airline pilots." Therefore, the report recommended that the Civil Aeronautics Board require the airlines to carry an engineer on the DC-6 "for all operations except day contact flight," when only two pilots would be required.

Action on the report was postponed in view of a CAB hearing on October 6, 7, and 8 in Washington. The three days of testimony during this hearing are the single most important source of the present, frantic crisis in airline-labor relations. Its purpose was to hear testimony on whether a full-time flight engineer, a full-time radio operator, and a full-time navigator were required on all four-engined planes then flying, or on future aircraft.

The pilots' union representatives wanted a third man and cited the increase in air traffic, the introduction of more complicated aircraft, the increasingly complex nature of traffic control procedures, the need for more constant radio communication, and the more difficult navigational problems as factors that increased pilot fatigue and, therefore, the possibility of accidents. The pilots did not exempt the DC-4 from their demand, stating that it was "only slightly less complicated than the 6" and citing numerous instances of accidents or near-accidents on both the military and the commercial versions of the DC-4.

Economics kept creeping into the hearing, despite the attempts of CAB Chairman James Landis to keep it out. At one point the pilots' union representatives said that with the new planes "some form of technological unemployment is now taking place in the industry," and noted as proof United's layoff of seventy pilots when the 6's were introduced, with another 200 men possibly to be laid off in the future. The pilots maintained that they would not attempt to specify what duties the third man should perform, but declared only that "We believe we need additional help in the cockpit."

Other labor groups also participated in the hearing: the navigators urged that the CAB insist on a navigator being carried on all domestic flights; the radio operators wanted all planes to carry one of their people; the engineers were equally firm that an engineer be added to the crew; and the Transport Workers Union urged the board to rule that all domestic flights be flown by a five-man crew, consisting of two pilots, a navigator, a radio operator, and a flight engineer. All of the union groups also shared the conviction of the pilots that the need for additional help was just as great on the DC-4's as it was on the 6's.

Except for Lockheed, all the aircraft manufacturing companies opposed adding more crew members. "The safest airplane is one that can be operated by a single person," an engineer for the Boeing Aircraft Company testified at the hearing. "Other things being equal, a two-man airplane is obviously less safe than is a one-man plane." The engineer was voicing a theory of aircraft design held by most of the industry: from the design viewpoint, the most efficient airplane is the one flown with the least number of crewmen, and neither the size of the plane nor the number of its engines should determine the size of the crew.

To back up his position, the Boeing engineer pointed out to the board that the introduction of a flight engineer's station on the B-29 military aircraft had "caused this airplane to be less safe" than if the plane had been built to fly without an engineer. Of course, Boeing's position on the size of the crew was no more disinterested or objective than that of the pilots' union, for if three men were to be required on the 377, it would have meant a re-designing cost that Boeing officials estimated at from $3,-

000,000 to $7,000,000.

Boeing's position was supported by the airlines: "The size of the aircraft should not dictate the number of crew members," said American, adding that the company recommended "against legislation which will de-emphasize the need for simplification of cockpit detail. To require the design of a flight engineer's station in all or some air carrier aircraft would most certainly remove the incentive to simplify the job of flying air carrier aircraft."

A more traditional management viewpoint was added to the already confused argument when the representative of the Air Transport Association, the trade organization of the airlines, insisted that "crew complement is inherently the prerogative of management" and the make-up of crews is a "responsibility which government should not attempt to regulate."

There was as much controversy at the hearing over facts as over opinions. The pilots from the union maintained that the DC-6 was more complicated than the DC-4, which was, in turn, more complicated than the DC-3; other pilots, now in management positions with airlines, took the opposite position. "All of us are agreed," said an Eastern Airlines pilot-official, "that the DC-4 is simpler to fly than the DC-3, and that no third crew member is required." An American Airlines pilot, then supervisor of flying for the airline, added: "Flying the DC-6 is easier than flying the DC-4." Delta Airlines reported that it had polled its pilots on whether a third man was needed on the DC-4's and their opinion contradicted the one expressed by their own union representative. According to the Delta official, 108 pilots said no engineer was needed, 22 had no opinion, and only 7 said yes.

For every accident or near-accident cited by the union groups as resulting from the lack of a third man, management cited accidents or near-accidents caused by the presence of the third man. The unions described hundreds of separate operations required for the normal routine flying of the DC-4 and DC-6 to prove that pilot fatigue was inevitable with two-man crews; the companies replied with statistics of millions of miles flown in the same planes and only the tiniest damage to aircraft chargeable to crew fatigue. United cited the C-54 operations of the Naval Air Transport Service, which had maintained a perfect safety record with two-man crews, and the union representatives countered with the Air Force practice of using engineers.

For the CAB, caught in eddies and crossfires between the conflicting interests of union groups, aircraft manufacturers, airline operators, and government agencies—conflicts of interest that not only separated the groups from each other but even split the individual groups themselves—the situation was an emergency. The real tragedy was that the extremely complicated problem of safety had to be decided in an atmosphere where judgments were inevitably distorted by fear of adverse economic or political consequences from whatever decision the board made.

There continued to be no respite from the accidents. Not long after the formal hearing ended, a United DC-6 plunged into Bryce Canyon, Utah, killing all the passengers and crew. On October 26, a Pan American DC-4 crashed in Alaska, leaving eighteen dead. Less than a week after that, another DC-6 had to make an emergency landing when a fire broke out in its baggage compartment. The CAB hurriedly grounded all the 6's until the planes were modified to lessen the fire hazard, which had been pinpointed in the fuel vent system, but the grim toll continued. In mid-November, a TWA Constellation making a check flight undershot the Wilmington Airport and slammed into the ground, killing its crew of five. On November 27, a DC-3, operated by a non-scheduled airline, crashed in Alaska, killing its eleven passengers and two-man crew. The year ended with another DC-4, operated by Alaska Airlines, careening off the runway at Seattle, after it had made an apparently safe landing, killing five passengers and one occupant of an auto which the plane hit as it swerved across the highway.

Finally, on April 14, 1948, the Board issued an order that all aircraft certificated for more than eighty thousand pounds on take-off would be required to carry a third man in the cockpit. His duties were to be solely those of a flight engineer. However, the DC-4, the plane most involved in the 1947 crashes, was automatically exempted from the third-man ruling since its weight was under the 80,000-pound maximum.

Was putting a third man in the DC-6 cockpit but not in a DC-4 a compromise answer to the political pressure in the situation? It seemed that way, and so no one was satisfied with the vague order that neither described the engineer's duties nor prescribed the training he should have for the job.

The pre-war concept of a flight engineer had been that he should have a mechanic's background rather than a pilot's, but, after the war, engineers were never a part of the crew of any airline flying domestic runs except for the lines using Constellations, which had been built with a flight engineer's station. Nevertheless, even though only a few hundred engineers were employed in the entire industry, they had begun to organize themselves into a union. Equally important, they were already thinking of themselves as a *craft,* as representatives of a highly skilled and important part of the flight crew. "I think," Chairman Landis had said at the October, 1947, hearing, "the position of the flight engineer is that they maintain they have a profession."

This belief received a great boost from the CAB order, and the engineers took the intent of the order to be that the third man should be one with a mechanic's background. Some pilots and companies assumed that the third man would be pilot-trained, but the wording of the order that limited the third man's work "solely" to that of a flight engineer seemed to mean that pilots could not be used as engineers.

American Airlines, which had a very large investment in the DC-6 equipment, petitioned the CAB in July, 1948, to suspend the new regulation, especially as it affected the DC-6, until after the board had conducted "scientific studies," which the company asserted were essential to the proper solution of the problem. To reinforce its point that no such studies had been made before the decision was reached, American Airlines pointed out that no member of the CAB technical staff, which was responsible for the certifications, had testified at the hearing. Further, said American, the assistant general counsel of the CAB had testified: "The administration does not favor a blanket regulation requiring that certificated flight engineers be required at all times on all four-engined aircraft," but only when design incorporated a separate flight engineer station.

American's action was supported by the Air Transport Association as well as by seven other airlines, which were equally worried about the additional crew cost. Besides the extra pay, the carriers were also concerned over who would bear the cost of modifying the DC-6 cockpit, which had been built for only two men, although there was an uncomfortable jump seat designed for the use of temporary observers.

The board, which by this time had lost four of the five men who had been members at the original hearing, responded merely with an announcement that the earlier decision was reaffirmed. The CAB files contain a report from the agency's DC-6 Type Certification Board analyzing American Airline's petition and disagreeing with it except in two very important respects: It agreed that "weight is no criterion" in determining whether an airplane should carry an additional crew memger, and it also admitted "that a thorough and competent scientific investigation into cockpit simplification and crew coordination would be of inestimable value to all concerned; however, it is imperative that the Administrator immediately determine the minimum crew requirement required for the DC-6 airplane in its present configuration."

The board justified reaffirming the earlier order by pointing out that flight engineers "can relieve the pilots of burdensome mechanical duties which if required to be performed when aircraft is being flown on instruments, when there are difficult navigational problems, when radio communications are erratic, or when pilots are attempting to follow complicated control procedures and accomplish instrument approaches, would be extremely onerous."

As another reason for its decision, the CAB stated that only three aircraft "now being produced or expected to be produced in the foreseeable future" would be affected by the order: the Constellation, the DC-6, and the Boeing 377. The board was

short-sighted in this assumption since only a few years later
there were DC-7's and two types of jets in the air, all of them
directly affected by the ruling.

The board did relieve the carriers' worry about the modifica-
tion of the DC-6 and 377 cockpits by saying that the engineer
"is able to perform important duties and add to safety of flight,
even when riding in the jump seat of a plane in which no flight
engineer's station has been provided," thus obliquely telling the
carriers that it was not necessary for them to add another seat
and a separate engineer's station to the DC-6 cockpit. Instead,
the engineer would have to be content with sitting in the awkward jump seat between and behind the two pilots.

The new order still made no attempt to be specific on the tick-
lish question of just which "burdensome mechanical duties"
should be performed by the engineer, or what background
training he ought to have, preferring to let each airline make
these difficult decisions for itself. The Board also avoided getting into the middle of a quarrel with the pilots, engineers, airlines, and aircraft designers by simply side-stepping the issue of
whether a flight engineer could do pilots' work in addition to
relieving the pilots of "burdensome mechanical duties." The
board "clarified" its original ruling in language into which anything could be read:

> The board in requiring a crew member for the perform-
> ance of a specific function intended to limit such a crew
> member to that function for the period of time during
> which it is required but the board did not intend to restrict
> that crew member from performing other duties at other
> times. It is intended, for example, that a flight engineer,
> when required, shall not be assigned other duties at the
> same time for which an airman certificate is necessary. On
> the other hand, an individual could relieve a pilot for part
> of a trip and at a subsequent time relieve the flight engi-
> neer, provided he held the appropriate certificates. . . .

In other words, don't look to us for much help. Fight it out
yourselves—which is what everybody did.

* * *

There was none of the usual bantering back and forth in the cockpit of the Constellation during take-off preparations—only a grim pilot and an angry engineer exchanging dirty looks. After the plane had taxied out to the runway, the pilot went through the usual procedures of running up the four engines. But he also made some of the checks customarily performed by the flight engineer. Then, satisfied that the engines were operating properly, the captain began the run down the strip. With the plane nearing the end of the runway, he called to the engineer for an increase to take-off power on the throttle controls. There was no response. Twisting around in his seat, the pilot looked back and saw the engineer sitting with his arms folded in front of him, doing nothing. Frantically, the pilot switched off all the power and aborted the take-off.

That incident was one consequence of the CAB's vague 1948 ruling about flight engineers—a dispute that resulted in an open conflict among the pilots, engineers, and airlines. As a direct result of this conflict, there have been, to date, at least six strikes, an unsuccessful attempt by the pilots' union to prevent Federal Aviation Agency inspectors from riding in the cockpit, the appointment of forty neutrals to presidential commissions and emergency boards which have been unable to resolve the problem, five commercial airlines flying with four men crammed into a cockpit designed for three, fist fights between crew members, and hundreds of grievances filed against each other—most of them, fortunately, not as serious as the row between the pilot and the engineer on the Constellation.

Because the CAB ruling had left the companies to decide the duties and background training of the flight engineer, widely varying patterns began to develop. Capital Airlines decided to use pilots as flight engineers; American and TWA chose mechanically trained men and United used men with both kinds of background. In deciding that its engineers would have to be pilots as well, Capital gave the following reasons:

1. The pilot group has asked that we make this requirement.

2. We feel that flight engineer experience is valuable to our pilots.

3. This will put all personnel in the cockpit on the same seniority list.

4. A flight engineer who is also a pilot should have a quick understanding of the pilot's problems as far as cockpit coordination is concerned.

Delta Airlines, too, decided to use pilots for flight engineers, a decision that the company said "was vigorously supported by all those pilots of Delta with whom the matter was discussed." Under the circumstances, the reaction of the Capital and Delta pilots was a perfectly natural one, because not only did the decision mean that the pilots had additional help in the cockpit, but, in addition, keeping the third seat warm for them meant that in case of layoffs there was another job open for a flier before he might have to walk out the gate unemployed.

The decision of some airlines to use engineers with mechanics' backgrounds was accepted with pleasure by the flight engineers, because increased employment opportunities thus were opened up for mechanics and, equally important, it strengthened the mechanic-engineer's feelings of self-respect and identity. The government had made them an essential part of the air crew.

On those airlines which consistently followed the policy of using pilot-trained engineers, there was no dissension in the cockpit or between the crews and the company, at least on this question. But when an airline used both pilot-engineers and mechanic-engineers, as did United, or just mechanic-engineers, squabbles, arguments, and strikes broke out.

The deterioration in cockpit relations actually began soon after the engineers had applied for admission to the pilots' union and were rejected by Behncke, then ALPA's president. The actions of the pilots' union often reflect a belief that men who fly are exalted over those who work on earth; many pilots look upon their engineers as not really entitled to wear wings because they are "just mechanics." Coupled with this was the pilots' fear of unemployment, or of cutback to the lower co-pilot status.

The question of technological unemployment returned to the pilots' agenda in 1949 when ALPA once again attempted to shift the basis for paying pilots from the number of hours they flew to the number of miles they covered. The battleground selected for this fight was the union's contract negotiations with American and United over the DC-6's. The union again insisted that the introduction of "more productive equipment would create technological unemployment," and therefore asked the companies to cut the flying hours per month to seventy and to set a maximum of 17,500 miles per month as the limit a pilot could fly. The union justified these two demands with three basic arguments:

1. Pilots had not shared in the increased productivities and economies which accrued to the carrier because of the introduction of faster, larger, and more complicated aircraft.
2. The job content on the new aircraft had become increasingly burdensome to the point that it amounted to a completely new job.
3. Pilots had suffered a loss in job opportunities, stability, and tenure because of the technological changes in aircraft.

Negotiations with the companies dragged on until, finally, in 1951, after many vain attempts by the National Mediation Board to settle the dispute, the companies completely rejected the pilots' demands. A partial strike took place at United with ALPA members refusing to fly the DC-6's. At American, after the disagreement had crept its tortuous way through the complicated and burdensome procedural paths of the National Mediation Board, a presidential emergency commission was appointed. But the 1951 settlements did very little to exorcise the specters of unemployment and cutbacks that haunted the pilots. For everyone knew that the real dispute was not over the DC-6's but over the new planes then being planned—the jets, which were going to fly far faster in far less time than the DC-6's. United's president, William A. Patterson, voiced the airline industry's viewpoint when he said that the pilots would have the right to be concerned about the jet planes and necessary adjustments in pay *only* when those planes arrived. "How can we be intelligent about a problem we don't understand yet?" he asked. "We can't settle tomorrow's problems today."

But tomorrow was today, for by 1952 the aircraft manufacturers were already beginning work on the jet planes, and in the plants at Seattle, Los Angeles, and San Diego mock-ups of the jet cockpits were already being built. In designing these cockpits, the manufacturers had to resolve several important problems. Because the weight and space problems in the jets were critical ones if the planes were to be economically useful, they first had to eliminate, insofar as possible, unnecessary duplication of instruments and controls; but this clearly was complicated by the CAB ruling that a third man was required on all aircraft over eighty thousand pounds, and by the differences among the airlines as to whether the third man should have pilot or mechanic background. The designers also had to build airplanes that would satisfy all potential customers, including the foreign lines which had indicated they might want to fly the jets with two-man crews. As a result, they tried to design a cockpit that, in the words of Boeing, "would accommodate, with minimum difficulty of change, the various preferences" of everybody. Jets were therefore made available in a choice of models, like new cars: without a third seat to foreign purchasers or to the Air Force (not under CAB jurisdiction) and with a third seat for those airlines required by the CAB to carry a third man. On the models that provided a third seat, it was necessary to provide for differing functions for the third man, depending on what kind of contract the company held with the unions involved.

Was the third man really necessary in the jet airplanes? The

Air Force decided he was not, and so the K-135 tanker, the military version of the Boeing 707, carries out its delicate work of refueling bombers high in the air with only two men in the cockpit. The eight-engined B-52 jet bomber and the six-engined B-57 jet bomber are also flown by an Air Force crew of only two, although they weigh many times more than eighty thousand pounds.

The operations of military and commercial aircraft are not really comparable. However, even in commercial operations, at least one airline, Trans-Canada, is committed to the idea that the way to achieve the safest and most efficient jet airline operation is by "reducing the work load on the pilots by means of basic detail design" rather than "by adding an additional member to the flight crew team." In carrying out its policy, Trans-Canada had its Vickers Vanguard turbojet planes made with 145 fewer instruments, controls, and lights than were in the DC-6 cockpit, and it claims that the plane "may be flown entirely by one pilot sitting in either the left or right seat." The same plane in U.S. operations must carry three men because its weight exceeds the eighty-thousand-pound limitation.

When it decided to buy pure jet planes, Trans-Canada wanted to extend its two-man crew policy to them as well, believing that "weight has really nothing to do with the situation [and] the need for a third crew member should depend entirely upon the design of the airplane's cockpit and controls." The company hoped that the introduction of the simpler jet planes "would afford an opportunity for the CAB to revise their regulations." But, according to Trans-Canada, "the situation had become too well entrenched from a labor standpoint to make a change, hence the rule based on weight would still stand. Under such circumstances, most manufacturers and airlines in the United States now adopt the philosophy that since they have to carry an additional crew member, they might as well give him something to do—hence the complex cockpits in most U.S. airplanes."

The result of the "circumstances" that existed in the United States, says Trans-Canada, was that "the Boeing Company [which had originally designed the 707 as a two-pilot airplane with *half* the instruments and controls of a conventional transport] had to re-design their cockpit to provide a flight engineer's station with its resulting multiplicity of controls and instruments. Needless to say, the Boeing Company was most disappointed because it believes the additional station is unnecessary."

Trans-Canada's version of the 707 development is disputed by the Boeing engineers, who maintain that from the start of the plane's design they had always planned for the commercial version to have a three-man crew. And, say the Boeing men who developed the 707, even though the 707 can be flown with only two men in the cockpit, the use of a third man there can certainly be justified, especially in dense air traffic, bad weather, or subnormal flying conditions.

It is true, say jet plane designers, that there are far fewer instruments to be watched in a jet cockpit than in a propeller craft, and it is also true that many functions performed by the crew in a propeller-driven plane are electronically automated in the jets. But they also maintain that, because of the great speed of the jet planes and the greater amount of radio communication required by the increase in air traffic, the third man may be extremely useful in emergency situations, especially since the jets, unlike the DC-3's, "forgive" very little on the part either of man or of nature. Since the amount of time available to correct an error in a plane moving at 650 miles per hour must be measured in fractions of a second instead of minutes, perhaps having a third set of hands in a jet cockpit is justifiable.

While the designers were trying to solve the over-all difficulties of the jets, the battle between the pilots and engineers took on new intensity and bitterness, with quarrels also breaking out within each union over their proper strategy. The crew dispute affected the negotiations between the two unions and all the companies, so that sometimes strikes took place over what appeared to be one question but was in reality the result of the pilot-engineer quarrel. The polite meetings of the Society of Automotive Engineers, which had established a committee on cockpit standardization, also became battlefields, with the engineers' group trying unsuccessfully to get representation on the committee before recommendations for cockpit designs were frozen.

The pilots established a Jet Study Committee to analyze the future operations of the jets, and the engineers' union set up a Future Aircraft Committee for the same purpose. Delegations from both unions kept making regular visits to the aircraft manufacturers in California and Washington, the engineers in a continual attempt to persuade the designers that for safety's sake flight engineers on the new planes should be given instruments that controlled engine power, and the pilots equally insistent that for safety's sake the third man's functions should be limited to monitoring dials.

"We didn't want to be just systems monitors, watching a set of dials but unable to do anything about it if we saw something go wrong," a former engineers' union official explained. "To be just a monitor would have been a completely emasculated position for us. What we wanted and believed we should have was control over engine power, over the electrical system. We wanted knobs and dials in front of us that controlled something at the other end. That's how we felt our special training could best be used."

The flight engineers were unsuccessful—the designers didn't give the engineer station any control over engine power. However, the designers refused to get caught in the middle of the arguments about whether the engineer should be a pilot or not. "The responsibility for and prerogative of establishing such crew member duties rightfully belong to the experienced airlines who will operate these aircraft," said Boeing.

It was obvious to everyone in the industry that at some point the dispute between the pilots and engineers was going to get beyond the stage of luncheon discussions with aircraft designers, or impolite wrangling over a table with airline industrial relations directors. The head of steam finally blew up into a jurisdictional strike at United Airlines in October, 1955.* It grew from

* The history of United's relationship with the pilots and flight engineers before the strike was an involved one, but, basically, it was charac-

the company's decision of the year before to hire only pilots as future engineers. As the company could have expected, the shift in policy created great resentment among those engineers with flying backgrounds. The flight engineers' union was determined to resist the new policy and demanded that all "future" engineers be taken from the ranks of the company's mechanics before the company could hire pilots as engineers. In addition, the union insisted that "all flight engineers' work belongs to flight engineers and to no other craft." United refused to accept these conditions, and so the flight engineers' union called the strike.

The strike dragged on for fifty-one days and ended only when the engineers accepted a compromise agreement. The fact that United was able to operate its flights during the strike, using pilots as engineers, pointed up the vulnerability of the engineers' union: as long as there were engineer-qualified pilots willing to go through another union's picket line, an airline could continue to operate. The fact that a great many pilots were glad to cross the picket line only added to the bitterness between the two unions.

By the next year, the war was on in earnest. In November, 1956, ALPA passed a resolution at its convention that had been proposed by its Jet Study Committee: for safety's sake on jets, "all members of the operating crew shall be pilot-qualified." In their contract negotiations with the companies, the pilots attempted to use their economic strength to make the new mandatory "fail-safe" three-pilot policy part of every agreement. The AFL-CIO made an effort to settle the dispute between the two unions, but, without the power to enforce a settlement, the federation officials were as unsuccessful as everyone else had been. The AFL-CIO urged the engineers to become part of the pilots' union, a suggestion the engineers completely rejected. They had not forgotten Behncke's earlier refusal to admit them when they had first sought membership in ALPA, and at any rate they

---

terized by shifting back and forth between favoring mechanic-engineers and pilot-engineers, with the result that by 1955 an utterly confused cockpit crew structure existed.

had by now built up institutional interest in their union and were loath to be swallowed up in the larger pilots' union with its barely concealed contempt for the non-pilot members of the flying crew.

The dispute came to a head again in the fall of 1958. American Airlines had ordered its jets earlier than any other company, and thus was in a position to get a six-month jump on its competitors. But the pilots were insisting that they would not sign a new contract with the company unless all three men in the cockpit of the new planes were pilot-qualified, and the engineers were equally adamant that their new contract with the company must give them the right to hold the third seat.

The first settlement American made was with the engineers' union. In exchange for a five-year contract, they guaranteed the third seat on the jets to members of the engineers' union, men generally without pilot training. The company decision was made at the time when a presidential commission, appointed to settle an earlier strike at Eastern Airlines on the same knotty point, was attempting to reach a compromise solution satisfactory to both groups. The effect of American's deal with the engineers' union was to nullify the possibility of a national formula being worked out—such as the one proposed at Eastern that provided for pilot training to be given by the companies to those engineers who were not qualified fliers. Once American had committed the third seat to the engineers, the company's negotiations with the pilots' union bogged down completely and a pilot strike seemed inevitable. C. R. Smith, president of the airline, complained to his pilots: "We do not believe that the flight engineer should be tossed out of his job, we do not believe that a third pilot in addition to the flight engineer is required. . . ."

The break in the deadlock came in the form of a company proposal to the pilots' union—the "featherbird" proposal. It took the company off the hook for a few months, let it reap the quick-profit harvest it sought over its competitors, and plunged the entire industry into chaos. What American Airlines proposed was that it would carry *four* men in the cockpit—

three pilots to satisfy ALPA's "fail-safe" demand, and an engineer to satisfy the requirements of the new contract with the flight engineers' union. And lest American be accused of creating an "unjob" merely in order to beat out its competition, the company immediately issued a statement that its action "was taken solely in the interest of the highest degree of safety," a complete contradiction of the statement Smith had made only a few months earlier to his pilots. American even attempted to persuade the government that it should force all the airlines to carry four men in the cockpit.

American got the jump on its competition, but at a high price. Their jets were flying with four men regularly crammed into a space designed to hold three. The only place for the third pilot to sit was on the forward one of two small jump seats originally designed for an observer to check-ride the crew. He could see the pilots' instruments only by peering over the shoulders of the two men in front of him, and he had only a tiny view out of the cockpit window. To the engineers he became known as the "featherbird pilot," a name pinned on him by the president of National Airlines.

The four-man pattern set by American was quickly followed by most of the other airlines having contracts with both unions. But those airlines which had always used pilots for their engineers planned to operate their jets with only three men in the cockpit, and so the third man theme soon grew sharp and discordant again. The engineers' union now even protested to the Federal aviation authorities that the third pilot was "unwanted, unneeded, and potentially unsafe." Those companies "who have agreed to carry such a featherbedding crew member have not exhibited the economical and efficient management required of them" under the law, the union said, asking that an investigation be made by the government into the policy.

By the end of 1959, when almost all of the airlines had received their jets and were flying them, there was utter confusion over the question of crew complement. Some airlines were flying with only three men in the cockpit; others, flying exactly the same routes, were using four. On interchange flights of two lines, one leg of the trip might be made with three men in the cockpit and another with four. Some companies trained their engineers to be pilots, some trained pilots to be engineers, some used both, and some had engineers without pilot training. The only point on which everybody now agreed was that the *fourth* man was absolutely unnecessary.

Then, in 1960, the pilots and the newly created Federal Aviation Agency became involved in a court fight over the fourth man. The FAA had assigned an observer to make a routine check ride with an Eastern Airlines jet crew. There was only one difficulty: the pilots' union refused to have the third pilot move out of the observer's seat. Since they had insisted that a third pilot was needed in the cockpit at all times, and the companies had agreed, how could they let the third pilot's seat be taken by an FAA observer, even if he was the man for whom the seat had been originally designed?

The pilots threatened to strike at Eastern, and did so for ten days, as well as at Pan American. Taking the ALPA to court in Chicago, the FAA attacked the union's thesis that the safety of the flight was endangered if the third pilot was forced to leave the forward observer's seat to make room for a Federal inspector. The third pilot is "a superfluous occupant of the cockpit," the FAA lawyer said, and asked the court to make the union produce the detailed report of the union's Jet Study Committee that had led to the adoption of the mandatory three-pilot "fail-safe" policy.

The pilots' union "requirement that the jet aircraft have a third pilot on the flight deck is not buttressed upon a consideration of safety, but is merely a device to assure that the technological advances brought on by the utilization of larger aircraft, with greater passenger capacity, will not adversely affect the employment of the defendant's pilots," said the FAA. The agency's lawyer also asked that the union produce the records of its pilots' council in Los Angeles, which, he said, included a resolution stating: "Experience has proved conclusively that a third pilot on jets is not needed (even less than on propeller-driven aircraft) for safety reasons or otherwise."

The strike ended after the judge warned the pilots of harsh legal penalties. Now, on check rides, the FAA man sits in the observer's seat while the third pilot squeezes himself into the second observer's seat near the rear of the cockpit, even farther away from the instruments and the windshield.

One airline, Continental, which, like American, had contracts with both the pilots and the engineers, decided not to put a fourth man in the cockpit but instead to have three pilots only, and so, in June, 1960, the engineers began a three-and-a-half-month strike against the company. The engineers lost because, again, the company was able to operate its flights with an all-pilot crew, as United had done in 1955. The loss of the Continental strike was an additional major blow for the engineers' union, which was still suffering from a presidential commission's recommendations at another airline that the mechanic-engineers on jet planes be given pilot training, and that any new engineers hired be pilots. Then, in January, 1961, came what the engineers took to be the most serious onslaught against them—a decision from a panel of the National Mediation Board, the agency set up to settle disputes and rule on representation questions arising under the Railway Labor Act.*

The pilots' union had petitioned in August, 1959, for an election at United Airlines to cover a new bargaining unit that would include the flight engineers and the pilots in one craft instead of keeping them separate. In the minds of the leaders of the engineers' union, combining the two groups into one craft would end their existence, because, with so many more pilots than engineers, the engineers' union was certain to lose; and whatever happened at United was sure to be repeated at every other airline where two unions represented the cockpit crew.

For more than forty days, a special panel of the Mediation Board heard testimony on the pilots' petition; 595 exhibits were introduced and there were 5,121 pages of transcript. The engineers' union claimed that the single union requested by the

* Originally, this Act covered only the railroads, but later it took on jurisdiction over collective bargaining on the airlines as well, even though its creaky machinery was hardly adapted to the problems of the new industry.

pilots violated the craft and class theory of the Railway Labor Act, while the pilots maintained that no real separation existed between the work of an engineer and a pilot. On January 17, 1961, the panel decided that "all flight deck crew members on United Airlines, Inc., in the job classifications of pilot or captain, reserve pilot, co-pilot and second officer or flight engineer constitute one craft or class" and should therefore vote on one ballot for their collective bargaining representative.

The National Mediation Board decision was, according to the engineers' union, "a complete deprivation of their rights to assemble into an organization of their own choice." They decided, therefore, to call a nation-wide strike in February against the seven airlines that still employed members of their union. Seven other airlines were not affected because they did not hold contracts with the engineers. In justifying this clearly illegal strike, the FEIA said: "The Flight Engineers were motivated to take such drastic action by their knowledge that if the Air Line Pilots Association took over the representation of their jobs, it would not simply mean that these members would be deprived of their rights to perform the job, but rather, that the job itself would deteriorate to a point which would adversely affect safety."

Four days after FEIA's illegal walkout, President Kennedy, in office only a few weeks, issued an executive order establishing a commission to examine the controversy. Secretary of Labor Goldberg stated that all the airlines except one, Western, had agreed that if the engineers promptly returned to work, no disciplinary action would be taken against them. The Secretary also announced that the pilots' union had agreed to maintain the *status quo* and not to press grievances or contract demands involving the crew complement if the engineers ended the strike. Two days later, the conditions were accepted by all the groups except Western Airlines, which, to this day, has refused to rehire the engineers who had struck and is flying its jets with three pilots. But at the other six lines, TWA, American, Eastern, National, Pan American, and the Flying Tigers, which is a freight line, the engineers returned to work and the three-man commission began its mediation task.

The first efforts of the commission were directed to trying to formulate an agreement acceptable to all the parties. But none of the disputants was willing to concede anything of importance. ALPA was adamant that its demand for three qualified pilots in the cockpit had to be met. FEIA had its fixed position from which it could not retreat: for safety's sake, the engineer ought not to be a pilot. To concede to the commission that mechanic-engineers needed pilot training would have made a mockery of all of the strikes they had called over this very question. They also knew that if they conceded that their members had to qualify as pilots, ALPA would petition for elections, and it would be the end of their organization.

The seven affected airlines, too, came to the commission with one idea prevailing: they were absolutely firm that any solution must somehow end with their eventually having only three-man crews, like their competitors. They saw the commission as an outside instrument that could rescue them from the mess they had put themselves in by copying American Airlines' proposal for a four-man crew.

The weeks went by as the three mediators held long discussions with all the parties. They met with them together, they met with them separately; they talked for hours on long-distance telephone and tried to keep in touch with developments on all of the airlines involved. But nothing they did could break the deadlock.

In a final attempt to exert governmental influence for a mediated solution, the Secretary of Labor, the aviation adviser to the President, the chairman of the National Mediation Board, and the commission chairman addressed the carriers and the union representatives. The four men pointed out the extreme seriousness of the conflict, how public confidence in free collective bargaining had been shaken, and how failure to reach a just settlement might very well end with a settlement being imposed by the government—a solution which "would constitute a major defeat for the institution of free collective bargaining in this country." All to no avail. On May 24, 1961, the commission, unable to fulfill its mission, issued a report to the President, not only making specific recommendations as to how the dispute might be resolved but including a number of pointed observations.

"The controversy has been marked throughout by irresponsibility and unreasonableness," said the commission. Their efforts had been "frustrated" by the "insistence" of the flight engineers' union "that the government, ALPA and the carriers must first capitulate to FEIA's position on the representation question."

The pilots' union, the commission said, "has declined to give serious and careful consideration to the fear of FEIA that ALPA, if it should become bargaining agent for both pilots and engineers on United or on the airlines before the commission, would seek to eliminate the flight engineers' craft as it presently exists and to eliminate jobs and job opportunities of incumbent flight engineers or, in any event, to jeopardize their future wages and working conditions."

The commission had something to say about the airline companies, too. "The carriers act like helpless victims caught in the crossfire between two hostile forces. To some extent, this is true. The erosion of the carriers' bargaining strength, however, has resulted in part from their failure to accept their managerial responsibilities and from their tendencies to temporize and to seek the expedient solution."

The commission's recommendations were worked out in some detail in the hope that the three parties would use them as a basis for conducting negotiations among themselves. But there were no real negotiations. ALPA was dissatisfied with the recommendation that mechanic-engineers who already held seats on jets should continue to do so without pilot training. In addition, the third pilots who had been added to the cockpit and now had a stake in those jobs were worried that in the shift to a three-man crew their seats would be taken by engineers who had pilot qualifications or would get them in the future. The leaders of FEIA, too, were unhappy with the commission's report, which, they said, "contains many features which militate against FEIA's position."

Since the report called for the gradual cutting down of the crew to three men, the carriers were more willing to accept it, and even commended the commission members "on their understanding of the many and serious problems presented to them" and expressed their willingness "to work toward a rapid, permanent and fair solution of the problem." But the carriers also proposed to the commission the "deferment" of all future collective bargaining between any company and any union on the issues with which the commission had dealt in its report. The carriers' position was bitterly opposed by the unions, especially by the flight engineers, who protested that "constitutional rights of the flight engineers have already been taken from them in this dispute. Even more have been threatened by responsible government officials."

The weeks passed into months, and no significant change in positions took place. Instead, as contract negotiations collapsed, emergency boards were set up at the separate airlines as provided by the Railway Labor Act. The boards reported, to no effect. In October, 1961, the commission issued an additional report, supplementing its earlier proposals and sharply pointing out that "the commission's goals will not have been achieved by providing a solution on paper. A solution in practice is what the commission has proposed and what the public has a right to expect. There is no occasion for further delay. Accordingly, the commission requests the parties . . . to arrange for prompt meetings for the purpose of implementing the commission's recommendations and completing agreements on all open contract issues."

Still nothing happened to break the three-way wrangle. Isolated groups of engineers and pilots on small airlines worked out merger agreements, but on the big carriers contract negotiations between the companies and the two unions continued to be deadlocked as strike deadlines again approached. To be sure, none of the parties wanted a strike. The pilots were reluctant because the complexity of the situation might easily make their demands seem outrageous to the public and, in any case, time was on their side. They had their three men flying and could afford to wait it out a little longer. The engineers were reluctant because they knew from their dismal experiences in the past that all it took to break one of their strikes was engineer-qualified pilots who were willing to walk through a picket line. Besides, they, too, had their man in the cockpit and this gave them a stake in the *status quo*. As for the companies, although they wanted to be done with the tedious business of long-drawn-out contract negotiations, they wanted even more to end the policy of having four men in the cockpit. At the same time they wanted to accomplish this without a strike from either of the unions. The government, too, was caught up in this sticky web. The President and the Secretary of Labor wanted a resolution of the dispute, also without a strike, if possible.

Finally, the dispute was resolved when three new arbitrators, who brought up to nearly forty the number of weary neutrals involved at some point in the dispute, ruled that Pan American could gradually reduce its crews from four to three men, that the engineers would be required to have pilot training, and that any new engineers hired would be pilots as well. That decision meant the end of the engineers' union, for it divided the union members among themselves: at TWA and ultimately Pan American, too, the engineers accepted the arbitration without a strike while at Eastern a walkout began that was doomed to defeat from the start.

Probably no labor dispute in the United States has been more complex and confusing than the one over who shall occupy the third seat of the jets. And probably in no other labor dispute have the real issues been so well hidden as in this one where all the parties so frequently invoke "safety" as an explanation for their actions. Surely, few words have been more overworked and misused. By now, it has been emptied of any real meaning; by now, it is impossible for the public to decide when a proposal made in the name of safety, as all of them are, is or isn't a cover-up, even when unconscious, for gaining some economic advantage.

III

*That machines do not, even at their first introduction, invaria-
bly throw human labor out of employment, must be admitted;
and it has been maintained, by persons very competent to form
an opinion on the subject, that they never produce that effect.
The solution of this question depends on facts, which unfortunately, have not yet been collected.*

—Charles Babbage,
Economy of Machinery and Manufacturers (1830)

Who is to blame for the continued existence of "dead horse"?
The responsibility must be distributed between the fearful
printers who vote to retain reproduction even though most of
them despise doing it and the newspaper publishers who publicly denounce reproduction but privately ask the union to force
their competitors to set the never-printed type.

Who is to blame for the "featherbird" in the cockpit? Again,
the responsibility must be shared. The Air Line Pilots' Association has used its economic power, in the name of safety, to demand three pilots in the cockpit; the flight engineers have been
equally adamant, again in the name of safety, that jets must have
only two pilots and a mechanic-flight engineer; the managements
of the seven airlines who bought themselves a little labor peace,
also in the name of safety, cannot adopt the pose of innocent victims; and, finally, the government must assume its share of the
responsibility because of the vagueness of its 1948 ruling.

More than anything else, however, the reason for "unwork"
is the workers' fear of permanent job loss or temporary layoff.
If an employee is given a choice between doing "unwork" or
not working at all, he will choose the "unwork." Once having
been trapped into doing something he hates, he seeks justification for it. He must rationalize that what he does is not only acceptable but necessary. If he does not do this, he cannot face
himself or a society in which work is so important. Soon, his
stake in "unwork" becomes as important to him as the economic

benefits he may derive from it.

We seem not much better equipped now to find a "solution of this question" than was Babbage 132 years ago, when he wrote that the facts "have not yet been collected." Economists are still arguing. The classical economists who justified the industrial revolution concentrated their attention on the effects the introduction of machinery had on wages, prices, and aggregate employment. There was a general assumption, then, that a neat, circular process took place: the price of a commodity produced in greater numbers by machine dropped, and the decrease in price caused an increase in demand for the product, thus eventually increasing the number of workers needed in the industry. If the process did not always operate perfectly and there was a reduction in the number of workers employed in an industry after new machinery was introduced, the loss of employment was not considered a serious problem. "A person trained to habits of industry and application can be easily moved from one employment to another," economist J. R. McCulloch wrote in 1830. "It is easy for a weaver of cottons to become a weaver of woolens or linen."

But nineteenth-century economic theories have only a very limited application to twentieth-century realities. The rapidly accelerating increase in the *rate* of technological change and the swift shifts in marketing patterns, public tastes, and styles made possible by the mass media have compounded a qualitatively different order of problem for society than existed in 1830. However "easy" it may have been then for a cotton weaver to shift over to work on wool or linen, it is extremely difficult for a displaced worker today to make such transitions. And, despite the continuous rise in the size of the total work force, no one is certain whether the statistics of the jobs lost to technology are accurate, nor does anyone really know whether technology is creating an equal number of new jobs to replace the old ones.

New techniques have to be found for determining what percentage of our unemployed are not working because of a temporary recession and what percentage are not working because their jobs have disappeared without replacement. There are serious statistical difficulties in trying to decide whether the unemployed are direct or indirect casualties of technology, but it should be possible to make a better evaluation of the data that do exist.

A new kind of industrial census might be in order, too: one that regularly samples not people but industries in order to discover whether new processes have been introduced and whether these processes have displaced workers.

The success or failure of the current retraining and relocation programs for unemployed workers needs to be carefully assessed. Some analyses of these programs show that the results have been far below expectations. If the comparatively small group of workers who have already gone through the retraining or relocation process either have not been able to find employment or can only work at a far lower skill and wage level, have we the right to assume that the same kind of program on a large scale will be anything more than a large-scale failure?

Even a successful program of this kind might prove to be too high a price to pay for too rapid a rate of technological change. The tensions that follow large-scale displacements of skill, the rupturing of family relationships involved in forced migrations, and the difficulties of adjustment faced by older jobless workers suddenly deprived of identity in a work-oriented society are still largely unknown. To all these unmeasured costs there must also be added the economic costs now being paid by the whole community.

All of the measures to relieve the burdens that come with unemployment are necessary because of an unchallenged assumption that management has an absolute right to automate its production system at all times. The newspapers attack union leaders who resist automation. "Management's right to manage must be preserved and as part of that right the unhindered, unqualified introduction of automation," a *New York Times* editorialist wrote. But who gave management its "right" to the "unhindered, unqualified introduction of automation"? If management's right to automate its property is an absolute one, then does not the union have an equally absolute right to resist automation in order to protect the workers' property—their jobs?

In fact, what fixed and absolute management or union rights are there outside newspaper editorials? Once, management insisted it had the "right" unilaterally to discharge an employee; now that right is considerably limited by public law and private contract. Once, management insisted it had the fixed and absolute right to move its plant where it pleased; now that right is becoming more and more limited by unions and the courts. Once, unions were free to keep out Negroes, but that kind of "freedom" is disappearing under the moral and legal pressures of the community. Ultimately, technology may force America to adopt a different set of axioms, based on an understanding that the acceptance of technology does not mean an unquestioning acceptance of its uses, products, and results.

We need new standards for assessing the effects of technology upon society. The total exploitation of oil fields made possible by technology is limited legally now whenever the interests of a stable price structure in the petroleum industry require it. Why then would it be improper to place limitations on those extensions of technology which *seriously* injure the human beings who work in oil refineries? Today, society must judge technology not only by what it brings in benefits of efficiency but also by the social costs, both hidden and open, that inevitably must be paid.

The existence of these social costs is being recognized and society is accepting some responsibility for sharing them with their victims. Yet retraining programs and unemployment insurance, important as they are, are not enough. If the oil industry is permitted a 27½ percent depletion tax allowance on the theory that oil extraction is a depletion of corporate assets, why, for example, should there not be a depletion allowance on jobs destroyed by technology? If corporations were given a technological tax allowance with the provision that the savings be used only for the development of new jobs, would not the community share more equitably in the benefits of technology and would not the corporation have a financial incentive for the creation of new jobs?

Until now, unions have led the attempts to ameliorate the effects of unemployment. They have restricted production, created "unwork," and even now are demanding a shorter work week. They have lobbied for increases in the amount of unemployment insurance. They have proposed guaranteed annual wages, supplementary unemployment insurance benefits, and improved pension plans. They have challenged the government to devise fiscal policies that will give greater impetus to the economy. But still, useful as these proposals may be, they are not enough.

Unions should take the lead in developing new standards for assessing the effects of technology. Their staffs are in a unique position to become the social ecologists of an industrialized society, the people who can best make judgments on the consequences of automation combined with feedback systems and computer controls. Once the consequences are assessed, even imperfectly, the increased efficiency gained through technology should be then weighed against other social values that may be important enough to justify limiting some uses of technology, just as the petroleum industry limits the amount of crude oil pumped from the fields. If we do not develop standards beyond the single one of efficiency for judging technological change, if we do not create new jobs by devising new economic instruments, and if we do not create new theories of industrial justice for the technological dilemmas of the twentieth century, only two alternatives may be open in the twenty-first century: either there will be so few jobs available that only an elite will be allowed to work while the remainder of society consumes, or the practice of "unwork" will need to spread. For the first alternative, a new social, cultural, and religious tradition will have to be substituted for the work-oriented one that we have now; for the second, many, many more "dead horses" and "featherbirds," with all of their unhappy, demeaning consequences.

INTRODUCTION

D U R I N G T H E winter of 1963, the trade union study sponsored by the Center for the Study of Democratic Institutions
was entering its final stage. As director of the project, which
was responsible for the publication of more than thirty books,
reports, pamphlets, and essays, I was asked to formulate my
own conclusions about the study.

"Old Before Its Time" describes some of those conclusions.
When they were published, Clark Kerr, president of the University of California, and chairman of the project's advisory committee, wrote an introduction to the essay in which he expressed
his disagreement with me. After the report was released, many
of my other colleagues on the project also dissented from my
views.

But I am convinced that collective bargaining in the traditional ways cannot operate successfully in coping with the
growing problems created by automation and unemployment;
that government intervention into collective bargaining will increase more and more; and that unions are faced with a
major internal crisis growing from their failure to understand
the nature of the Negro demand for job equality.

"Old Before Its Time" is not a definitive statement of the
work done by the Center trade union study, for not all the
work has been completed. But it does highlight some of the ur-
gent problems connected with the present state of the unions.

OLD BEFORE
ITS TIME:
COLLECTIVE
BARGAINING
AT
TWENTY-EIGHT

(1963) O N SIXTEENTH Street across the park from the White House is an eight-story, squarish, marble building, set back from the sidewalk. A curving driveway leads up to its imposing entrance lobby, which is dominated by a huge mosaic mural spread out all across the wall. The heroic-sized figures in the mural are all workers; the building is the national headquarters of the AFL-CIO.

Inside the building men and women go to their floors in automatic elevators, soothed by discreet music, and do their work in comfortable, well-lit offices. The men who dominate the life of the building, the high officials of the AFL-CIO, deal almost exclusively in their outside work with their counterparts, the high officials of American government, whose offices are located in the sprawling Department of Labor headquarters on Constitution Avenue, or with the business leaders whose buildings of identical glass walls and steel frames now make the downtown section in every large city of the country look alike.

A man in a mended jacket, unpressed but clean pants, and cracked shoes trudges up the steps of a small, dingy building just off Mission Street on the edge of Skid Row in San Francisco.

At the top of the stairs, he goes to a grilled window marked DUES and stands on line. When he gets to the window, he gives the woman behind it a few tattered dollar bills stuck in a little black book and tells her he wants to pay his dues for one month. She makes a notation on a yellow card in a file case behind her, licks a little stamp, and puts it in his book. Then he moves around to another window under a sign that says DISPATCHER. But the man who sits behind that opening shakes his head from side to side, for there are no jobs to which the members of Miscellaneous Culinary Workers Local 110 of the Hotel and Restaurant Workers Union can be dispatched. So the man shuffles over to sit down, wearily, in one of the chairs that are spread out along the dirty windows overlooking the street below.

"Miscellaneous Culinary Workers" is a euphemism for dishwashers, bus boys, and porters. In San Francisco, the Filipinos, Chinese, and Negroes, the bulk of the local's membership, receive from $13.70 to $14.70 per day when they are employed at the dirty, sloppy jobs every restaurant, big or small, needs done. When they are unemployed, they sit in the union hall waiting their turn to be sent out, by seniority, on a job. In the evenings, they return to their furnished rooms, with single-burner gas plates, in the crowded Negro slums, or to the brown hotels along Mission Street that advertise "Free TV in the Lobby" but have only one toilet to a floor.

Vast distances, social and geographic, separate the members of Miscellaneous Culinary Workers Local 110, San Francisco, from the men and women whose offices are in the marble AFL-CIO headquarters on Sixteenth Street, the monumental Labor Department offices on Constitution Avenue, or the rectangular glass-box buildings favored by the corporations. But, despite the distances and differences, the high union, government, and corporate officials have always been linked to the "catchers" of Local 110, the men and women who work in the kitchens shifting hot plates, cups, saucers, and glasses from the conveyor belt of the dishwashing machines to the dollies that get pushed into the restaurant. The link has been a collective bargaining system in which unions and employers have dealt directly with each other, free of outside intervention. In this system, the government has played a hands-off role, acting only as a referee or as a mediator when disputes have broken out in certain key industries.

Now, however, the collective bargaining system is collapsing, and with its collapse the unions that have been so integral a part of it face a dim and uncertain future.

I

Some symptoms of the breakdown of collective bargaining are obvious and attract immediate attention. Others remain obscure. But all point toward two fundamental alterations in industrial society today: first, the system of collective bargaining, which has operated successfully since the passage of the Wagner Act twenty-eight years ago in 1935, has proved less and less adequate for the solution of some basic problems now faced by unions and management and, second, an increasing number of workers remain outside the system, with very little possibility that they will ever come into it.

Union-management collective bargaining could not and did not end the New York newspaper strike nor the dramatic strike of airline flight engineers; it cannot and will not resolve the national collision of the railroads with the railroad unions, for in that confrontation an industry with declining revenues desperately seeks relief far beyond the scope of collective bargaining: it proposes that the unions with which it deals bargain their members out of jobs and their organizations out of existence.

So, too, the once-proud coal miners of Pennsylvania, now learning to bend over sewing machines, and the once-skilled packinghouse workers of Chicago, now sloshing suds on auto headlights in car-wash sheds, are visible and tragic human symbols of the limits of traditional collective bargaining.

Automation and the *particular* unemployment it brings to a *particular* plant are problems obviously beyond the capabilities of union-management collective bargaining. No one can reasonably expect management to continue employing unneeded workers, but no one can reasonably expect unions to concede that they and their members have become superfluous. No one can expect management to absorb all the costs of moving and training displaced workers, but no one can expect the workers to bear those costs themselves. And so the problem of automation and particular unemployment cannot be kept inside the confines of traditional collective bargaining; the government must share the responsibility for its solution, and perhaps assume the major share. True, machines have made workers unemployed before, but it has never happened at such a rate. Even if the rate were not so alarming, America has passed the point where workers who become unemployed through no fault of their own can be left to shift for themselves and somehow to scrabble out a miserable existence.

The perpetual ice age brought on by the cold war has also imposed new limits on union-management collective bargaining in the growing number of military industries. One of the first acts carried out by Arthur Goldberg after he became Secretary of Labor was to force an end to the disputes that had been plaguing production in the missile industry. In the entire aerospace complex, some form of government intervention occurs the moment a serious dispute flares up. Within the Defense Department the division to help avert labor-management disputes that threaten production of military goods, or to bring the pressure of the Department to end those that do erupt, has been strengthened. Only a truncated form of collective bargaining exists in these cold war industries.

Just as the permanent cold war has become accepted as a fact of our lives, so the permanent unemployment of millions seems on its way toward being accepted as natural and normal. While collective bargaining cannot be blamed for an economy that moves from "stagnant" to "sluggish" to "moderate," and back again, unemployment has the effect of weakening bargaining by taking more and more people out of its purview. The union means very little to the unemployed lumber worker of the Northwest who sits in the state employment office waiting for a job that will not come. The millions of inexperienced teen-agers leaving school today to look for jobs that do not exist never even have the opportunity to join unions, and in a few years they will be only unskilled and unemployed adults for whom the process of collective bargaining will have no significance or meaning.

The large-scale removal of workers from the direct effects of collective bargaining is also taking place in other ways. The very nature of the work force is changing as a shift occurs from manufacturing industries to service trades and government, from blue-collar to white-collar workers. The union button pinned on the side of a cap is giving way to an identification photo pinned on a jacket lapel. Even within some important manufacturing industries there has been a noticeable shift from blue-collar work to white-collar jobs. In the mining industry 60 percent of the production jobs disappeared from 1947 to 1959, and in railroad and bus transportation they went down 40 percent. The textile industry lost 30 percent, and the primary metal indistries and rubber had 15 percent fewer opportunities in the manufacturing classification. From 1951 onward, more than one-third of the national unions suffered membership losses—losses that have not been replaced.

If unions have no members they cannot function, and if they do not function neither does collective bargaining. It is true that the shifts in the employment pattern are no more the responsibility of the unions than is unemployment. Nevertheless, unions must accept the responsibility for not attempting to overcome the dangerous consequences of the shift and for not attracting into membership any sizable number of the white-collar and technical employees who are rapidly replacing the blue-collar workers. Even apart from these professional and technical workers, an increasing number of production employees also show little enthusiasm for union membership. Just as one example, the union shop elections held recently in the aerospace industry (elections once considered so certain to be decided in the union's favor that the original provision of the Taft-Hartley Act requiring them was dropped at the suggestion of Senator Taft) ended in a defeat for the United Auto Workers and the International Association of Machinists.

These fundamental changes in the nature of the work force and in the attitude of workers toward unions have received more recognition outside the unions than inside them, despite their weakening effect on unions and consequently on collective bargaining. As late as May, 1962, George Meany, AFL-CIO president, was saying, "Some people are worrying about the future of the American trade union movement, complaining that we don't have the same zeal, the same drive we had in the early days. Well, things have changed since those early days. We are perhaps more businesslike and maybe we don't get as excited." But, he maintained, "the American trade union movement is not dying of dry rot, it is not suffering from hardening of the arteries . . . it is very much awake and very much alive."

The contrast between these sentiments and reality is startling. Meany seems unaware not only of present-day attitudes of workers toward unions but even of what is going on inside his own office building. There the social dynamism that once attracted idealistic men and women to union service has dribbled away to such a degree that recruiting union professionals becomes more difficult each year, and many who remain would leap at the opportunity to follow their former colleagues into government service.

In retrospect, it is possible to see why the social energy that made unions so attractive in the late thirties has now disappeared, to the detriment of the bargaining system. World War II and the cold war converted unions from a militant stance to unquestioning acceptance of the status quo. Although union membership doubled during the war, reaching more than thirteen million by 1945, the new members knew little and cared less about past history. Since the war, the political and economic role of the unions has been one of continuous and unquestioning alignment with the national authority. The expulsion of the Communist-dominated unions from the CIO was carried out not only because CIO leaders believed the Communists were manipulating the unions they controlled to further the interests of the Soviet Union, but also because anti-labor feeling among the public was high and the CIO felt that the Communist stigma might seriously damage its reputation. Although both reasons were good ones, an inevitable consequence of the expulsions was to bring all serious political debate inside the CIO to a standstill. In some unions it became a habit to brand as a Communist anyone who opposed the leaders, and unions could be counted on to give automatic approval to any action undertaken by the government in its struggle with world Communism. Thus, ultimately, the stakes that unions developed in the economy extended to the political arena and made them prisoners of the present rather than innovators of the future.

Labor leaders show very little concern over the weakening of the links that once held liberals and labor together. Neither do they seem very troubled because the favored position unions once held among social welfare groups has been lost. This lack of social vision, as well as the change in the nature of the work force and the problems engendered by automation in a stagnant economy, have been analyzed at great length in a variety of public forums for the past five years. All three factors, developing at about the same time, have been causes for the breakdown of collective bargaining. But it is not only the failure of the unions to adapt to the new circumstances that has contributed to the present crisis: the past economic success of unions and a lag in the public understanding of the role that unions play in a technological society have also been important factors in the present failure of bargaining.

Past union success in the economic area does not mean that labor has acquired too much power vis-à-vis the employer and that the pendulum must now swing back to favoring management. In fact, unions have too little power of the proper kind. They cannot cope with automation or unemployment using economic tools. Their goals are too narrowly economic at a time when economic power is relatively useless and when a much wider spectrum of political goals is called for.

During the early part of the nineteenth century trade unions were oriented to political reform. And in 1886, when the AFL was organized, its constitution clearly demonstrated a belief in the existence of an American working class with a special identity and a special role: "Whereas," read the preamble to the first AFL constitution, "a struggle is going on in all the civilized world between the Capitalists and the Laborers which grows in intensity from year to year. . . ." But as the economic strength and power of unions grew during the first fifty years of the twentieth century, their commitment to political goals grew progressively weaker.

It is true that because workers were often still at the mercy of employers the struggle of the unions for better economic conditions gave them moral strength even without commitment to political reform. When workers were being shot or imprisoned for trying to organize or for striking, it was not just money but justice that was at stake. Before there were unions, an employee was at the mercy of supervisors, from foremen on up to the company president. Before there were unions, a worker could have been fired for reasons that ranged from being injured on the job to not lending money to the foreman. He worked the hours set by the employer under conditions determined by the employer. Then unions came in to establish the first condition of industrial justice: bilateral determination of wages and working conditions, bilateral determination of discharges. The issues were moral issues then. By now, however, that fight is over for the most part, and the unions, having played the decisive role in bringing industrial justice to the plants, have found nothing to take the place of their moral fervor. Unions are now part of the industrial system. Once the resistance of employers to unionization ceases at the level of principles, the union, through its contracts, becomes part of the plant government, not only a force for justice but also an integral part of the system of authority needed to operate the plant.

There has never, of course, been any guarantee that industrial justice would prevail without unions, unless the government, through law, were to take a much greater role in the protection of the rights of workers against their employers than it has taken so far. In a society that has always functioned by responding to the pressures of countervailing forces, it was necessary and proper to vest unions with some effective legal means of opposing the power of the corporations. That power has been the right to strike, accompanied by the power to control entry into the job market and to bargain both for their own members in the plant and for those who are not union members. It is this capacity for sharing legal control of the labor supply that differentiates unions from other organizations in American society, and it is the right to strike that makes them unique.

Until recently the right to strike has always been considered an essential part of collective bargaining. Now, public sanction of stoppages is being withdrawn, and the concept of compulsory arbitration seems to be growing as the popular cure-all. There is a grave danger, in fact, that shortened tempers and heightened political pressures will push Congress into considering compulsory arbitration as an instrument for preventing strikes. Quite apart from the important policy questions that a prohibition against strikes raises for a free society, and quite apart from the fact that forbidding strikes may make second-class citizens of the workers in the affected industry, another consideration must be taken into account: it is impossible to carry out such a policy in America.

All the experience in this country indicates that compulsory arbitration succeeds only when the parties to the dispute would be disposed to agree without it. Union members can always find other ways than the formal, legal strike for achieving their purposes even over the opposition of their leaders. If they are sufficiently ingenious, they can always slow down operations legally, and if this is done by enough employees it will have the same effect as an actual strike. Compulsory arbitration of industrial disputes does not *resolve* disputes; it merely seeks to impose a truce upon the combatants. But either the need for such truces must be understood and accepted, or the state must have the police power to enforce them. A society that forces men to work by use of police power cannot be called free.

No sharper illustration of the gaps in public knowledge about unions can be found than in the fondness presently being expressed for compulsory arbitration. If new methods must be developed for maintaining industrial justice, a widening of public knowledge about unions and their functions is essential.

II

Union government and union political processes are as unknown to most Americans, including many union members, as is the way of life pursued by aboriginal tribes living in a distant Australian wilderness. But if the maintenance of some form of collective bargaining is essential to public policy, if industrial justice is to continue for workers like the dishwashers, porters, and bus boys of Local 110, knowledge about unions must replace the myths that circulate today.

Some of the most extreme public misconceptions about collective bargaining grow from the natural tendency to think about *THE* union, as if the 186 international unions and 78,000 locals in the AFL-CIO made up some kind of homogeneous entity. The varying characteristics and many shapes of union governments in the United States are determined not only by their constitutions but by the contracts they sign and the markets within which they operate. Indeed, the "constitutions" that "govern" the operations of the international unions are for the most part not so much constitutions as administrative manuals. The Constitution of the United States, for example, establishes the basic principles of American government and its fundamental law; union constitutions are much more concerned with such details as how members may transfer from one local to another, who shall issue seals to locals, who shall edit the union's paper, and how per capita taxes shall be paid. In fact, if union constitutions alone were taken as the criteria that reveal the character of the unions, the judgment would be a dismal one: a study of seventy international union constitutions,* the formal instruments that rule a membership of almost sixteen million workers, shows among other things that in most of those seventy unions power is generally concentrated in the hands of the international presidents, with few restraints placed upon them, that discipline may be enforced against union members with little regard for due process, and that opposition to the incumbent administrations is almost impossible.

But so grim a view of union government, based on the partial, imperfect guide of union constitutions, would be no more accurate than discussing unions as *the* union. The contrasts between industrial unions like the Steelworkers and craft unions like the Carpenters must also be taken into account in assessing union government. Even within the same industry wide variations can exist among local unions: some locals of the Oil Workers Union, for example, have a long history of militancy; others, only a few miles away, whose members work in the same kind of refinery, are weak and dominated by the company. Within all national unions some locals cannot afford the rent of even a small office; others are so large that they can and do duplicate the functions of their national organization. In the Retail Clerks International Association, Local 770 of Los Angeles has eighteen thousand members and operates as a little international, complete with its own welfare system, nine different departments, and even a political action organization of its own. It holds its compulsory quarterly meetings in an American Legion stadium; monthly membership meetings of another local of the same union are held in a small room rented for the evening.

Union government actually begins in the shop. The "shop" may be a steel girder seventy stories up where a riveter and his helper sit, out in the open air, legs dangling in space; or it may

* *Union Constitutions,* by Leo Bromwich. Center for the Study of Democratic Institutions, Santa Barbara 1959.

be inside a huge building without windows, an air-conditioned and artificially lit cavern, where men in hard hats crawl over huge, sleek missiles. The shop may be the noisy city room of a newspaper, the bridge of a ship, the dishwashing room of a cafeteria. Wherever men and women work, there is a "shop."

At these millions of work places the enormous range of occupations, the different technologies, the variations in physical layouts, the kinds of people who work in them, all affect the character of the union, its government, and its relationship to management. Railroaders, even though they are employed by different companies, still see each other often in common freight yards, and this continual contact marks the character of the railroad unions in a special way, differentiating them from the International Union of Electrical Workers, whose members at General Electric may never meet those at Westinghouse except perhaps at union conventions. The motion-picture projectionist, sitting alone by his whirring machine in a small town, has a different kind of union from the auto worker who spends a frantic hour getting ahead of the assembly line so that he may spend a few minutes talking with the man next to him on the line. Oil workers are different from hodcarriers because oil companies for years hired only white high school graduates. Printers visit with each other away from work far more than do freight handlers, who usually know little more about their fellow workers than their names. And while it is possible to get all the steelworkers in a plant together for a union meeting, it is never possible to do this with over-the-road truck drivers, who meet their fellow drivers only in one or another of the thousands of diners scattered out along the highways.

The single most important determinant of the form that a union government assumes is its jurisdictional claim, for this establishes the market in which the union operates. This is the union's warrant for existence.

"This organization has jurisdiction over. . . ." "The work and workers covered by the jurisdiction of the. . . ." "This organization shall include all persons working in the. . . ."

These words are from the most important clauses in any

union constitution, for they define the union's particular and special jurisdiction—the jobs and the job holders over whom it claims authority. Sometimes the jurisdictional claims are very detailed; it takes almost five and a half pages of fine print in the Machinists' constitution to spell out all the hundreds of jobs over which the union claims control. Sometimes the claim is very briefly worded and all-encompassing. "Any person who has performed, or is performing, or is about to perform, in motion pictures" is the one sentence relating to jurisdiction in the Screen Actors Guild constitution. But, whatever form the claims take, one of the most important purposes of union government is the preservation—and, when possible, the expansion—of this jurisdictional sovereignty.

In this country union solidarity extends to the jurisdictional line but little further. Justice has been achieved through the efforts made by each of the unions to bring benefits to the workers in *its* jurisdiction rather than to "the workers" as a class. Sometimes, in fact, justice by jurisdiction is achieved only by destroying the interests of other workers in other unions, equally deserving but less powerful. Jurisdictional autonomy has always been sacred to the craft unions and only slightly less important to the industrial unions. Until very recently each affiliate of the AFL-CIO has regarded itself as a separate duchy, free to control its jurisdiction in its own way with a minimum of interference from any central power. The compact binding the duchies of the federation together is minimal, and lacking in enforcement provisions—for few unions have been willing in the past to cede to the central body any degree of real authority.

A few years ago the AFL-CIO did establish a procedure (which has worked remarkably well) under which a permanent outside arbitrator was given authority to decide certain types of jurisdictional disputes. But only when there has been great fear of public opinion has the federation attempted to interfere with the autonomy of its members, as when the Teamsters were expelled because of corruption. Where no great public pressure is evident, the federation is reluctant to act, especially against a strong union like the Carpenters, some of whose officers have been found guilty of bribery and contempt of Congress or have been charged by the McClellan Committee with serious misuse of union funds.

The tradition of non-interference is reinforced by union leaders who recognize that although affiliation with the AFL-CIO carries benefits it is also possible to survive very well without it. The Teamsters have grown, despite their expulsion from the AFL-CIO; the unaffiliated West Coast Longshoremen have maintained their tight grip on the docks and warehouses of California, Washington, and Oregon; and the leaders of the East Coast Longshoremen were able to beat off the attempt of the AFL-CIO to take over their membership despite the fact that they had been expelled for racketeering.

Jurisdictional sovereignty is, of course, achieved and maintained through the contracts with the employers, and so the preservation of contracts is a dominating factor in every aspect of the relations between union leaders and members and, equally, between the employer and the union.

The latter relationship, although not necessarily exposed to the public, is somewhat like the one that exists in a manufacturing plant between the production and inspection departments. In the plant the function of the production department is to turn out the products; the job of the inspectors is to protect standards of quality by rejecting production, if necessary. Clashes between the two departments are inevitable; but, as a general rule, both groups recognize their long-run dependence upon each other. In labor-management relations dependence sometimes takes the form of economic alliances between employer associations and the unions that control the source of the labor supply. The Bituminous Coal Operators Association and the United Mine Workers have been charged with a conspiracy to force small coal operators out of business by setting high contract rates. In this way, it is alleged a dual employer-union monopoly is set up that gives the union members high wages by minimizing marginal competition within the industry. Small trucking companies have made similar charges against Hoffa's

COLLECTIVE BARGAINING   (271)

Teamsters and big companies.

The contract, therefore, is all-important. Over the years the necessity to preserve it has not merely converted radical union leaders into supporters of the Establishment, or simply provided unions and management with mutually satisfactory economic relationships; it has come to take on a life of its own, an existence separate from the parties to it and not dependent upon them. The contract has become an institution itself. It has given rise to a system of informal governance at the plant level under which the rights that the contract originally established have been transmuted in the minds of the workers into *natural* rights.

Seniority rights, for example, are almost always brought into existence solely through the union contract, but once workers have them they resist, often very bitterly, any subsequent changes that the union may make in them. Sometimes, in fact, when workers are dissatisfied with union decisions affecting seniority rights they go to court to fight the union. This has happened particularly in the airlines and street transportation industries when two or more companies, which have been in business for different lengths of time but are under contract to the same union, merge and the union is made responsible for the complicated task of consolidating seniority lists of workers with different periods of service.

Before collective bargaining existed, an individual employee was theoretically free to make any kind of contract he could with his employer, and it was assumed that if he did not like the conditions of his employment, he could bargain for better ones or, if still not satisfied, leave his job. In fact, however, such a process rarely operated except for highly skilled workers, or when labor was in very short supply. Without equality, a contract is not a free agreement between free men but only the formalization of dependence. Through collective bargaining the unions changed this imbalance between worker and employer, but the equality achieved has been collective, as the very phrase indicates, rather than individual. Unions bring rights to the group, not to the person. As a result, union government, from the shop level on up, is forced to reconcile the varying demands and needs of union members vis-à-vis each other as well as group needs vis-à-vis the employer.

One of the most important and least understood functions of local union government in collective bargaining has been the continual reconciliation of differing interests in the shop. Sometimes contradictory interpretations of the contract create a conflict between the informal government of the shop (or the washroom) and the formal government of the local union. No completely satisfactory way has yet been found to determine the equities involved in a conflict of interest between an individual union member and his local union. In most locals the leaders are the ones who decide a dispute among workers, with some kind of ratification given to the decision by a majority of the members. Unfortunately, this sometimes means that the jury making the determination of rights is itself going to be affected by the outcome and so has a vested interest in its own decision.

Many such clashes of interest develop. Day workers quarrel with night workers over what bonus shall be paid for the midnight to 8 A.M. shift; skilled workers dispute with semi-skilled men over how much of a differential there shall be between their wages; younger workers argue with older ones about seniority systems. Such arguments can grow extremely bitter, especially when the economic stakes are high. Still another kind of conflict occurs when an individual worker acts in a way that both the company and the union officials disapprove of. The leader of a wildcat strike may have the support of his fellow workers, but if the company and union leaders agree, informally, that he ought to be fired, he is. The union then either makes no attempt to press his grievance or, if forced to do so by internal politics, does it in such a half-hearted fashion that failure is guaranteed. If there is informal agreement between the union officials and the company that a worker is a troublemaker, he has very little protection.

The rights and duties of union members are also difficult to disentangle in other situations affecting collective bargaining. Sometimes union officials believe correctly that the rights of a member have been violated, but the worker involved refuses to process his grievance. Who owns a grievance—the union or the worker? Should the union have the right to process grievances even over the opposition of the employee affected? Or, at the other extreme, a union member may believe he has a grievance against the employer, but the union leaders or other members disagree with him and side with the employer. Should the worker have a right to process his grievance anyway, and, if so, how is this to be done?

These problems, some more serious than others, arise because one of the most important consequences of union efforts on behalf of workers as a group is to reinforce the belief of the individual worker that he has a vested stake in his job existing outside the union contract. Union government has not yet caught up with the new concept of job rights that workers now hold.

Whatever form union governments take, whatever varying factors have molded them into their varying shapes, they all have one common function in the United States: achievement of economic ends through contract. In this respect all union leaders are alike, too, whether they be David Dubinsky, who now lives on the glories of a militant past; or A. J. Hayes of the Machinists, who, despite the constitution of his union that still calls for "organization founded upon the class struggle," stodgily attacks those who he thinks still believe in class struggle; or Jimmy Hoffa, filled with cynical contempt for those who speak of unions as a social movement; or Walter Reuther, caught in the dilemma of a union leader whose ideals of social welfare have inevitably been diluted by the need to maintain contracts with the employer.

But the economic purposes that unions seek to achieve through contracts are far too limited for the solution of current problems. The entire collective barganing process is thus of only very limited use.

III

Like every other institution in American life, unions are caught in the contradiction between the ideals of participational democracy and its practice. The popular conception of collective bargaining assumes the existence of the ideal American trade union—an organization in which the members exercise complete control over their officers and policies. And it is true that the right of union members to run their own affairs, make their own decisions, and freely elect their own officers still has considerable vitality in the local unions, much more than in the international ones. The discussions about a forthcoming election among the members of Culinary Workers Local 110 as they sit around a table in the restaurant waiting their turn to wash up at the end of a work day or as they stand at the back end of the local union hall have very few counterparts at the national union level.

Nevertheless, although there is very little hardening of the bureaucratic arteries in the local unions and self-government flourishes, the fact is of little consequence in the crisis collective bargaining now faces. Power, effective power, to cope with the important issues rests with the national organizations, not the local ones. This is partly the result of the structural changes that have taken place in union government, reflecting the centralization of industry and the growing concentration of large capital investments. Company-wide negotiations and now, as in the railroads, even industry-wide ones are becoming more common, as more efficiency in bargaining is demanded of both unions and management. Local unions may argue with the local managements about whether the company is going to supply work gloves to some groups of employees, but over-all union-management policies are determined at the national level and, as in the General Motors agreement, no local agreement "shall supersede or conflict" with the national one. As collective bargaining encompasses broader areas, more and more specialized skills are required of the negotiators. Only the largest union locals can afford to pay the actuaries, health plan experts, and pension advisers who now flank the negotiators on both sides of the table. Local unions can do very little to stave off the collapse of collective bargaining.

The normal accumulation of power by leaders, characteristic of all organizations, takes place in unions, too, and inhibits the rise of new leaders who might deal with the present crisis in new ways. This concentration of power does not necessarily mean that the international unions are badly administered, even if they are badly led. On the contrary, most American unions are well administered. Even when they are not, union members show little interest in changing their leaders. In any event, unless a split takes place among the top leaders, the structure of most unions makes it very difficult for the members to replace an incumbent union administration. Even without specific controls, in most unions it is the president who customarily appoints the staff members, controls the union newspaper, and dominates the union convention. Incumbent leaders also have a great financial advantage over their potential opponents, for their salaries and expenses continue to be paid while they carry on their political activity at local, district, and state council meetings; their opponents, on the other hand, must continue to work in the shop. No Hatch Act operates during union election campaigns. Leaders can call special meetings for one purpose and use them to push their own positions: when David J. McDonald was opposed for the presidency of the Steelworkers, his candidacy was pushed at six conferences, which were estimated to have cost the union $1,000,000.

No niceties are observed when a fight for office breaks out among union leaders. When that happens, and an incumbent union administration faces possible defeat, the struggle for power becomes very grim. "Rip this cancer out of your bowels," David McDonald entreated the delegates to the 1958 convention of the Steelworkers where he was determined to wipe out his opposition. No traditions of "fair play" exist in most unions, and there are no codes of ethical election behavior to which either side is committed. The stakes, of course, are high; defeat in a union election could mean returning to the grim monotony of factory work. In some instances, it is true, the defeated group may still retain enough strength to protect its adherents from punitive actions, and in unions like those of the typographers or the railroad trainmen, where opposition is a more normal part of life, fewer purges take place. But, usually, defeat— for either the incumbent or the challenger—means complete obliteration.

This often affects the staff members too, for high officers frequently demand that the organizers, business agents, and representatives take an active part in their campaign; if they refuse, their loyalty is in question, and if they accede and their side loses, they are usually jobless. The Textile Workers Union was ripped apart by such an intra-leadership battle. In the Machinists Union the entire West Coast staff of Grand Lodge representatives was discharged for supporting a vice-president who unsuccessfully opposed the administration; yet, if they had not campaigned for him in their area and he had won the election, they might have been fired at the first opportunity the successful candidate had to punish them.

Unlike the civil servant who keeps his job no matter what party is in power, a union staff man is damned either way in internal power struggles. As a result, more and more staff members have organized unions of their own, despite the resistance of their officers, in an attempt to protect themselves from being kicked around or even discharged as a result of a factional fight.

The stultification of union leadership in this period of crisis for collective bargaining is not explained, however, simply by the control they exercise over their administrative machinery. The fact is that most members view their unions as limited-purpose economic institutions and not as a movement. The concept of opposition groups among the membership becomes increasingly alien to the rank and file as their unions grow older and more successful. Even the traditional two-party system of the International Typographical Union appears to be dying out. American workers are not divided on religious or political grounds as they are in European countries, where Catholic, Communist, and Socialist unions vie for the allegiance of the workers. When opposition groups do spring up in the United States, they usually have some specific economic purpose, such as getting a better share of the work or a higher proportion of union jobs. That purpose achieved, they almost always go out of existence.

When opposition groups do exist, they cannot be successful today unless they formulate their program in economic terms. When the Communists dominated some of the old CIO unions, they were supported by the non-Communist members not because the members had any allegiance to the political program but because the program was disguised as an economic one. The experience of the Catholic Church with these members is revealing. It was only when the Catholic members of Communist-led unions grew dissatisfied with the *economic* conditions for which their leaders were bargaining that they changed leaders. Until then they had ignored all the sermons from their priests calling for change.

Most public discussion of the relationship between union democracy and collective bargaining is limited to the right of union members to speak on issues, to run their own affairs, to make their own decisions, to elect their own officers freely. This view is based on an assumption that the more responsive union leaders are to their members, the more responsible the leaders will be. It is striking that so little is said of the possible consequences that this sort of supposed participational democracy has for collective bargaining. It was a democratically determined vote of photoengravers that kept the New York newspaper strike of 1962-63, itself the result of a democratic vote by printers, continuing even after all the other unions had settled with the publishers. Vesting the rank and file with authority often poses greater economic problems not only for employers but for the public than may be created by the most autocratically run unions.

When John L. Lewis retired from the presidency of the United Mine Workers, he was heaped with lavish praise by the mine owners and the press. It was a far cry from the days when editorial cartoons all over the country portrayed him spouting fire as he defied law and order. In the intervening years Lewis had become a "responsible" union leader, even a labor statesman, and in all the newspaper editorials that lauded him on his retirement, in all the speeches made at the banquet honoring him, Mr. Lewis's iron control over his union was never even mentioned, much less criticized. There was a good reason for the silence, for it was Lewis's autocratic domination of the union, exercised at some points by imposing trusteeships for years over entire districts of the UMW, that permitted the coal industry to automate without resistance from its workers. It was because Lewis was *not* responsive to his membership—indeed, because he was protected from them—that the price of coal to the consumer was kept down and the mine owners were enabled to make profits at the cost of permanent unemployment for many mine workers.

The conflicts that grow from idealizing union democracy but rejecting the consequences of it result in contradictory demands on union members and their leaders by the public. The members are exhorted to take an active interest in electing leaders who will protect them on the job and get greater benefits for them from the employers. Congress has even made failure of the leaders to do these things the cause of possible action against them. At the same time the leaders—and members, too—are asked to act "reasonably" in the interests of the employer and the public, despite the fact that such action may conflict with even the limited mission of the union. In view of this confusion, it is not surprising that Congress has thus far been of very little help in coping with the collapse of the bargaining system.

In the face of such contradictions, the Declaration of Findings, Purposes, and Policy of the Landrum-Griffin Act offers only the truism that "the relations between employers and labor organizations and the millions of workers they represent have a substantial impact on the commerce of the nation" and the obscure suggestion "that in order to accomplish the objective of a free flow of commerce it is essential that labor organizations, employers, and their officials adhere to the highest standards of responsibility and ethical conduct in administering the affairs of their organization, particularly as they affect labor-management relations."

To whom do labor organizations and their officials owe "responsibility"? To the members of the union? To the public? To the employers? And when all three groups are in conflict, as often happens, to whom do labor organizations and their officials then owe "responsibility," and how do they go about carrying it out?

To these admittedly difficult questions there is no answer in the Declaration or in the Act itself. While Congress is to be commended for having established a bill of rights for union members, it must be recognized that in doing so it ignored any consideration of the fundamental dilemma of democracy in government: more democracy for union members is frequently not compatible with efficiency for the enterprise.

Ignorance of the facts of economic life is equally prevalent outside the halls of Congress. When the New York newspaper printers voted to reject a contract with the publishers, New Yorkers went without newspapers for nearly four months. This may not have been a catastrophe, except for the advertising agencies and waste-paper dealers. In fact, if the indispensable *New York Times* had not been one of the papers involved in the strike, the public hullabaloo would probably have been less, as it has been in cities like Cleveland and Portland, Oregon, where much longer newspaper strikes have taken place without any great outcry. But what if it had not been their newspapers but the subway that New Yorkers had had to do without? Would this have been a mere inconvenience? No, clearly it would have been a catastrophe. Does this mean, therefore, that subway workers must be deprived of the rights guaranteed to other employees? If so, what do they get in exchange?

A society with a strong sense of national purpose can voluntarily subordinate its industrial conflicts to that purpose. But

America's pride is that its consensus votes for pluralism, for a society in which various countervailing interest groups—like unions and management—somehow work out their problems by butting heads. There is something to be said for this theory, to be sure, and one thing that might be said is that it has, until now, worked rather well. But "until now" is the key phrase, for an overwhelming sense of dislocation and uneasiness has come over all of American society, coupled with a growing belief that pluralism in industrial relations is getting to be a luxury that the nation can no longer afford.

Technology has freed America from much harsh and routine labor and greatly improved its living standards, but it has also made the people so interdependent that no one of them is free from the consequences of another's actions. What has been missing is a political theory that tries to bind together the tradition of collective bargaining without government intervention and the needs of a technologically intertwined society trying to survive in a world of extraordinary internal and external pressures. In the absence of theory it was inevitable that traditional collective bargaining would become useless.

IV

Many people, including some without any vested interest in collective bargaining, do not agree that traditional collective bargaining patterns have become archaic. They point to the new, continuous bargaining relationship that has developed between the United Steelworkers and the steel corporations as an indication of the adaptations that the collective bargaining system can make to new situations. They look at the existence of thousands and thousands of peaceful agreements between local unions and management as proof that collective bargaining operates reasonably well at the plant level. But even those who still believe in the basic vitality of the present collective bargaining system agree that some issues are beyond its capabilities.

George Meany, AFL-CIO president, who maintains his confidence in the traditional methods, concedes that some basic problems raised by technology and automation are not susceptible to solution in the manner to which his own union, the Plumbers, has been committed. There are other labor leaders, too, who, without finding basic flaws in the system, have become aware of the dim future that they and their members face. They sense that, unless some decisive actions are taken immediately, unions will become victims of the crisis in industrial relations, as extinct in the future as the Industrial Workers of the World are today. But their reluctant recognition that a grave crisis exists may have come too late, and their conception of it is certainly too narrow.

Despite the present breakdown of collective bargaining, industrial justice still depends upon the existence of unions, at least in the immediate future. However, if unions are to survive, they must discard their outmoded methods and attitudes. It is obvious that the organizing techniques they have been using for so long are no longer effective enough. The white-collar and technical employees who provided the margin of defeat for the union shop in the recent elections in aero-space plants are typical workers of the future. For years the AFL-CIO has summarily dismissed the associations that claim the allegiance of these white-collar, technical, and professional workers as "company unions," but it is they, not the AFL-CIO, that represent a growing number of workers and appear to be far more responsive to the needs of the new semi-professional employees. Union leaders must study the operations of these organizations. Unions also should become a voice for the great mass of unemployed workers. No one has seriously tried to do this, and unless the unions fill the vacuum a dangerous spokesman may arise who will use the discontent of the unemployed for vicious political purposes. The farm workers are still unorganized, too, and this should also be a task of the unions, despite the great difficulties involved.

Perhaps unions would have a better chance of taking a significant place in a new bargaining system if the AFL-CIO merger were dissolved. The marriage between these two groups has never been very happy, and whatever advantages it might have had are gone. Neither groups really wants the alliance any longer, even though they feel unable to free themselves. When the AFL and the CIO were separate entities, each had a special identity, a special behavior as an organization and as an organizer of workers. The federation has no identity; it is as amorphous and characterless as the dull resolutions perfunctorily discussed and apathetically approved at its conventions. With the loss of identity has come a sharp drop in staff morale; one of the few things that engenders some excitement among union officials of both groups is the thought of a split.

To be sure, improving staff morale, important as that is, is not enough by itself to justify the break. But there are other purposes that a separation might serve. A more sensible consolidation than the present one would be to follow the natural lines of work rather than the present cumbersome groupings of criss-crossing jurisdictions. The building trades have a natural affinity, for example, since carpenters, bricklayers, hodcarriers, and the other construction crafts are together at work. It seems equally foolish for newspaper printers, stereotypers, and engravers to be in separate unions, for they are part of one continuous work process. So, too, the transportation unions and the industrial unions are linked at work. Unions like that of the machinists, which are both craft and industrial, are more difficult to place into such a framework, but the future development of this union seems to be toward the industrial type. The Teamsters is the only real general union in the United States encompassing all kinds of jurisdiction. No other union seems interested in or capable of following this pattern.

Even now, the internal organization of the AFL-CIO reflects the natural work grouping in some ways. There is a building trades department, an industrial union section, a metal trades division. More power rests with these separate groups than with the parent federation. The people in them are more comfortable with each other than they are with the men and women whose work is strange to them. But the minimal pact that holds these groups together inhibits them from developing their own organizing and operating style. The fact that the industrial union section of the AFL-CIO is now undertaking its own organizing campaign indicates that some recognition is being given to the need for freeing the potential energies bottled up within the AFL-CIO. An authentic split might be the impetus for a surge of activity in which many unions would participate far more energetically than they do in the lackadaisical atmosphere of the AFL-CIO today.

Other advantages would accrue from a split. Workers might be better represented if there were active competition for their allegiance. Major social problems might get more attention. The old CIO policy of organizing into single unions all the workers in the mass industries—including Negroes—was one of the strongest influences that opened up the AFL to more Negroes. When bargaining rights were at stake and Negro workers were in a position to influence elections, the patterns of discrimination in both unions were considerably shaken up.

If a split did take place within the AFL-CIO, it might be necessary to minimize if not eliminate jurisdictional strikes by forcing more unions to merge. This would be difficult because of the special interests that develop within unions, but perhaps the process could be speeded up by the use of legislative authority. Competition between unions might pose a problem for employers, since changes in union representation are often accompanied by instability in labor relations and new contract demands. The new union and the employer would have to break themselves in, as it were, and develop new ways of getting along together. But this would not be impossible, and it might even have the advantage of cutting down the mutuality of interest that often develops between union and company officials, sometimes to the detriment of their respective constituencies. In any event, initial instability in union-management relations is not too high a price to pay for the advantages that would accrue from a split in the AFL-CIO.

There would be political advantages in separate federations. Today the lobbying of the AFL-CIO is hampered by the contradictory political pressures exerted by the jurisdictional groups within it. The bitterest complaints about labor lobbying often come from labor-supported legislators faced with the conflicting demands made upon them by different unions or groups of unions. There is no reason why separate federations could not join together in their political activities when their mutual interests are identical and lobby separately, as they do in fact now, when their interests are different.

V

A collective bargaining system that excludes a huge group of workers is clearly not fulfilling its purpose, and so the acute dilemma forced on unions by the rapid change in the tempo of race relations in America demands attention all by itself. At a time when the energies of unions should be engaged in efforts to create a new bargaining system, they have drifted into a serious conflict with the Negro community.

The contradiction between the stated ideals of the country and its practices with regard to discrimination and integration of Negroes in American society is reflected in the unions and has always been there. Take these three quotations:

"The sentiment of organized labor in the country is decidedly in favor of maintaining and encouraging the recognition of equality between colored and white workers. . . ."

"To the union of the trade belongs absolute jurisdiction on all matters connected with the trade."

"If the colored man continues to lend himself to the work of tearing down what the white man has built up, a race hatred far worse than any ever known will result. Caucasian civilization will serve notice that its uplifting process is not to be interfered with in any way."

The same man, Samuel Gompers, founder of the AFL, wrote all three of those statements, and the conflicting sentiments are still apparent in unions today. Gompers maintained that he was opposed to racial discrimination by unions. But he also believed that the "absolute jurisdiction" of the autonomous unions affiliated with the AFL included their right to carry out discriminatory policies. Goaded by the actions of Negroes who became strikebreakers because it was the only way they could get jobs normally controlled by the unions, Gompers would lash out at them, not understanding the resentment they felt toward an organization that promised them the future in convention resolutions and deprived them of the jobs they wanted in the present.

An embarrassing parallel exists between Samuel Gompers and George Meany; between the old American Federation of Labor, which was craft-union-oriented, and the AFL-CIO, which is still dominated by many AFL traditions. Like Gompers, Meany says he is opposed to racial discrimination. But, just as Gompers thought the fledgling AFL had to accept the affiliation of unions that discriminated against Negroes, so Meany believes he cannot expel discriminatory unions from the AFL-CIO without serious consequences. In both cases the justification is the same: the time-consuming effort to eliminate discrimination is better accomplished if the unions are inside the structure of the federation than if they have been refused admittance or have been expelled.

Just as Gompers once bitterly accused Negroes of "tearing down what the white man has built up," Meany sometimes loses his temper when the AFL-CIO is attacked by Negroes today. "Who in hell appointed you the spokesman of the Negro people?" Meany shouted in 1959 at A. Philip Randolph, president of the Brotherhood of Sleeping Car Porters, when Randolph protested the failure of the AFL-CIO to take decisive action against unions that were still discriminating against Negroes.

Meany has vented his full bitterness in his counterattacks against the NAACP. He points to the changes that have come about under his leadership: the drop in the number of unions that openly exclude Negroes; the establishment of a civil rights committee by the AFL-CIO; and his own personal efforts to break down discriminatory practices, including even an offer to recruit non-union Negro electricians for a construction job in Washington if the electrical workers' local in that city continued to ban qualified Negroes.

Meany's indignation is shared by many other labor leaders who believe that they are being unfairly attacked solely for demagogic purposes. There are certainly differences between the condition of the AFL under Gompers and that of the AFL-CIO under Meany: whereas many AFL unions openly and formally excluded Negroes, only one in the AFL-CIO still has a constitutional bar against Negroes, and although discrimination is still prevalent within individual unions, it is slowly easing. But most union leaders have proved incapable of understanding that it is precisely at the moment when unions relax their racial bars, indeed precisely *because* the bars have been lowered, that they become subject to even more intense pressure from Negroes, who suffer far more seriously from unemployment than do white workers.

"What other institution in the country has voluntarily done as much for the Negro as the unions?" ask the leaders, pointing to their lobbying for civil rights legislation in Congress, their support of the Supreme Court decision on school segregation, their cooperation with Fair Employment Practices Committees, their resolutions of praise for the NAACP, and their financial aid to the Negro cause. They cannot understand why they, sometimes the only friends of the Negro, should be the ones now to come under such severe criticism. The indignant quality of their response to the attacks, the hurt tone that has now grown into impatience, reveal a great deal about the nature of the separation between the unions and the Negroes.

Union leaders do not comprehend that it is now a mark of status for Negro students to have served jail sentences, that pan-Africanism has moved from the gin mills of Greenwich Village to the auditoriums of Oakland, California, that Negroes are no longer prepared to be "patient." Today no Negro leader can survive without adopting a posture of action against the white world. The Negro intellectual has come back full circle to where he started: once again he is a black man first who may also happen to be a writer, a painter, or an auto worker. Union leaders also fail to recognize that the attitude of articulate Negroes toward union leaders in their roles as white liberals is different from the attitude of these Negroes toward the rest of the white community. When Negroes deal with open Southern segregationists, the rules of behavior for both groups are well established and understood, even if detested. But, in their personal and organizational relationships with liberal union leaders, Negroes are rarely sure of the reaction they are going to get; there is always the fear that, under certain stresses, the liberal will turn white.

It is because union leaders have committed themselves for so long, on paper, to raising the standards of the Negro that Negroes now demand that they live up to their claims. Union leaders are discovering that if you give minority groups a finger, they want a hand—as indeed they should.

The change in the level of aspiration for Negroes in unions is most marked in their growing rejection of the token Negro on the union staff, the black man to whose office the overseas visitors are directed. For a long time, when they had nothing else, Negroes had to be content publicly, no matter how they mocked privately, with these token Negroes, these "Cousin Toms" who possessed no real power in the union because their status depended on white union leaders. Now Cousin Tom has become a symbol not only of white paternalism but of Negro shame, and there are great pressures in the Negro community to open up the union job hierarchy to people of their own race.

No union is completely free of these tensions, but there are marked differences in how the leaders see the problem and what steps they take to cope with it. The leadership of the United Auto Workers, with more Negro staff members than any other union in the country, cracks down hard on local unions that attempt to maintain either separate seniority lists or separate facilities, but until its last convention it had resisted the pressures to add a Negro to the Reuther slate of officers. The United Packinghouse Workers is probably the only one with a mixed membership that has elected many high officials who are Negroes. At the other extreme are the unions in which Negroes are even denied membership, much less union office; others with segregated locals; some, especially in the South, that maintain separate seniority lists; and still others that block the entrance of Negroes into apprenticeship programs.

Between the two poles, a wide range of practices exists, depending upon the technical character of the industry, the social composition and traditions of the union, and the amount of autonomy granted to its locals by the international union. In some, the relationship of the locals to their central headquarters almost duplicates the autonomy granted to the international unions in the AFL-CIO. In several large locals of the International Longshoremen, for example, Negroes are so numerous that they constitute a major political force. But even in this "progressive" union there is at least one local that excludes Negroes, and the only justification that Harry Bridges, the international head, can cite for the failure of the international union to act is that his locals have a very high degree of autonomy.

Bridges's argument is a powerful one when the alternatives seem to be either allowing the local union to continue its discriminatory practices, however reluctant the international may be, or expelling it. The provocation for expulsion has to be very great before any union will voluntarily give up a bloc of members, and, clearly, discrimination against Negroes is not enough to warrant that action even in the ILWU. The excuse given by some industrial unions either for organizing segregated locals in the South or for not resisting discriminatory hiring and promotion practices is that otherwise the entire organizational battle might be lost. There is some truth to the argument, for unions have been defeated in bargaining elections in the South because the company raised the race issue. However, unless unions are organized initially on a nondiscriminatory basis and unless they continue to operate on a nondiscriminatory basis, they are forced to carry the burden of segregation from then on. It is a hard fact that unions no longer have much room or time for compromise with principle.

Eventually the pressure of the NAACP upon the AFL-CIO will ease up, and then the next phase in the complicated history of the Negro in unions will begin. It could be another extremely difficult period, for the success of the Negro in gaining power and status inside the unions will then depend on how quickly competent Negroes can develop within unions. At the moment no new major figures have appeared as articulate, capable voices of the Negroes inside unions. Herbert Hill, NAACP labor secretary, and the most outspoken critic of the AFL-CIO, is outside the union structure. But when "Cousin Tom" leaves, someone has to take his place.

VI

New but still very shadowy concepts of industrial justice are beginning to emerge from the wreckage of collective bargaining. It is impossible to imagine, for example, that America could ever return to the kind of labor-management relations that existed before the passage of the Wagner Act, when the employer was given all the authority for determining the relations between himself and his workers. The days are also past when the government's role in labor-management relations was merely that of a referee. Today, whether union leaders and management spokesmen like it or not, government is entering directly and increasingly into these relations. Both the courts and the legislature have begun to involve themselves deeply in areas that were once considered inviolate.

Until recently, the courts maintained the traditional attitude toward unions: they were voluntary associations whose internal life was their own affair. They were given the right to dispense justice to their members, free of outside interference. The relationship between the union and its members, formalized in the union constitution, was regarded as a contract, with all of its conditions enforceable by law. Now, however, the courts—and the legislature, too—are maintaining that the exclusive bargaining rights granted to American unions, along with the variety of other membership-enclosing devices, have reduced to polite fictions both the old voluntary association theory and the legal theory that the union constitution is an enforceable contract between member and union.

One important reason for the change in the legal attitude toward unions is that due process is still in a very primitive stage in most American unions. Sometimes union laws are so vague as to cover almost any offense—in the Carpenters Union, for example, expulsion is possible for "an attempt to create dissension among the members"; in many other unions "conduct unbecoming to a union member" may serve as the sole basis for charges. Frequently the procedures for hearings and trials are lacking in those safeguards against bias and self-interest which are normally found in civil or criminal law. Despite these weaknesses only three unions—the United Auto Workers, the Upholsterers, and the Packinghouse Workers—have established independent boards outside the union to review cases of members against whom either a local or the national organization has taken action.* What is worse, no other unions have even shown any signs of pursuing voluntarily the path that these three unions have opened up.

As a matter of fact, there is not much real evidence that wholesale violations of due process are taking place in unions. Despite the lurid publicity given to the "thousands" of complaints allegedly received by the McClellan Committee, American union leaders seem easily able to govern their organizations without resorting to suppressive devices on a mass scale or to the establishment of trusteeships. But the potential for punitive action by union leaders against union members exists, for unions still have control over an important part of their members' lives, and in the absence of adequate principles of due process workers must necessarily look outside union administration and collective bargaining for their ultimate protections.

* See *Democracy and Public Review,* a study of the UAW Public Review Board, by Jack Stieber, Walter E. Oberer, and Michael Harrington. Center for the Study of Democratic Institutions, Santa Barbara (1960).

As the legal attitude is changing about the rights of union members vis-à-vis their leaders, so there is a growing change in the views of workers toward rights in their jobs. Although the right not to be fired arbitrarily, the right to bargain collectively for wages, the right to help determine working conditions, and the basic right to hold a job are derived initially from the terms of the union contract, workers eventually begin to look at these rights as having an existence apart. Every union representative and management official must deal with this phenomenon. "This job is *my* job," the worker maintains as he fights off other workers, the union, the employer, and sometimes even the government whenever an attempt is made to take the job away from him. The airline flight engineer who is replaced by a pilot, the railroad fireman who is taken out of the cab, or the steelworker who loses his job to another union member with more seniority because of an operational merger is fighting not only for a job, for the right to make a living, but for the particular job at which he has been employed.

No one, no local union president, no international union officer, no company vice-president of personnel, no arbitrator, no government official, no judge, has come up with a solution that satisfies all the conflicting interests in such situations. Here, again, union-management collective bargaining is of little use, for its limited and special nature, its dependence on "collective" action, prevents it from being a useful tool to assess *individual* rights. Government, through the law, will be required to assume the burden of developing a theory about job rights.

The most serious weakness in traditional collective bargaining, however, is its incapacity to deal with the economic conditions that are making unemployment a permanent way of life for millions. Once upon a time Americans were blithely secure in the belief that their future was unlimited: the economy of abundance was just over the horizon and that government was best which governed least. The depression of the 1930's eroded the core of that belief so severely that only a few ultra-conservatives were opposed to the actions that government took then to mitigate the disaster. Now, more and more Americans are becoming discontented with the view of a future in which a high rate of unemployment is accepted, in which other countries equal and sometimes exceed our once untouchable rate of growth, and in which an accelerating technology makes each of us increasingly dependent upon the other. The concept that government is there not just to help when economic catastrophe strikes but to avert the catastrophe, whenever possible, before it begins, is widely accepted today. More, rather than less, government seems inevitable.

No precise predictions can be made about the long-term replacement for the obsolescent tool of traditional collective bargaining. The development of social institutions is so continuous and changing a process, so susceptible to unforeseeable pressures, and so dependent upon the imagination of man that it is impossible to do more than hazard a few guesses.

One development probably will be the replacement of crisis negotiations between unions and management, carried on under the tremendous pressure of contract deadlines, with continuous bargaining under the watchful eyes of public representatives. The process of continuous negotiation would actually be an extension of the daily resolution of conflict that takes place now at the shop level. Gradually, also, unions may give up the right to take certain kinds of strike actions against employers, but the speed and willingness with which this takes place will depend directly on how willingly corporations give up what they have always considered their sacred rights to set unilaterally the size of the work force and to determine the distribution of profits. Some national consensus about both jobs and profits will have to emerge, however, before unions or workers will ever abandon the right to certain strikes.

The place of unions in the structure of industrial justice will continue to grow smaller unless unions return to the political function that once was primary with them. They will need to design new political tools and new forms of political participation, for it is clear that future union-management relations will depend less and less on sheer economics and more and more on political instruments and political techniques. When the potential of unions was being more fully realized, it was not just the legal right to strike that made them unique. So long as their economic function brought dignity to workers like the men and women who comprise Miscellaneous Culinary Workers Local 110, unions rightly commanded the respect of the community and the allegiance of their members. Unions freed workers from worrying about being fired arbitrarily. They provided the means for many workers to hurdle the barrier raised by lack of formal education and to become eminent citizens. They instilled the principles of industrial justice so deeply in the society that no one seriously questions them any longer.

Now unions must move on from the simple economic level. In Israel, in the Scandinavian countries, in England, and in many other foreign lands unions are an integral part of the political system, not onlookers as they are in America, where the simplistic AFL tradition of rewarding friends and punishing enemies in the political arena is still dominant. The tragedy of American unions is that those that did so much to create the old collective bargaining system are taking so minor and unimportant a role in developing a new one. It may mean their death.

Would it be a tragedy if American unions disappeared? Would they be missed? The answer can only be "yes" to both questions. Unions have the potential to be a unique political force: they are the only institutions in society that bind together men who spend an important part of their lives together, sharing the common experience of work. Even if unions disappear, industrial justice may survive, but still the loss will be felt, not just among workers like the Local 110 "catchers" on the dishwashing machines but among all the people of America.

POSTSCRIPT

I RETURNED to Minneapolis a few years ago for the first time since I left the city in 1938, and it was as if I'd never been there before. It had become a strange place to me, with new high shiny buildings and streets that were sadly unfamiliar. I wandered around looking for the Trotskyist headquarters where I had spent so much time, sitting in meetings, talking with the comrades, and worrying about whether I was conducting myself as a proper Bolshevik should. But I couldn't find the building. Perhaps it has been torn down, or perhaps it is still there and I no longer recognize it.

The people I knew then were gone, too, or unrecognizable, and I felt cheated, felt as if somehow there should have been some distinct mark left on the city by the presence there once of the Dunne brothers, of Farrell Dobbs, and of the other Trotskyists who ran Local 544 of the Teamsters.

I last saw Ray Dunne, the smartest and the most awesome of the brothers, seven or eight years ago in the audience at a meeting in Los Angeles where I was making a speech. Physically he was unchanged, except that his hair was gray and cropped much shorter than I had remembered it. He stared up at me on the platform as he always looked at everybody, his eyes seeming to measure me against his rigid standards of behavior. And I felt as if, once again, I had failed to meet the test.

I spotted Dobbs, too, one evening a few years ago, standing on a street corner in downtown Manhattan. As I walked toward him, I saw that he was studying a sheaf of papers under the street light. He must have been waiting for someone, for he kept looking up from the documents to scan the sidewalk. As I came abreast of him, his eyes passed over me without any recognition in them and I walked by without speaking to him. He seemed a wraith to me, a figure without reality, still living in another time.

And, although I could find no physical marks left in Minneapolis of the Dunne brothers, Farrell Dobbs and the other Trotskyists, their presence there once is still felt throughout the country. They, especially Dobbs, were the first to understand both the key role truckdrivers were to play in the American economy and how the drivers should be organized. Ironically, while Dobbs and Dunne live on in their shadow world of revolutionary working-class politics, Jimmy Hoffa builds on the structure of their legacy, the largest, nonpolitical, middle-class union in the country.

That's the irony of it all, the joke on all the radicals who, because of their commitment to the revolutionary aspirations of the working class, helped to build union strength. For what we did—sometimes in important ways and more often not— what we did was to help create a new middle class of placid workers.

Well, is that such a bad thing to have helped create? No, I guess not, even if it isn't what we wanted nor expected. The tragedy of American unions isn't so much in their present state as it is in what they could be, and aren't. But then, isn't that the plight of America, too?

San Francisco, 1963

INDEX

AFL constitution, 264
AFL-CIO: and Communists, 17; disadvantages, 282; and farmworkers, 171, 193-194; founding, 156; headquarters, 257; and Hoffa, 65, 66-67; jurisdiction, 8-9; McClellan Committee, 58; NAACP, 162-166; Negroes, 156-158, 161, 285-289; non-affiliates, 270; number of unions, 266; if split, 281-284; Teamster expulsion, 269
Admiral Radio Corp., 22
Aeromarine West Indies Airways Service, 219-220
Aerospace industry, 260; unions, 281
Agents, see Business agents
Agricultural Workers Organizing Committee (AWOC), 193
Agriculture: fatalities, 173; workmen's compensation, 180, 186-187
Air Force jets, 238
Airline crews, 229-230; strikes, 221, 222, 225, 235, 236, 240-241, 244, 246, 250
Air Line Pilots Asociation, 220-221, 245-250
Airmail Act of 1934, 223
Air Transport Association, 229, 232
Alaska Airlines, 230
Allied Industrial Workers, 33
ALPA (Air Line Pilots Association), 220-221, 245-250
American Airlines, 229, 232, 234, 246; 1958 compromise, 242-243; strike, 236-237
American Farm Bureau Federation, 181
American Friends Service Committee, 190
American Labor Party, 123
American Newspaper Publishers Association, 210, 216
Anti-Semitism, 134-136
Appleton, Shelley, 126
Apprenticeships and Negroes, 288
Arbitration, compulsory, 265-266
Archer-Daniels-Midland Co., 16

Area agreements, 13, 14, 23
Areas, farm workers', 176
Arizona Cotton Growers Association, 182, 185
Associations, white-collar, 281
Attendance at meetings, 57, 149-150
Attorney General and citizens, 87
Automation, 60; and coal industry, 278; and jets, 239; and management, 253-254; Negroes, 160; newspapers, 253-254; unemployment, 260; unions, 264; "unwork," 199, 201
Autonomy, local, and Negroes, 288
AWOC (Agricultural Workers Organizing Committee), 193-195

Babbage, Charles, quoted, 251
Baird, Joseph, 211-213
Bargaining, collective, 271-275, 276-280; automation, 260; flaws, 278-280, 281; future, 292-293; limits, 259-261; missile industry, 260; unions, 265; Wagner Act, 259
Bartenders Union, 154-155, 169
Beck, Dave, 11, 25, 36; business interests, 18-19; early years, 13-14; Ethical Practices Committee, 43; Fruehauf, 18; Hoffa, 6, 17-18; ILA (International Longshoremen's Association), 16; Kennedy, 74; trucking industry, 38
Behncke, Dave, 220, 222, 242
Bellino, Carmine, 82
Bender, ex-Sen. George, 48-49
Bituminous Coal Operators Association, 270
Boards, public review, 104, 108, 290
Boeing Aircraft Co., 228-229, 230-240; jet cockpits, 237; Teamsters, 35
Boeing 377, 226, 232-233
Boeing 707, 238
"Bogus," 199; squabbles over, 213-215; undone, 209-218; see also Reproduction

PAUL JACOBS

Born in New York City in 1918, Paul Jacobs briefly attended City College of New York and the University of Minnesota. He first became active in the union movement as an organizer and later served as an international union representative, co-publisher of a labor paper, and a labor consultant. He is on the staff of the Fund for the Republic's Center for the Study of Democratic Institutions and is associated with the Institute of Industrial Relations of the University of California at Berkeley. A regular contributor to *The Economist* of London, Mr. Jacobs also has written for *The Reporter, Commentary, Commonweal, Atlantic* and *Harper's*. He lives in San Francisco, California.